1929

A crisis that shaped
The Salvation Army's future

by

John Larsson

Salvation Books
The Salvation Army International Headquarters
London, United Kingdom

Published by Salvation Books
The Salvation Army International Headquarters
101 Queen Victoria Street, London EC4V 4EH, United Kingdom

Printed by UK Territory Print & Design Unit

Contents

Foreword

NOBODY likes having their dirty linen washed in public, still less if it is the 'linen' of a Christian organisation anxious to retain a reputation for Christlike integrity. This being so, it is a matter of no little surprise that so many books and other published accounts have been written about the most unfortunate events of 1929 which culminated in the brilliantly gifted General Bramwell Booth being removed from holding The Salvation Army's highest office.

Bramwell Booth was an outstanding Salvationist leader. In an address to Salvation Army officers on his 80th birthday, General William Booth wrote of him: 'He possesses capacities for government in all its branches, whether those of leadership or administration, in a remarkable degree … . He is dear to you all on the ground of his practical godliness.' The Founder went on to refer to his son's 'unswerving impartiality in dealing with officers the world over', his 'unflagging energy' and his 'capacity with details'.

This is the man who is the central figure of the story told between these covers. He made an inestimable, unmatched contribution to the life and mission of the Army, unsurpassed except by that of his father. The revered General Frederick Coutts, in his 1973 Volume Six of *The History of The Salvation Army – The Better Fight*, describes Bramwell as a man of 'holy imagination'. Of all those playing a significant role in the saga of 1929 Bramwell Booth is one of the very few who emerged with dignity intact. When it was all over, *The Times* newspaper concluded that 'the reputation of General Bramwell Booth as the faithful guardian and zealous enlarger of his father's inheritance is secure.'

General John Larsson (Retired) has painstakingly created a further narrative of the 1929 debacle by synthesising many of the published records, adding data to be found in already known unpublished materials, and drawing upon some new sources searched out by him. His enthusiasm for, and fascination with, his subject comes through in every chapter of the book. The result is a well-researched, clear and comprehensive, balanced version of what some still see as the shameful happenings of 80 years ago.

This book is all the more interesting for coming from the pen of one who has occupied the office of General. Readers will gain from the insights thus afforded. However, even after eight decades have passed and after all the main players are no longer alive, there will inevitably still be some feeling that in publishing yet another book about the 1929 High Council we are re-opening old wounds. To a large extent I share that feeling. Nevertheless, this latest analysis is a model of impartiality as between the various protagonists, highlighting past errors that we must never repeat, and showing how the Army has moved on and matured into an era of consultative leadership without sacrificing principles foundational to our polity and heritage.

Therefore I record thanks to the distinguished author for this diligent and orderly account. His work helps us to learn from things past, and serves to caution us that, even among godly people, sometimes the right thing is done for reasons and motives unworthy of the sacred, higher cause at stake.

Shaw Clifton
General

London, August 2009

Preface

IN 1929 a constitutional storm that had long been gathering suddenly burst, sweeping from office General Bramwell Booth, the son of and successor to William Booth. The crisis stunned The Salvation Army. So traumatic was this event that for many years '1929' – for that is how it was known – was only talked of in hushed tones in Army circles. The telling of what happened was left to those from outside the Army family.

General Albert Orsborn envisaged that one day the full story of the crisis would be told by a Salvationist writer. He therefore in 1947 asked the surviving members of the 1929 High Council to let him have their personal recollections of the event and the lead-up to it, so that 'an accurate account can be prepared in order that history may be correctly recorded'. Sadly, already by that time there were few key members still alive and most of them were of advanced years. The yield was therefore meagre.

By 1958, when General Orsborn wrote his autobiography, he wistfully concluded that 'the history of the first High Council will never be fully told; most of the private correspondence of the chief participants was destroyed by them'. He could well have added that much of what the participants did not themselves shred went up in flames when International Headquarters was destroyed by fire in the Second World War.

However, extensive archival research in several countries has revealed that more documentation has been preserved than was realised. This work is therefore a far fuller telling of the history of the constitutional crisis than might previously have been thought possible, and includes much material that has not previously been published. Eighty years after the events it describes, it is also the first comprehensive account of those momentous times written by a Salvationist author.

While the story of the 1929 crisis, with all its astonishing twists and turns, is a tale full of human drama it is a drama without villains. In this respect it is like the incident recounted in Acts 15 in which Paul and Barnabas had a 'sharp disagreement' about whether John Mark should accompany them on their missionary journeys. So acute was their dispute that they parted company. However, Paul and Barnabas were good people and respected leaders of the Church – and they were no less good and no less respected because they disagreed about John Mark.

In the same way, *1929* is the story about good and revered Salvation Army leaders who disagreed sharply as to the best way forward for The Salvation Army – but who were no less good or less esteemed because of their dispute about the Army's constitution.

What shook the Army also shaped its future. Through those events of long ago the Army was set on a path of reform that continues to this day. *1929* is part of our heritage.

John Larsson
General (Retired)

Prologue

Breaking the News

IT was New Year's Day 1929. As the car inched its way along the icy London roads on the 100-mile journey towards Southwold, the small east-coast community near Lowestoft, Commissioner Catherine Booth looked out on the wintry scene and prepared her mind for the distressing task ahead.

She was the bearer of bad tidings for her father, General Bramwell Booth. The General, aged 72, lay ill in 'Crapstone', the villa in Southwold that he and his wife Florence had used for many years as a hideaway whenever they needed to escape from the swirl of events. General Booth of The Salvation Army was a celebrity figure in Britain, but in Southwold they were known simply as 'Captain and Mrs Bernard' and nobody asked intrusive questions. Thus undisturbed by public attention they had often enjoyed the peace and beauty of the Suffolk coast to return refreshed for the demands of the next day.

Bramwell Booth had been General for 16 years. When he became General upon William Booth's death in 1912 he was 56 years of age and previous to that had been second-in-command to his father for 40 years.

According to the Army's constitution it was the duty of every General to choose his successor by placing the name of the person selected in a 'sealed envelope' to be opened upon his death. When William Booth died everybody knew that the only possible name in the envelope was that of Bramwell Booth, the Chief of the Staff, and so it turned out to be. When the envelope was opened on 25 August 1912 Mr Bramwell, as he was always known, became General

1

Bramwell Booth. It was the first rank he ever held. He was never a commissioner.

In the press there was widespread speculation at the time whether the Army would survive the death of its founder. Was The Salvation Army an iridescent meteor that had brilliantly lit up the sky during William Booth's lifetime but which was destined to fade and die with him?

Salvationists had no such fears. They knew their Bramwell! His succession was greeted with universal acclaim. Harold Begbie, who was later to become the official biographer of William Booth, got it right when in his obituary of the Founder he wrote: 'General William Booth has always been the Army's heart and soul, its dreamer and its inspiration. The brains of the Army are to be looked for elsewhere … Bramwell Booth is the mastermind directing all those worldwide activities. And but for Bramwell Booth The Salvation Army as it now exists would be unknown to mankind.'[1]

However, could the mastermind change gear, could he lead with heart and soul, could he dream dreams and inspire the Salvationists of the world to even greater things now that he was to be the captain of the ship rather than its builder? Some observers wondered, but not for long. For Bramwell blossomed in his new role. His was not the charisma and flamboyance of his father. Vachel Lindsay could never have written of Bramwell:

> 'Booth led boldly with his big bass drum,
> Are you washed in the Blood of the Lamb?'

Only William Booth could give that kind of a lead, but Bramwell Booth took hold of the helm with assured hands and in his own way steered the Army towards horizons that his father could only have dreamt of.

After 16 years of his leadership the Army's work had extended to a further 25 countries, the number of officers had almost doubled, and worldwide the Army had become a force to be reckoned with. Kings and princes, presidents and prime ministers honoured Bramwell Booth and sought his advice.

In Britain, where Bramwell Booth was in effect the 'territorial commander', the work had grown to unprecedented size and influence. With 5,000 active officers and 150,000 senior soldiers at work in 1,500 corps and 220 social centres, the Army in the land of its birth had never been bigger.

There were visions for even greater things. The plans for the William Booth Memorial College being built at Denmark Hill – the fulfilment of the Founder's dream of a University of Humanity – envisaged a yearly intake of 700 cadets.[2] The sessions of cadets had been growing larger each year. The 1928 session had actually begun with 700 cadets, and there seemed no reason why this should not become the annual intake figure.

The British Salvationists loved and admired General Bramwell. Not one of them could remember a time when Bramwell had not been there in the front line to lead them on. They admired him for what he had achieved and they loved him for what he was. They applauded him for not letting deafness get in the way of his ministry. He had been hard of hearing since a teenager, and the sight of Bramwell on the platform turning his horn-shaped ear trumpet towards the speaker was all part of the Army scene. Hearts were often warmed at the sight of Bramwell counselling seekers at the mercy seat and listening attentively to their every word through his acousticon.

The pressure of events had now laid the giant low. By the first day of 1929 General Bramwell Booth had been ill for more than seven months. His condition had taken a serious turn for the worse at the beginning of November 1928 when it was feared that he might die. After two weeks he had begun to regain strength and the doctors were now hopeful that in time he would make a complete recovery. William Booth had led the Army vigorously until his death at the age of 83. Bramwell was only 72 and had made it clear that he anticipated leading the Army for at least another decade.

As the car picked up speed on leaving the outskirts of London, Catherine Booth wondered how best to break the fateful news she was bringing. 'I felt that the words I must speak would be his death,' she later recalled.[3] It was a fear that Bramwell Booth's doctors shared. They had insisted that he must not be told until his condition had improved and he was out of danger. For more than six weeks his wife and daughter had withheld the information from the stricken warrior, but the doctors had now pronounced him well enough to bear the shock.

The bad news

The shattering news Commissioner Catherine Booth bore was that at that very moment the 63 most senior leaders of The Salvation Army were converging on London by ship and train from around the world to adjudicate whether General Bramwell Booth was to be removed from office.

Six weeks before, seven London-based commissioners had taken hold of a little-known emergency provision in the Army's constitution whereby a General who had become 'unfit for office' could be removed. They had jointly written and signed a letter addressed to the Chief of the Staff requesting that the High Council of The Salvation Army be called to judge whether Bramwell Booth was unfit to be General. As the 'joint requisition of not less than seven commissioners' was sufficient to trigger this constitutional provision, the Chief of the Staff had summoned the Army's leaders to gather in London for the first ever meeting of the High Council. The Council was to convene on 8 January 1929. That was now only seven days away.

Commissioner Catherine Booth knew how utterly devastating this news would be to her father. Bramwell Booth had played a large part in the writing of that part of the constitution, and more than anyone else would know that the intention of the provision was not to remove a General who had become 'unfit for office' through illness. The provision was intended, as William Booth had plainly said, to make it possible to remove a General 'who for some calamitous reason had been proved incapable for, or unworthy of, his position'.[4]

Catherine Booth also realised how distressed her father would be at the public spectacle of the Army's leaders from around the world coming to London to sit in judgment on him. The very fact that they had been summoned carried a stigma. He knew each of them personally, knew their families, knew their hopes and their concerns. He had promoted and appointed virtually all of them to their current ranks and appointments. They were his spiritual brothers and sisters, and the bonds of mutual affection were genuine and strong. Now seven members of this family of leaders had set in motion a constitutional crisis whereby all members would have to judge whether he was fit or unfit to be their General. The pain for Bramwell Booth might prove to be too much.

The only word of comfort that she would be able to offer her father was that it seemed unlikely that the requisitioning commissioners would be able to secure the necessary number of votes at the High Council to depose the General. The constitutional threshold had deliberately been set high. Three out of every four members of the High Council had to vote the General 'unfit for office' for him to be removed. If such a majority was not obtained, the General would remain in office, the High Council would be declared closed, the members would return to their ships and trains and head back to their territories, and the seven commissioners who had requisitioned the calling of the High Council would be left with a great deal of explaining to do. The stakes could therefore not be higher. Bramwell Booth might yet be vindicated.

Darkness had fallen by the time the car arrived in Southwold and drew up outside the house. Mrs Booth, as she was always known, had been anxiously awaiting the arrival of Catherine. As they caught up with each other's news and discussed recent developments, any observer would have been left in no doubt that together they made a formidable team.

Wife and daughter

Mrs Booth, aged 67, exuded energy and authority. As 19-year-old Lieutenant Florence Soper she had accompanied William and Catherine Booth's eldest daughter Catherine, *La Maréchale*, when she opened the Army's work in France. Since her marriage to

Bramwell Booth, she had been a role model of how to combine successfully support for her husband in his appointments, hold significant responsibilities herself, and be a good wife and mother.

The young Mrs Bramwell Booth had opened the Army's first rescue home for women, had founded and was for many years the leader of the Women's Social Work in Britain, and had pioneered the Home League, a ministry destined to become the world's largest movement for women. In later years she had become a commissioner in her own right and as the British Commissioner had directed the Army's evangelistic work in Britain for six years between 1919 and 1925.

Mrs Booth was the author of several books, was a frequent and effective speaker at youth councils, officers councils and large national events, had campaigned independently in the USA, Canada and several European countries, and had preached in famous pulpits including some never before occupied by a woman. She was currently responsible for overseeing the training of Salvation Army officers worldwide, was World President of the Home League and of the Life Saving Guards, was a Justice of the Peace, and a Visiting Magistrate of Holloway Prison.

In addition Mrs Booth shared in not only the General's public ministry but also, behind the scenes, in the executive decision-making process. This controversial aspect had become particularly pronounced during the General's long illness. While the Chief of the Staff was in charge, and consulted with the General when he was well enough to attend to business, Mrs Booth was highly influential, not least as the Praetorian Guard at the General's bedroom door who decided who and what he could see.

Catherine Booth, born 20 July 1883, was the first of seven children born to Bramwell and Florence Booth. She was also William and Catherine Booth's first grandchild, and as she grew up she was very close to them both. After Catherine Booth, the 'Army Mother', died in 1890, when Catherine was seven years of age, William Booth seemed to draw special comfort from spending time with this new Catherine who so resembled his own beloved wife.

Their special friendship continued as Catherine moved into her teens and following training, which began at the age of 20, became an officer.

Catherine Booth was dogged by ill health during her early years of officership – a disappointment as much to her as to her parents. Her first appointment after training was sick leave for six months to recuperate her strength. Following two corps appointments she was transferred to the training garrison staff, where during a 10-year stay she rose to become the second officer in charge of women cadets. Even there her service was interrupted by sick leave of two months. She was then appointed to International Headquarters as a major, to be under secretary in the Foreign Office.

In September 1922 adversity struck. Lieut-Colonel Catherine Booth was diagnosed with tuberculosis. Once again it became necessary for her to take sick leave. This break in her service was to last a full four years and was for her a very dark period. However, on making what was hoped to be a full recovery she was appointed Leader of the Women's Social Work in May 1926 – the work that her mother had founded.

Commissioner Catherine Booth, by now aged 45, had inherited the steel of her mother – and of her grandmother Catherine, the Army Mother. It was said that she almost sensationally resembled her grandmother in mental capacity and spiritual calibre. By nature she was drawn to a contemplative life, and being of a shy disposition she was not a natural mixer. Throughout her life she found public work very costly, but she could be remarkably powerful on the platform.

Catherine adored her father, and such was her devotion to him that in 1930 she was to change her name by deed poll to Catherine Bramwell-Booth.

Breaking the news

Now, on New Year's Day 1929, Catherine and her mother steadied themselves for the difficult task that lay before them. They entered the room where the General lay and Catherine kissed her father. He spoke cheerily, telling her that he was 'on the mend' – he had not seen her for some time. Then, before she could say anything, he looked steadfastly into her eyes and said:

'They have called the High Council.'

She recoiled. 'His words struck me like a blow,' she later recorded. 'So God had told him! I could not speak. I nodded.' There was a long pause.

'Did Hurren sign?' he asked.

Catherine nodded again, and once more a silence fell.

Commissioner Samuel Hurren was the spiritual son Bramwell Booth loved the most. Bramwell Booth had been his mentor ever since Samuel as a young lad had entered training from Camberwell Corps. He had watched carefully over him and encouraged his development. Samuel Hurren was a brilliant financier and at an early age Bramwell Booth had promoted him to the rank of commissioner and made him Chancellor of the Exchequer at International Headquarters. Then, with inspired insight, Bramwell had recognised the prophet within Samuel Hurren and had appointed him British Commissioner.

After a moment Bramwell broke the silence:

'Yes, I felt they would take advantage of my illness. I wonder what they really think in their hearts?'

Then question followed question: 'Where is the Chief of the Staff in all this?' 'What is Frost's attitude?' (William Frost was the Army's legal adviser.) 'How have the officers and soldiers reacted? What about the press?' Mrs Booth and Catherine began to brief him on all that had happened since the doctors had imposed their news blackout in the middle of November. After a time Mrs Bramwell Booth left the room, and Bramwell at once said to his daughter:

'If I die, Catherine, remember, there must be no bitterness. I forgive. You and the others must forgive too. They want to change the General's plan.'

The General's plan he was referring to – he always called William Booth the General when speaking to his children – was the plan whereby Generals appointed their own successors.

'They want to change the General's plan,' he repeated, and then added: 'They must know I shall never agree.'

Mrs Booth returned and joined in the conversation. 'With only seven days before the High Council would assemble,' recalls Catherine Booth, 'there was much to be done.'

The confirmation of his worst fears had clearly taxed Bramwell Booth's strength, and as his wife and daughter tucked him up for the dark night hours ahead they could not escape the foreboding that the calling of the High Council would sooner or later be his death.

It was a tragic crisis – for the Army and for Bramwell Booth personally. The seed of it had been sown many years before, even before the Christian Mission became The Salvation Army.

Chapter One

Laying the Foundation

ON a wintry spring day in the year 1878, William Booth, accompanied by his 22-year-old son Bramwell, made his way across the quiet squares of the Inns of Court in the City of London. Climbing the stairs they found themselves in the gloomy, candlelit chambers of an eminent counsel in the Temple, who later as Lord Cozens-Hardy, Queen's Counsel, was to be Master of the Rolls. Mr Cozens-Hardy sat behind a table piled with papers, and having just come in from court was still wearing a wig grey with dust.

William Booth explained that he had come because he wanted to annul the constitution for the Christian Mission that he with Mr Cozens-Hardy and Mr Thomas Whittington, solicitor to the Mission, had drafted three years earlier in 1875. He wanted to write a new one. As Mr Cozens-Hardy listened to William Booth describing the shape of the new constitution he had in mind, the lawyer became increasingly restive. In the end he blurted out with some acerbity:

'Mr Booth, you want me to make you a pope, and I do not think it can be done.'

Never at a loss for humour, William Booth retorted:

'Well, Mr Cozens-Hardy, I am sure that you will get as near to it as you suitably can.'[1]

The new constitution would be the third attempt made by William Booth to get the right constitution for the Christian Mission. The first constitution was written in 1870 and was what the official history of The Salvation Army describes as 'a self-denying ordinance on the part of William Booth' in that Conference – the annual assembly of the evangelists and other elected members – 'was made the final authority in the affairs of the Christian Mission'.[2]

The second constitution of the Christian Mission was written in 1875 and was the first constitution to have legal authority. It had been executed as a deed poll – a binding declaration executed by one person only – and had been enrolled for safekeeping in the Close Rolls of the Chancery where it was open to public scrutiny.

This 1875 constitution still recognised two 'authorities' in the management of the Mission – the General Superintendent and Annual Conference – but a significant shift in their respective roles had taken place. Conference continued to have wide-ranging executive and legislative responsibilities and powers, with the General Superintendent being required to refer most matters to it before he could act, but in the 1875 constitution William Booth gave himself the power of last resort to override any resolutions of the Annual Conference with which he was in disagreement. The final authority in the affairs of the Mission was therefore no longer Annual Conference but William Booth as the General Superintendent.

However, whether under the 1870 or 1875 constitution, the system of government remained cumbersome. William Booth had worked hard at giving the Annual Conference its rightful place in the management of the Mission ever since he founded it, but working the system required from both the General Superintendent and the members of Conference an enormous investment of time and energy. Frustration with the often interminable discussions on seemingly irrelevant matters eventually boiled over.

Just before Christmas 1876 a deputation of senior evangelists headed by Bramwell Booth and George Scott Railton, Secretary of the Mission, approached William Booth.

'We gave up our lives to work under you and those you should appoint,' they said, 'rather than under one another.'

'You tell us what to do,' added William Ridsdel, later a commissioner of The Salvation Army, 'and we'll do it. I can't see the good of a lot of talk, with one wanting one thing and another another.'[3]

As a result William Booth called a meeting of the Conference Committee – a sub-committee of the full Annual Conference – but invited *all* the evangelists to attend. They met on 23 and 24 January 1877. William Booth addressed them on 'The Constitution and the Future of the Mission' and a lively discussion followed.

The conclusions reached without a dissenting voice were that government by committee was too slow, that decisions were continually required on important personnel, finance and property matters, that the General Superintendent must be free to take action on these matters, and that the Annual Conference should no longer be a legislative body but a 'council of war'.[4] William Booth immediately began to work to the new plan.

However, the full Annual Conference itself – which only two years previously had formally adopted the 1875 constitution – remained to be reckoned with, but with William Booth having taken the precaution of inviting all evangelists to the January 1877 meeting of the Conference Committee, the ground was already prepared.

The Annual Conference 1877

When the full Annual Conference met in June 1877 for its yearly meeting, William Booth candidly admitted the failure of his plans as embodied in the 1875 constitution. He spoke of the general frustration felt, and said: 'It became evident to me we were drifting in a wrong direction. I confess I have been much to blame in this matter. Under the idea that teaching my brethren management and law-making would increase their sense of responsibility and unite us more fully together, I launched Conference on a sea of legislation which all came to nothing.'[5]

William Booth then explained that the Annual Conference would in future years take the form of a council of war on the military pattern whereby 'the commander-in-chief calls the principal officers around him to receive information and counsel from all … and then … resolves upon a programme of operation'.

He also announced the abolition of the Conference Committee, but added: 'If any great question involving the happiness of us all were to arise, the only plan would be, it seems to me, to call together the most experienced of our brethren, and if need be all the others. But for all ordinary purposes it seems by far the simplest way, the only mutually satisfactory plan, for me to deal with the brethren personally and when possible face to face.'

William Booth was going to be the Christian Mission's commander-in-chief. 'This is a question of confidence as between you and me,' he thundered, 'and if you can't trust me it is of no use for us to attempt to work together. *Confidence in God and in me are absolutely indispensable both now and ever afterwards.'*

It is clear that the 65 members present at the June 1877 Conference had confidence in both God and in William Booth, for in a 'heartily endorsed' resolution they confirmed that the General Superintendent would in future have the freedom to act without the restraint of Conference.

William Booth's bold new style of executive leadership resulted in new evangelists joining the Mission, new stations opening and new converts being gained. A powerful new dynamic was at work. The Christian Mission was on its way to becoming The Salvation Army.

Yet legally the 1875 constitution was still in place. Legally there were still two authorities – the General Superintendent and Annual Conference. William Booth knew that the changes in the governance of the Mission that he had brought about had to be formalised by changes to its constitution.

He saw the meeting of the Annual Conference to be held in August 1878 as the opportunity to make those changes. He announced it as a 'Council of War', and planned that during its course the members of Annual Conference would be asked to vote to revoke the 1875 constitution and vote to adopt a new one.

That is why on a spring morning of 1878 William and Bramwell Booth were in the office of Mr Cozens-Hardy. They had before them the current 1875 constitution that was about to be revoked, and reviewed its provisions together. It was a remarkable document. Though annulled at the 1878 War Congress, a number of its provisions have since been reactivated and are now part of the Army's present-day constitution.

The 1875 constitution

The constitution of 1875,[6] after describing the history of the Mission, confirming its name as the Christian Mission, and setting out the 11 points of doctrine, declared that: 'The Christian Mission is and shall be hereafter for ever under the oversight, direction and control of some one person', but there would 'always be an annual assembly called the Conference'. Its members were the Mission's 'life evangelists' named in the deed together with other appointed delegates.

William Booth had unique and exceptional powers. He was to be the General Superintendent 'for the term of his natural life, unless he shall resign or unless he shall be by disease or some other cause disqualified for discharging the duties of such office, such disqualification to be declared by the unanimous sentence of the Conference'.

William Booth could therefore be removed from office, but only if the members of the Conference *unanimously* agreed. Just one solitary supporter would be enough for him to remain in office. Considering that his wife Catherine and son Bramwell were among the 46 'life members' of Conference listed in the 1875 constitution, his deposition was something of an unlikely prospect.

William Booth had power of veto over Conference, enabling him 'to set aside all or any of the decisions and resolutions of Conference'. He also had the power to appoint his own successor 'by deed'. Appointing the next General Superintendent by legal deed enrolled in Chancery would be like anointing his successor publicly, and there is no indication that William Booth ever did so.

Crucially, William Booth had the power of annulling or altering anything in the 1875 constitution 'with the concurrence of three fourths of the members of the Conference'.

Future General Superintendents would have fewer powers than William Booth. Only William Booth was able to appoint his own successor. Future General Superintendents would be elected by Conference.

Only William Booth and his immediate successor would hold office for life. Beyond that, all future General Superintendents would be 'appointed for a term of five years' but could be 're-elected to the same office for the same term'.

Only William Booth had absolute veto power over Conference. Future General Superintendents would 'have power to set aside or veto any resolution or decision of the Conference', but Conference would be able to overturn the veto by a two-thirds vote. Conference would therefore have the last word.

Future General Superintendents could be 'removed from office by a vote of three fourths of all the persons composing the Conference after a fair investigation by the Conference'.

By far the longest section of the 1875 constitution was devoted to the executive and legislative powers and responsibilities of Conference. These included accepting and appointing evangelists, and writing and updating the 'Rules and Regulations' of the Mission. Legally the Mission was a charitable trust and the members of Conference were its trustees. As such they were legally responsible for holding and managing the Mission's property and financial assets for the furtherance of its purposes.

Very significantly, the 1875 constitution also mandated Conference to review the constitution and government of the Christian Mission periodically in order to consider whether any improvements could be made. The first review was to take place after five years and subsequent reviews were to be held at 10-year intervals. Changes to the constitution could be effected by Conference if a two-thirds majority in two consecutive annual meetings was in favour. Certain subjects were exempted, for example the doctrines of the Mission, the powers of the General Superintendent, and the right of women to hold *any* office within the Mission.

When Mr Cozens-Hardy and his two visitors had completed their review of the 1875 constitution, the lawyer listened and made notes as William Booth outlined in detail the changes he wanted included in the new constitution.

During the next few weeks Mr Cozens-Hardy worked on the text, and when he next met with William and Bramwell Booth it was a very different document that lay on the table. What hit the eye immediately was its brevity. It was only a third as long! The differences were dramatic.

The 1878 constitution

The constitution of 1878, reproduced in full in Appendix I, is at the heart of the story told in this book and we therefore need to pause to examine it. Following a brief survey of the history of the Christian Mission the constitution consists of six clauses. *'Firstly'* deals with the name of the Mission. *'Secondly'* sets out its doctrines. Then follows:

Thirdly
That the Christian Mission will 'always be under the oversight, direction and control of some one person, called the General Superintendent'. The General Superintendent is to be the sole legal trustee of the Mission's property and funds, but can be assisted by other trustees, and must annually publish an audited balance sheet.

Fourthly
That William Booth will 'continue to be for the term of his natural life the General Superintendent of the Christian Mission' unless he resigns such office.

Fifthly
That William Booth and every General Superintendent who succeeds him will 'have power to appoint his successor to the office of General Superintendent', with 'all the rights, powers and authorities of the office' vesting 'in the person so appointed'. The successor will take up his appointment 'upon the decease of William Booth or other General Superintendent appointing him, or at such other period as may be named in the document appointing him'.

Sixthly

That it is 'the duty of every General Superintendent to make in writing, as soon as conveniently may be after his appointment, a statement as to his successor, or as to the means which are to be taken for the appointment of a successor, at the decease of the General Superintendent, or upon his ceasing to perform the duties of the office'. Such statement is 'to be signed by the General Superintendent and delivered in a sealed envelope to the solicitor for the time being of the Christian Mission, but such may be altered at will by the General Superintendent at any time during his continuance in office upon a new statement being signed by him'.

What is most significant in the 1878 constitution is what disappeared from its 1875 predecessor. Gone are all mentions of Conference and references to the relationship of William Booth and his successors to that body. There is now only one authority – the General Superintendent. Gone is the concept of multiple trustees being legally responsible for the Mission's assets – there is now only one legal trustee, the General Superintendent. Gone is the mention of William Booth being uniquely empowered to appoint his successor 'by deed', and that this immediate successor will serve for life. Gone is the reference to subsequent General Superintendents being elected and serving for a renewable term of five years. Gone is any indication whatsoever as to how a General Superintendent might be removed from office. Gone is the clause giving power for the constitution to be revoked or varied.

Instead *all* General Superintendents – not only William Booth – are given the power either (a) to appoint their successors, or (b) to make a statement 'as to the means which are to be taken for the appointment of a successor'. The system to be used is no longer that of a legal deed but of a 'sealed envelope' – the contents of which can be altered at any time by the General Superintendent – which will become operative on his death or 'upon his ceasing to perform the duties of the office'.

A surprising feature of the 1878 constitution is the open-endedness of the second option for selecting a successor, the option whereby the 'sealed envelope' would contain instructions 'as to the means to be taken for the appointment of a successor'. These means – which would not be revealed until the envelope was opened – could be anything from, say, certain senior evangelists being delegated to elect the successor, to all members of the Mission being given a vote, or to the Archbishop of Canterbury being asked to select the next General Superintendent!

The existence of this second constitutional option for selecting a successor was never publicised. *Orders and Regulations for Field Officers* published eight years later in 1886 simply stated that 'the General must and will appoint his successor' – and it became the accepted assumption that this is what the constitution required him to do.

What is even more surprising in the 1878 constitution is that William Booth did not retain for himself or his successors the power to change or revoke the constitution. In the 1875 constitution William Booth had given himself the right to vary the constitution 'with the concurrence of three fourths of the members of Conference'. In the same constitution he had also mandated that Annual Conference *must* review the constitution after five years and then at 10-yearly intervals. Changes could be made if two thirds of members at two successive annual meetings of Conference concurred. In the 1878 constitution there was no longer a Conference to undertake such a task, but astonishingly in the new constitution William Booth retained no powers of amendment whatsoever, not even for the General Superintendents.

William Booth had been very explicit in his instructions to Mr Cozens-Hardy. He did not wish the new constitution to include power for it to be revoked or varied in any way, whether by himself or by any of his successors. This was so out of the ordinary that we can be sure that Mr Cozens-Hardy would have pressed William Booth hard on the point. We do not have his exact words, but one can almost hear him saying:

'You do realise, Mr Booth, that if you do not include a clause giving you or your successors power to vary the deed, the constitution can be changed by only one higher authority – by the

British Parliament itself. By this deed you are creating a charitable trust of which you are the sole trustee. I cannot emphasise strongly enough, that unless there is a clause that gives power to vary the deed, a trustee cannot alter the trust at will. He cannot vary the deed even if there are good reasons for doing so. I therefore beg you to consider this point very carefully.'

William Booth, however, remained insistent. There would be no variation clause. One can hear Mr Cozens-Hardy trying again:

'Mr Booth, may I respectfully remind you that you wrote a constitution in 1870 only to rescind it five years later. Then in 1875 you wrote another constitution, and now three years later you wish to annul that one. How can you be sure that you will not want to amend or revoke this new 1878 constitution in time? No one knows what the future may hold. Would you not be wise to include a clause giving you power to vary this constitution?'

Bramwell Booth looked quizzically at his father, but William Booth was adamant. This constitution was to be set in stone, and to be set in stone for all time. It was not going to include a clause giving power for it to be changed or revoked.

It is difficult at this distance in time to know exactly why William Booth felt so strongly on the matter, but we can try to enter into his thinking. The 1878 constitution contained what he felt was a divinely inspired plan for the Mission. It is therefore likely that he did not wish to empower his successors to tamper with that plan, or to give them the possibility of changing the doctrines, abandoning the concept of one-person control, or altering the way in which General Superintendents would be selected. Furthermore, having abolished Conference there was no other 'authority' whose concurrence for any proposed variations could be stipulated in the deed.

Whatever his reasons, William Booth made the 1878 constitution non-variable. The official history of The Salvation Army records this momentous decision in one brief sentence: 'Power to alter the constitution was not retained, consequently the [1878] deed poll can be varied only by an Act of Parliament.'[7]

It was a decision William Booth was to live to regret.

The War Congress 1878

A few months later, in August 1878, the evangelists of the Christian Mission met in London for what was to be the last meeting of the Annual Conference. George Scott Railton, in his editorial in the May 1878 edition of *The Christian Mission Magazine,* had prepared the hearts and minds of the evangelists for what was about to transpire. 'There have been more than enough conferences, and congresses, and committees and deliberations,' he wrote. 'It is time to act. There is not a moment to lose.' The evangelists were going to gather for a conference to end all conferences. In the War Congress the commander-in-chief was going to meet with his principal officers, receive their counsel, set out his plans – and lead the attack; and so it turned out. The 1878 War Congress was a watershed event in every way.

The devotional meetings saw spiritual outpourings as never witnessed before in the life of the Mission. The business meetings changed history. These sessions took place at the Mission's headquarters in 272 Whitechapel Road, with about 200 evangelists and other delegates present.

William Booth's first address was on 'The Past of the War' and he said: 'Let us try to look at the flaws of the past. Let us never be ashamed to learn. And let us say to all our critics, "Be merciful to us." We are travelling along a road on which none ever trod before … I was brought up amongst Wesleyan Methodists … I have had much to unlearn, and it is very difficult to unlearn being a Methodist. But I think I have almost got out of my last skin. I see the land. Sometimes when you are out at sea the sailors see the land ahead a long time before you can. And if any of my brethren are inclined to say they don't see where we are going, I would say to them, I see the land if you don't. Trust me. Have faith in me and be happy.'[8]

Preparing the ground for becoming sole trustee, he spoke sharply about unauthorised expenditure by stations and unwise decisions regarding property. 'Nobody shall run me into debt. There has been a great deal of this.' He was critical of evangelists who had let out Mission halls for non-religious purposes. 'I never let our property be touched with impunity, and I am going to have a thousand times more power to protect it in the future than in the past.'

The formal addresses at the congress were interspersed with testimonies and accounts of the advances that had been made during the past year. William Booth for the first time presented a statistical report for the previous year – which not surprisingly was 'interrupted by prolonged and repeated shouts of thanksgiving'. Three of these sets of figures are of special interest to us. They show not only the marked upturn in numbers since William Booth had in practice taken full charge in early 1877, but also the relative smallness of the Mission at the time that the 1878 constitution was adopted – a point that was to be reiterated in years to come.

	May 1877	30 June 1878	Increase
Stations occupied	29	50	21
Evangelists	31	88	57
Members	2,669	4,400	1,731

William Booth then spoke on 'The Future of the War'. 'Dwelling upon the difficulty of the task undertaken, to overthrow the kingdom of Satan and establish the kingdom of God,' reads the official report, 'he showed the necessity for the utmost possible force, and therefore for adopting God's plans of organising a force upon a thoroughly military system.'

On Wednesday 7 August 1878 the Annual Conference 'in order to secure greater freedom for effectuating and furthering the principles of the Christian Mission' formally resolved 'to wholly and absolutely annul' the 1875 constitution. It thereby voted itself out of existence. With Mr Thomas Whittington, the Mission's solicitor, in attendance, William Booth sat down at a small table in front of them all and signed a deed poll to this effect. The 1875 constitution was no more.

William Booth then, 'with the unanimous and hearty concurrence of the Conference', held up the new constitution for all to see and with a flourish of his pen executed the new deed poll establishing the constitution of 1878. It was one of the most fateful documents he ever signed. By this Deed Poll of 7 August 1878 William Booth legally became the commander-in-chief, sole trustee and only 'authority' of the Christian Mission. Both the annulment deed and the foundation deed were duly enrolled in the Close Rolls of the Chancery on 13 August 1878.

Swept away also was the plethora of committees at local level where as many as half a dozen different official bodies might meet every week. 'The poor convert', wrote George Scott Railton, 'who had been brought to the penitent form two months since must appear trembling before an elders' meeting. If he ventured to aspire to public speaking he must pass another examination before the exhorters' meeting. Did he wish to distribute tracts, then he must see the tracts committee. If the tract distributor came across a case of extreme need, then he must apply to another committee for the shilling or two which he might be allowed to give', and quarterly there were the local preachers' and elders' meetings. 'Oh, those elders' meetings,' sighed Railton, 'prolonged till midnight many a time!'[9]

Perhaps it is little wonder that George Scott Railton, in looking back on the War Congress of 1878, could write: 'I do not believe when that congress ended there was an evangelist or delegate whose heart was not full of joy and satisfaction.'[10]

Within a few months of the War Congress, the move towards a military style executive was given the greatest impetus of all when William Booth changed the name of the Christian Mission to 'The Salvation Army'. From that point the work exploded into a new dimension. By 1886 – just eight years later – the 50 stations in Britain had become 1,006 Salvation Army corps, the 88 evangelists in Britain had become 2,260 Salvation Army officers, and the Army had commenced operations in 12 other countries!

The change of name was formalised by an endorsement to the 1878 deed dated 24 June 1880. Curiously and inexplicably this endorsement was not enrolled in the Supreme Court of Judicature until 26 years later, on 20 April 1906.

The first 'sealed envelope'

In the new 1878 constitution William Booth had committed himself to make in writing as soon as convenient a statement regarding his successor or the means to be taken for the appointment of a successor. Early death by disease or accident was a permanent factor of life in Victorian times. There was now no electoral body to elect his successor should he fail to discharge this responsibility, and should he suddenly die the Mission would be left in chaos. The matter could not long be delayed.

It is evident that from the earliest times William Booth saw Bramwell Booth as his successor, but in August 1878 Bramwell was only 22 years of age. However brilliant he might be, did he have the experience and acceptability to step into the breech immediately should William meet with an untimely death?

William Booth waited for 13 months before committing himself,[11] but on 29 September 1879, unbeknown to the 23-year-old Bramwell Booth, William Booth wrote a statement in his own hand:

> In pursuance of the power entrusted to me by the Deed Poll of the Christian Mission, now known as The Salvation Army, I hereby will and decree that in case of my death, my son William Bramwell Booth shall take my place as General Superintendent of the said Christian Mission or Salvation Army, and I wish him to posses all the power and influence now possessed by me in the said Army according to the covenants and provisions of the said Deed Poll, and I hope and desire that all my faithful people will receive him and love him and follow him as they have received, loved and followed his father in the name of the almighty God, so that they may be led on to further victory and blessing. Amen!
>
> William Booth
> General of The Salvation Army

William Booth asked Mr Thomas Whittington to witness the statement. He then placed it in an envelope, sealed the envelope and handed it to the solicitor for safekeeping.

In the early 1880s Dr Washington Ranger and his younger partner Mr William Frost were appointed legal advisers to The Salvation

Army in succession to Mr Whittington. The 'sealed envelope' was therefore transferred for safekeeping to the office of the new solicitors.

When after some time William Booth privately described for Dr Ranger the style of the statement within the 'sealed envelope' – written as a will – the legal adviser suggested that it should be replaced by a more formal legal document. Dr Ranger therefore prepared the necessary document and on 21 August 1890 met with William Booth in his office together with two witnesses. On this day – 44 days before Catherine Booth was promoted to Glory – William Booth confirmed his choice of Bramwell Booth to be his successor by inserting his name into the document. He signed the statement, folded it so that the two others present could sign to witness his signature but without seeing the name he had written, placed it in an envelope, wrote the date on the outside of the envelope, and then sealed it. The new 'sealed envelope' was once again entrusted to Dr Ranger, and the previous envelope was destroyed.

As Chief of the Staff, Bramwell Booth knew of the existence of the 'sealed envelope' and William Booth frequently hinted to Bramwell and to others – even publicly – that Bramwell was the chosen successor, but at no time did he say so outright.

Soon after confirming Bramwell's nomination by signing the new legal document in 1890, William Booth began to have second thoughts about the succession arrangements he had established by the 1878 constitution.

Even popes can change their mind.

Chapter Two

Second Thoughts

'NOW, excuse my asking,' said Mr William Gladstone with a serious and somewhat apologetic air as he gazed intently at General William Booth, 'but I am sure that the question of the successorship to the very important position that you hold will have occupied your earnest attention. Will you tell me whether any arrangements have been made for filling up this post when the time arrives for your removal from it?'

William Ewart Gladstone, now in his 88th year, the most impressive statesman of his day, four times Prime Minister under Queen Victoria, an Oxford scholar and a leading churchman, was living in retirement at his country seat of Hawarden Castle, North Wales. William Booth had suggested he might call on Mr Gladstone following weekend meetings he was conducting at Keighley Corps. They were seated together in front of a roaring fire in Mr Gladstone's library. It was Monday afternoon 21 December 1896.

Mr Gladstone, famed for his incisive mind and effortless command of language, was keen to learn as much as possible about William Booth and his Army. The conversation ranged widely, from the Army's militarism and the Anglo-Saxon factor in its worldwide spread, to the Army in continental Europe, experimental religion, the sacrifices made by Salvationists – and the succession to the office of General.

The interview was so significant that William Booth published an account of it some months later in a slim but meaty hardback entitled *A Talk with Mr Gladstone at his own Fireside.*[1]

William Booth's description of his response to Mr Gladstone about arrangements made for his succession gives us an insight into his thinking at that time. With the assurances given to Mr Gladstone comes a hint of further thoughts, and the first ever mention of what later was to be known as the High Council.

'In as few words as possible,' wrote William Booth, 'I endeavoured to describe the arrangements that have been made for this important business. That it was the first duty of the General for the time being to nominate his successor in writing, such nomination being placed under cover in the hands of the solicitors for the Army, whose duty it was to deposit it, unopened, in a place of security. That its contents need only be known to the General himself, whoever he might be, he having the power to change the appointment at any time, as his judgment might direct.

'Mr Gladstone listened to these statements, and then asked whether there were any arrangements made which would give legal force to such a procedure. Was there a deed? "Yes," I said, "a deed drawn after much thought, settled by eminent counsel, and enrolled in the High Court." "That is well," he responded.

'He was evidently gratified that the matter had received the careful attention which its importance demanded, but then his mind reverted to the novelty of the methods employed.

'He seemed to wander over the whole world, looking in upon every work – religious, philanthropic, and secular – at present in existence, and turning back upon the centuries past in order that he might find an instance similar to, or illustrative of, the method adopted for arranging the successorship, as he termed it.

'It was a peculiar position, he said, that we had taken up. "Even the Pope is elected by a Conclave of Cardinals, and I think we must go back to the 16th century to find an example of a system of personal nomination by the person occupying the post of authority, similar to the one you have chosen."

'He appeared to closely sympathise with me when I described the anxiety with which I had regarded the question, and how, for years, it had steadily been considered.

'He was still further interested when I mentioned a scheme, now being completed, for providing against the possible contingency of a General passing away who had neglected the appointment of his successor, or who, for some calamitous reasons, had been proved incapable for, or unworthy of, his position, and for soliciting a new General in an Assembly of all our commissioners throughout the world.

'I named one or two of the possibilities that might occur, and he added, "Yes, and the possibility of heresy would come under that category."'

Seeking safeguards

William Booth left Hawarden Castle with much to think about. He had for some time become increasingly concerned that the succession arrangements outlined in the 1878 constitution might at some time go wrong. Not only might a General fail to complete a 'sealed envelope', but his appointed successor might refuse office. Furthermore, what if the General and the person he had appointed as his successor were to die together, say, in a train or car accident?

The Founder's concern about the potentially precarious nature of the succession arrangements was given an unexpected impetus a few days after his return to London. He was driving with Bramwell from International Headquarters to King's Cross Station when, near Mount Pleasant Post Office and too close to the horse and cab for comfort, a bomb exploded – the work of political extremists. A shaken Genereal leant over to his son and whispered, 'What a mess the Army would have been in had we both gone to Heaven at the same time!'[2]

William Booth had also become concerned that the 1878 constitution provided no way of removing from office a General who, as he had put it to Mr Gladstone, 'had been proved incapable for, or unworthy of, his position'.

Should any such situation arise it would have serious consequences for the Army. William Booth had therefore been working on a scheme to rectify these omissions in the 1878 constitution. For him, the interview with Mr Gladstone became the tipping point. A General who had become a heretic? He shuddered at the thought. Some safeguard had to be built into the system, but how?

One of William Booth's favourite sayings was: 'What I have done, I can undo' – but by his own decision the 1878 Deed Poll could neither be revoked nor varied. He remembered how Mr Cozens-Hardy had urged him to include a clause that would give him power to change it. He had chosen not to have such a clause. Only Parliament could now vary the 1878 constitution. What he had done, he could not undo.

To William Booth an appeal to Parliament was out of the question. He was determined not to place his living, spiritual movement called The Salvation Army in thrall to a secular institution. For the Army to ask the British Parliament to legislate on the General's succession was as unthinkable as the Roman Catholic Church asking the Italian parliament to determine how the Pope should be chosen.

William Booth had the preliminary outline of a scheme in his mind. He had discussed it with Dr Washington Ranger and Mr William Frost, but however much they turned the matter over the dilemma remained: the 1878 Deed could not be varied.

The legal advisers suggested that the three most eminent constitutional lawyers in Britain should be consulted. The Booths always considered money spent on getting the best available legal brains to be money well spent. Therefore Mr Herbert Asquith, afterwards Prime Minister of Great Britain, Mr Richard Haldane, afterwards Lord Chancellor, and Mr Charles Sargant, afterwards Lord Justice, were retained.

These expert constitutional lawyers agreed that the 1878 Deed could neither be revoked nor varied, but after studying the matter in depth they arrived at the conclusion that an 'amending deed' might be possible, as long as its provisions did not in any way vary the original deed but only amplified or supplemented it. It would be a delicate project, for if the amending deed actually varied the provisions of the original deed in any way it would not be legally valid.

The legal team, after many months of work and many discussions with Bramwell Booth as the Chief of the Staff, drew up the draft of a 'supplementary deed' and presented it to William Booth. The deed had all the hallmarks of the brilliant legal minds that lay behind its drafting. It was long. The supplementary deed was in fact three times longer than the original 1878 Deed. The annex being added to the house dwarfed the house itself. However, the supplementary deed would ensure that there could never be a breakdown in the succession to the Generalship, and provided means for removing a General from office.

The supplementary deed was ready by late 1897, but William Booth had hesitations about signing it. He in fact hesitated for a full seven years. During those years, wherever he travelled in the world he discussed the draft deed with his senior leaders, incorporating into the text suggestions made, but he still drew back from executing the deed.

William Booth hesitated for two reasons. Firstly because he feared that the provision for removing a General from office might be misused. The law of unintended consequences had to be reckoned with. Secondly because he feared that the supplementary deed would not be legally valid. Had Mr Cozens-Hardy not emphasised that 'the trustee of a charitable trust cannot alter the trust at will'? It seemed to him that with the proposed supplementary deed he was coming very near to doing precisely that. By the terms of the 1878 Deed it was not possible to remove a General from office. With the proposed supplementary deed it would become possible. Did that merely amplify the original deed or did it change it? It was a debatable point.

The three constitutional lawyers had recommended that the deed should be approved by a meeting of officers representing all the countries in which the Army was at work as this would help to cement its legal standing. The International Congress planned for 1904 was to be followed by an International Staff Council two weeks later at which senior officers from all over the world would be present. The staff council could provide an ideal opportunity to present and explain the deed and to execute it.

After seven years of delay William Booth decided to grasp the nettle. He asked Bramwell Booth to get the final text of the deed prepared by the legal team. He also asked him to obtain final confirmation from the three eminent counsel that it was legally in order for him to proceed with the execution of the deed and that its validity would not some day be challenged in a court of law. The three top constitutional lawyers of the day responded:

> In our opinion the executing of an Amending Deed in the form of the draft which is identified by the writing of our names in the margin, would be a reasonable and expedient act on the part of the General of The Salvation Army.
>
> It is not indeed competent for the General by the execution of any deed, or the adoption of any other means, to completely effect any alteration of, or addition to, the trusts of the original Deed of Constitution.
>
> All the proposed changes, however, are in the direction of limiting rather than increasing the powers of the General for the time being, and of more completely ensuring the carrying on of the trust in the various contingencies referred to. And we are of the opinion that the provisions of the Amending Deed are not only likely to lessen the occasions of uncertainty in the future, but will as time goes on become invested with much added authority.
>
> We accordingly advise the execution of the Amending Deed as it now stands.[3]

The way was clear to proceed. As Bramwell Booth himself was later to sum it up: 'The 1904 Deed was designed for the purpose among others of minimising the possibility of doubt, dispute or litigation as regards the succession to the office of General of The Salvation Army', and that thereby 'provision was made for filling vacancies in the office of General of The Salvation Army, supplementing but not in any way curtailing or restricting the power for that purpose conferred by the [1878] Deed of Constitution.'[4]

The 1904 supplementary constitution

The constitutional crisis that engulfed The Salvation Army in 1929 hinged on the 1904 Supplementary Deed of Constitution, and we therefore need to examine in what ways it 'supplemented' the original 1878 Deed of Constitution.

The 1904 Supplementary Deed in fact only supplements one clause of the 1878 Deed – the sixth – the clause that deals with the 'sealed envelope' and the 'appointment of a successor at the decease of the General Superintendent or upon his ceasing to perform the duties of the office'.

To avoid any problems with the succession of a person named in the 'sealed envelope' by reason of 'the death, incapacity, refusal or unwillingness of an individual', the 1904 Deed supplements the 1878 Deed by decreeing that the statement in the 'sealed envelope' is to be 'succeeded as soon as possible by one or more alternative statements numbered in the intended order of priority'. Such alternative statements can 'be revoked or altered at will by the General at any time', and are only to be opened 'in the event of the prior statement failing to result in the appointment of a successor', and otherwise are to be 'destroyed unopened'.

Supplementing the 1878 Deed to allow for a General to be removed from office was a harder assignment for the constitutional experts for, as noted, the text of the 1878 Deed does not include an explicit provision for removing a General from office. All it says is that the 'sealed envelope' becomes operative either 'at the decease of the General Superintendent *or upon his ceasing to perform the duties of the office'* (my italics). It does not explain the circumstances under which a General Superintendent might cease 'to perform the duties of the office'.

The constitutional lawyers could not 'vary', they could only 'supplement'. So with great ingenuity they took hold of the italicised phrase above, and like a preacher who starts with what seems an unpromising text but manages to preach for an hour on it, they produced a complete 12-page scheme by which a General of The

Salvation Army might 'cease to perform the duties of the office' *because he has been removed from it.* The entire scheme was by way of 'supplementing' the one short phrase 'upon his ceasing to perform the duties of the office'.

Clause 2

The key section of the Supplementary Deed 1904 that deals with the removal from office of a General is Clause 2 and its three subclauses. These clauses were to be microscopically examined in the lead-up to the 1929 crisis.[5]

'Every General', declares Clause 2, 'shall be deemed to cease to perform the duties of the office within Clause 6 of the [1878] Deed of Constitution and to vacate such office upon the happening of any of the following events.' The three subclauses set out the possible 'events' that will result in a General having to vacate office.

Subclause 1

A General shall be deemed to cease to perform the duties of the office and to vacate it:

> If a majority of commissioners of The Salvation Army in active service 'amounting to at least four in five declare by writing under their hands that they are satisfied that the General is of unsound mind or permanently incapacitated by mental or physical infirmity from the adequate performance of the duties of his office. ... Any such declaration may be made by one or several documents and need not be signed simultaneously so long as there shall not be an interval of more than three calendar months between the first signature and the last.

If the General is 'of unsound mind or permanently incapacitated mentally or physically from the adequate performance of the duties of his office', a majority of four in five of the commissioners of The Salvation Army can remove him from office by a 'write-in', without them having to meet together.

If the General is removed from office on these grounds, the 'sealed envelope' containing the name of his successor or

34

instructions as to how he shall be chosen remains valid, as long as, in the case of *mental* incapacity, the envelope is dated earlier than one month from when he was declared to be of unsound mind.

Subclause 2

A General shall be deemed to cease to perform the duties of the office and to vacate it:

> If all the commissioners of The Salvation Army or a majority of such commissioners amounting to at least nine in ten declare by writing under their hands that they are satisfied that the General is in consequence of bankruptcy or insolvency, dereliction of duty, notorious misconduct, or other circumstances unfit to continue to perform the duties of his office.

Should such a regrettable situation arise, a majority of nine out of ten commissioners can remove the General from office, again by a 'write-in', without them needing to assemble. If the General is removed from office under the provisions of this subclause the 'sealed envelope' becomes null and void.

Subclause 2 lists a number of specific contingencies which give grounds for removing the General from office, but in the best legal tradition ends with a 'catch-all' phrase. If nine out of ten commissioners are satisfied that the General 'in consequence of ... *other circumstances*' is unfit to continue to perform the duties of his office, he has to vacate office. This very open-ended phrase was to be minutely examined as the storm clouds gathered in 1929.

In Subclauses 1 and 2 a new 'authority' within the Army appears – the commissioners in active service. With the abolition of Conference in 1878, the General had been left as the sole 'authority' within the Army. However, in the 1904 Supplementary Deed William Booth limits the powers of the General. Instead of the Conference with its evangelists it is now the commissioners who in certain very defined circumstances can act as a second and counterbalancing 'authority' within the Army.

Subclause 3

Subclauses 1 and 2 deal with cases where the unfitness of the General on health or moral grounds is absolutely clear-cut. Subclause 3 deals with less clear situations in which the fitness or unfitness for office of the General is a matter that has yet to be established. According to Subclause 3 a General shall be deemed to cease to perform the duties of the office and to vacate it:

> If a resolution adjudicating the General unfit for office and removing him therefrom shall be passed by a majority of not less than three-fourths of the members present and voting of the High Council of The Salvation Army hereinafter referred to.

The mention of the High Council in Subclause 3 in connection with adjudicated unfitness is the first reference in a constitutional document to that Council. It introduces yet a further alternative 'authority' within the Army. It is not only the commissioners who constitute an alternative 'authority'. The High Council is also such an 'authority'.

The High Council

The three words 'hereinafter referred to' in Subclause 3 pave the way for a full description in the 1904 Supplementary Deed of the powers and responsibilities of the High Council. Key points are that:

- The High Council is an adjudicatory body charged with the responsibility of judging whether the General is fit or unfit to continue in office.
- The summoning of a High Council is triggered by either the Chief of the Staff and four other commissioners, or seven commissioners not including the Chief of the Staff, jointly requisitioning (requesting) that a Council be called.
- The very act of the High Council being requisitioned invalidates the 'sealed envelope', but if the High Council

adjudicates the General fit for office the 'sealed envelope' is reactivated.

- The High Council is also an electoral body responsible for electing the next General if the previous General has been removed from office, or has failed to leave a 'sealed envelope' with the solicitor, or has become ineligible to appoint his successor, in which case the 'sealed envelope' is to be destroyed unopened.
- The membership of the High Council is to consist of all commissioners and 'all the officers holding territorial commands in the Army in any part of the world, whatever their rank in the Army'.
- The High Council is not an executive or legislative body, but stands dissolved *immediately* a new General is elected and accepts office.

Clauses excluded and included

None of the three subclauses in the Supplementary Deed of 1904 dealing with ways in which a General would be deemed 'to cease to perform the duties of the office' covers the most obvious way of all – namely that he might vacate office by voluntarily resigning from it. The right of a General to resign from office is mentioned in passing later in the deed where it states that the 'sealed envelope' is valid 'if the vacation of office of General shall take place through death *or resignation*', and must have been considered too self-evident to merit a separate statement. However, the lack of an explicit statement granting successors to William Booth the right to resign from office – absent not only in the 1904 Deed but also in the original 1878 Deed – was to lead some to question in 1929 whether it was legally possible for a General to resign.

Significantly, a variation clause was this time included in the deed. The 1904 Supplementary Deed of Constitution could be varied or revoked by William Booth or any succeeding General – but only with the consent of two thirds of the commissioners, one of the two new 'authorities' within the Army.

All of these provisions in the 1904 Supplementary Deed were made, according to the three eminent constitutional experts, without legally 'varying' the 1878 Deed, only 'supplementing' it. The constitutional lawyers earned every penny of their fee.

The International Congress and International Staff Council 1904

Salvationists from the four corners of the world converged on London for the third International Congress to be held from 24 June to 8 July 1904. The Army had grown and extended beyond all recognition from when it had 4,400 members in 1878. Worldwide there were now 14,291 officers and around 260,000 soldiers, recruits and adherents.[6] The Army was at work in 49 countries.

A special International Congress Hall, seating 5,000, was erected in the Strand in Central London. It was after washing his hands in a bucket of water when checking the completion of work on this building that General William Booth was received by His Majesty King Edward VII at Buckingham Palace. Commented the *St James's Gazette* after this royal recognition: 'General Booth wears no inverted commas round his title now.'

The congress made an immense impact on its participants and the people of London alike. When the series of public meetings ended, William Booth met with 1,000 officers in the Clapton Congress Hall for the International Staff Council. He asked Mr William Frost to be present for the second morning session on 26 July 1904, informing him that he wished to sign the Supplementary Deed in the presence of the officers at the close of that session and before lunch.

When the session ended, William Booth explained the background to the Supplementary Deed of Constitution and briefly summarised its content. Quoting from the preamble to the deed, he emphasised that its purpose was 'to minimise the possibility of doubt, dispute or litigation' in the succession of future Generals. He then asked Commissioner Frederick de Latour Booth-Tucker (Commander of the American Forces), Commissioner T. Henry Howard (Foreign Secretary at International Headquarters), Commissioner Ulysse Cosandey (Territorial Commander for France, Italy and Belgium) and Commissioner Adelaide Cox (Commissioner for Women's Social Work in Great Britain) to come and stand by him.

William Booth offered fervent prayer and then, seating himself at a table on the platform as he had done when signing the 1878 Deed, he executed the 1904 Supplementary Deed while everyone watched. Mr William Frost and the four commissioners signed as witnesses.

The Army's leaders and senior officers from around the world, recognising that they were present at an historic turning point in the Army's development, burst into prolonged applause. While the ovation continued, William Booth, ready as always to add a touch of humour to even the most serious moments, said with a grim smile to those nearest him:

'I have just signed my own death warrant!'[7]

He hadn't, of course. Yet unforeseen consequences were to flow from the events of that day.

Chapter Three

A Smooth Transition

DOCTOR Washington Ranger and Mr William Frost, the Army's solicitors, arrived in good time at International Headquarters for the 4pm meeting. It was Wednesday 21 August 1912. William Booth had been promoted to Glory the night before at 13 minutes past 10. Since then The Salvation Army had been without a General. In his briefcase Dr Ranger carried the 'sealed envelope' which William Booth had lodged with him in 1890.

The meeting was to be held in the Chief of the Staff's office, and those invited began to assemble some minutes before the appointed hour. Present were the Chief of the Staff and Mrs Bramwell Booth, Commissioner Mrs Lucy Booth-Hellberg – Bramwell's sister – and nine London-based commissioners, among whom were Commissioner Adelaide Cox, Leader of the Women's Social Work, Commissioner T. Henry Howard, Foreign Secretary, and Commissioner Edward Higgins, the recently appointed British Commissioner.

After prayer, Dr Ranger produced the 'sealed envelope' and passed it round for inspection. It bore the endorsement 'The appointment of my successor. William Booth, 21 August 1890'. Bramwell Booth immediately grasped the significance of the date. The document had been signed while his mother was still alive. If the name in the envelope was his, she must have approved of his appointment. Only later was Bramwell Booth to learn that he had been the designated successor from as early as 1879.

Exactly 22 years to the day after the envelope was sealed it was opened by Dr Ranger. If those present were expecting to see a small slip of paper with a name on it they were in for a surprise. The envelope contained a full-sized handwritten legal document which quoted the relevant portions of the Deed of Constitution of 1878 and provided a space for the insertion of a name.

Dr Ranger, who had been blind from the age of 14, asked his partner to read the statement. When Mr Frost reached the words 'I do hereby nominate and appoint ...' the only surprise was the triple identification William Booth had given to his nominee in order to ensure that there could be no doubt as to his intention. 'I do hereby nominate and appoint *my son, William Bramwell Booth, the Chief of the Staff of The Salvation Army,* to be my successor and to succeed me as from the time of my decease in the office of General Superintendent and Commanding Officer of The Salvation Army.' Bramwell Booth had been his father's right-hand man since he was 16. No one in the world was more qualified to be the General than he was.

At the end of the reading, Dr Ranger asked Bramwell Booth if he accepted the appointment his father had made, and a deeply moved Bramwell Booth responded that he did. 'The solicitors thereupon handed such appointment to the new General,' reads the official statement that everyone present signed before leaving, 'and advised that by virtue of such appointment and acceptance, the said William Bramwell Booth had become and was now the legally appointed General of The Salvation Army.' No further formality was needed. The Army had a new General.

In his will William Booth had appointed his successor as his executor and 'the effect was to vest the legal title of Army property in the next General without the necessity for transfers of deeds or orders of court'.[1] The Army had a new sole trustee.

Two days later General Bramwell Booth, as required by the Supplementary Deed of Constitution 1904, executed a deed confirming that he had accepted office not only on the terms of the Deed Poll of 1878 but also on the terms of the Supplementary Deed Poll of 1904. Little did Bramwell know as he signed his name to the deed that his signature on that document was to prove decisive in a constitutional crisis that was to erupt 17 years later.

When Bramwell Booth had spoken his words of acceptance at the 'Opening of the Envelope Ceremony' on 21 August 1912 at International Headquarters, all of the commissioners spoke briefly, pledging their allegiance to the new General. As the meeting began to break up, word soon spread through the building and was quickly broadcast to the Salvationist world by cable: the Army had a new General and his name was Bramwell Booth.

After everyone had left and Bramwell Booth was alone in his office, there was a diffident knock on the door. It was Colonel Theodore Kitching, William Booth's trusted aide. After greeting and congratulating the new General, Colonel Kitching handed him an envelope. Bramwell Booth immediately recognised the handwriting. It was his father's. The envelope was addressed to 'My Successor in the Generalship of The Salvation Army'. William Booth had written the letter many years previously, but some weeks before he died the now blind Founder had asked Colonel Kitching to read it to him. In so doing he entrusted to his aide the knowledge of who he had chosen as his successor. Some circumstances had changed since William Booth wrote the letter, but after listening to it being read to him he had decided not to alter anything in it, and had asked Colonel Kitching to hand the letter to Bramwell at the appropriate time.

Bramwell Booth stayed late at the office that day. He often did. It was not unusual for him to be still working at 9 pm. Well-wishers had to be greeted. Messages had to be responded to. The funeral arrangements for his father needed his urgent attention, but when at last quietness settled on International Headquarters, Bramwell Booth sat down in the armchair in the corner of his office and opened the envelope that Colonel Theodore Kitching had given him. He unfolded the papers. There were two letters. The first was a letter addressed to him. The second was a letter addressed to his brothers and sisters. Both letters had been written 17 years previously and were dated 16 August 1895.[2] He made a mental note to send a copy of the second letter to each of his siblings the next day. In the first letter he read:

43

Some Counsels for the guidance of my successor in the Generalship of The Salvation Army. To be read and considered after my death.

My dear Bramwell,

I write the following in view of the possibility of my being taken away by some sudden stroke, which will not give me an opportunity for giving any parting advice in view of the position for which I have chosen you ... These counsels contain my mature convictions on the subjects treated of, and I lay them upon you with all the authority of my last commands ... I begin with a few general directions as to the selection of a successor.

The first duty of a General will be to name his successor according to the requirements of the Deed Poll.

a) In attending to this important duty he must seek help from God and make his choice as in his very presence. No given task as important ever engaged his attention before.

b) He should most seriously consider, that in view of the uncertainty of life, and the great trouble and inconvenience that would be caused to the Army should he die without having named a successor, he must name the person who in his mind at the moment appears most likely to efficiently fill the position. If *not quite satisfied* with his choice, he should consider further, until quite satisfied that he has selected the best qualified officer within his knowledge.

William Booth then lists in some detail the desirable qualities of a General. 'He should be an Army officer in good and full standing with unblemished reputation ... He should if possible be of mature age ... it is difficult to imagine many instances where an officer could be found suited to so important a position under 30 years of age ...'

He should be godly, a good and hearty believer in the doctrines, an enthusiastic Salvationist, he should be healthy and vigorous, and should 'possess the capacity necessary for the occupancy of such a post'. He mentions platform ability and business skills, and adds: 'For the continuous aggression which is the life of the Army, on which its continued existence largely depends, *a General must be a fighting man.*'

He must also be a prudent one. Prudence 'is indispensable. A rash and heedless General might do irreparable injury before he has been in office many months. Indeed the most important duty that will lie before any succeeding General will be the wise guidance and control of the mighty force which will be at his disposal.'

William Booth then moves on to a delicate point:

> Now it will be good if these qualities, or any considerable number of them or meet in the direct heir of the General for the time being. That is if the best man for the position happens to be the son or daughter of the General himself, or should they meet in any prominent member of the family. But the General in making his choice of any members of his own family must beware of passing over any other officer who he has reason to believe would be more suitable for the position and more acceptable to the holiest, the wisest and the most energetic officers and soldiers in the Army. *He must be impartial.*
>
> A woman if otherwise qualified is equally eligible with a man.
>
> Under no circumstances should a General divulge the name of an officer on whom his choice has fallen.
>
> If at any time after a General has made his choice he is convinced that he has been mistaken in some important particular, or should a more likely officer for the post be presented to his mind, he must at once change his selection and do so in due form.

William Booth then indicates that he will give further personal counsels to Bramwell – but immediately reverts to the matter of the succession. One hears not only the father speaking to the son but also the General speaking to his Chief of the Staff:

> You will follow the general directions just given as to the selection of your successor. So far as I at present know the Army, I think in the first instance your choice should fall upon Herbert …
>
> If God should spare you for many years from the date at which I write this, as I trust he may, other officers even more capable may rise up, or officers who may from the fact of their being younger and more vigorous, be better adapted for the position. I must leave the choice in

such circumstances entirely to your judgment. In which case the responsibility of the selection will rest entirely upon you. It may be that God may raise up a member of your family duly qualified for the command.

With regard to the grandchildren I cannot say more than ask that they may be dealt with in the spirit of what I have asked of their parents, that is that impartiality may govern all their appointments. They will however have largely to take the same chance as the children of other senior officers.

William Booth then adds 'a serious word or two' about Bramwell's relationships with members of the family. 'In this matter,' he writes, 'I think I have set you a fair example. I have endeavoured to treat you all with affection and yet not shown you any favour as it regards the honours and positions of the Army, that is, I have not promoted you without due regard to your capacity and devotion. I fully expect that you will follow in my steps. I believe you will.'

He adds further words of personal counsel. Among them: 'Persevere on the lines of *aggression*. Beware of *stagnation*.' To this he adds with the insight of a father who knows his son well: 'Set a watch against the natural conservatism of your character – you must go forward on the lines of conquest or you must perish.'

Seated in the armchair in his office, Bramwell Booth reflected for a moment on what he had just read, and then turned to the letter William Booth had written to all of his children. Bramwell had seven brothers and sisters, and the letter is an appeal for them to remain true to their highest ideals, to love each other – and to support the brother who has been chosen to be the General:

You will, I feel sure, cordially accept him. Although I have never in so many words said as much, still the selection has been an open secret. Hence his appointment will not come upon you as a surprise in any way. And about your assent to it there will be no question. *But what you do I want to be done heartily.* You will do this. Because he is my deliberate choice.

He will, I believe, be generally accepted. If the entire Army were polled I have no doubt his selection would be unanimously approved. Having accepted him heartily, support his authority …

Cordially second the efforts of the new General. They will not all meet with your highest approval. They may not always be such as you would put in action if you were in his place. Nevertheless you must give him credit for the best motives and support him with your influence and co-operation.

Have patience with him – he will be sensitive to your criticisms, therefore don't make unfavourable remarks on his actions, or exaggerated repetitions may reach his ears signifying far more than you intended, thereby not only inflicting pain on him, but leading to other mischief.

Bramwell Booth arrived late that evening at their home 'The Homestead' in Hadley Wood, north of London. There were a thousand things to discuss with Florence. He always talked everything over with her. Despite the advanced hour, he showed her the two letters. They reflected together on how much had happened in the 17 years since the letters were written.

The succession

Whenever there was a brief lull during the next few days, Bramwell Booth thought about what his father had written concerning the succession. He knew that within a few days he would have to decide on his own successor and place the name in a 'sealed envelope'. With the uncertainty of life, he also knew that it would have to be someone ready to step into his shoes now. If necessary he could later choose someone else. He pondered his options.

Should it be a member of the Booth family? William Booth had consistently made it clear that the Generalship was not hereditary. Yet there seemed also to be an ambiguity in his thinking. It was as if he was saying: the Generalship is not hereditary but it could be advantageous for the Army to be headed by a Booth. This slightly muffled sound from the trumpet had been heard as early as in 1882 when he addressed the great crowd of Salvationists assembled for the marriage of Bramwell to Florence:

> People are saying, 'What will happen when the General is gone?' By the blessing of God, although the Generalship of the Army is in no sense hereditary, and it is not contemplated to make it such, nevertheless, in the possibilities and probabilities happening in this direction, after the General the son would step into his place; and should he do so, there would rally round him, I believe, as cordially and as thoroughly the hearts of thousands and tens of thousands composing this organisation as they have rallied around me.[3]

The fact that the Generalship was not hereditary had been proclaimed ever since. As recently as in 1910 *The Salvation Army Year Book* had stated: 'The succession to the position of the General is not in any shape or form hereditary, nor is it intended ever to be so.' Successive editions of *Orders and Regulations for Officers* had made the same statement and had added: 'Every General will be under the most solemn obligation to select that officer to succeed him who, in the circumstances of the time, he considers best adapted to fill so important a position and most likely to use the great power and influence associated with such a command in a manner that will promote, to the largest extent, the glory of God and the salvation of the world.'[4]

Hereditary it was not – and yet?

Something of the ambiguity already noted reveals itself in the letter written by William Booth to his successor – the letter which Bramwell had recently read. After strongly making the point that the most qualified officer for the position must be chosen, and listing some of the qualities required, William Booth had gone on to say that 'it would be good if these qualities or any considerable number of them, meet in the *direct heir* of the General for the time being – a son or daughter of the General himself – or meet in any prominent member of the family.'

However, he quickly returns to his main thrust – that the position is not hereditary, and that the General '*must be impartial*' (his

48

italics) in his choice – but then goes on to add: 'I think in the first instance your choice should fall upon Herbert.'

This was a bold choice. In the male succession he was bypassing his second son, the brilliant but volatile Ballington, and was focusing on his equally brilliant but steadier and very popular third son, Herbert, who was six years younger than Bramwell. Even so, the choice of Herbert was to be only 'in the first instance'. In other words, Herbert was ready now, and a change could always be made later.

Herbert Booth, however, was no longer eligible to become General.

The Founder had suffered grievous losses in his famously gifted family since writing his 'counsels for the guidance of my successor' in 1895.

In 1896 his son Ballington, 'the Commander', then in charge of the work in the USA, had resigned his officership together with his wife Maud and had commenced a rival organisation, Volunteers of America.

In 1902 his daughter Catherine, *La Maréchale,* whom Florence had accompanied to France, had resigned together with her husband, Commissioner Arthur Booth-Clibborn. They had been in charge of the work in The Netherlands.

In the same year, 1902, his son Herbert, 'the Commandant', then the territorial commander for Australia, had also resigned along with his wife Cornelie.

The next year, 1903, his daughter Emma, 'the Consul', had died in a rail crash in the USA. She was married to Commissioner Frederick Booth-Tucker, and they had jointly headed the Army's work in that country since Ballington's departure.

William Booth's daughter Marian had been an invalid since childhood. She held the rank of staff-captain but was never active as an officer.

Therefore when Bramwell Booth became General only two of his siblings remained as officers, his sister Commissioner Mrs Lucy Booth-Hellberg – married to Commissioner Emmanuel Booth-Hellberg, a Swedish officer whose health was fast failing – and his sister Evangeline Booth, 'the Commander', since 1904 responsible for the Army's work in the USA.

Lucy, who was William and Catherine's youngest daughter, had been territorial commander in India at the age of 24 with her husband, Emmanuel Booth-Hellberg, as chief secretary, and had been joint territorial commander with him in France, but both were now on sick leave because of his declining health. Following the promotion to Glory of her husband, Commissioner Mrs Lucy Booth-Hellberg was subsequently to become territorial commander for Denmark, followed by Norway and then South America, but though gifted, she was not seen as a potential General.

However, Evangeline Booth was. Of all William Booth's children, Evangeline was the one most like him. She had flair, drive and passion, was a born leader and could hold an audience spellbound with her dramatic oratory. She was the darling of British Salvationists who loved her flamboyant ways and would flock to hear her whenever she was announced to speak.

As a young commissioner, aged 31, she had rescued the Army in the USA when her brother Ballington resigned in 1896. Despatched by her father to try to persuade him not to resign his commission, she arrived in New York to find herself locked out from a meeting at the headquarters in Fourteenth Street in which he was seeking to persuade the officers to follow him into the new organisation. Swift in decision, like her father, she dashed into Thirteenth Street and, passing through a house whose yard backed on to the Army's property, climbed up the fire-escape, crawled through a window, and made a dramatic appearance on the platform. Demanding to be heard, she made an impassioned appeal for the officers to remain true to the Army of William Booth. She won the day. The officers decided to stay with the international Army. Ballington Booth left headquarters alone, never to return.

When she later addressed a hostile crowd at Cooper Union, she heard hisses from the audience. She immediately seized an American flag, flung it about herself and shouted: 'Hiss that if you dare!' The abashed mob became silent.

After briefly holding on as leader in the USA until the arrival of the Booth-Tuckers, Evangeline Booth was appointed in command of Canada, where she remained for the next eight years. In 1904, when Frederick Booth-Tucker no longer felt able to shoulder the responsibility for the work in the USA after the death of Emma, she returned to New York as 'Commander' for the Army in the USA. By the time of William Booth's promotion to Glory in 1912 she had already been the USA Commander for eight years and was recognised by all as an outstanding leader – indeed, a General-in-waiting.

Nine years younger than Bramwell, hers was the most obvious name to be placed in the 'sealed envelope' instead of Herbert's, even if only for the time being – 'in the first instance' as his father had put it.

Yet it is unlikely that Bramwell's thoughts went in that direction. His relationship with Evangeline was strained, as it was to some degree with all of his brothers and sisters. His personal closeness to his father, his role as his father's 'chief executive', even the fact that he was the epitome of a headquarters officer whereas his brothers and sisters had been appointed to the front lines of service, had occasioned a degree of sibling rivalry that grace did not always overcome. Bramwell and Evangeline appreciated each other's gifts, but their views about the future of the Army had already begun to diverge. It is therefore unlikely that Bramwell saw Evangeline as his successor.

His options were surprisingly limited. He had already decided to appoint Commissioner T. Henry Howard to be his Chief of the Staff. Commissioner Howard was older than Bramwell, a safe pair of hands, but not a future General. Commissioner Edward Higgins, the recently appointed British Commissioner, had not yet become as prominent as he later was, and would therefore also have been an unlikely choice. No other names of leaders younger than himself – other than Evangeline's – stand out in the list.

What about his direct heirs? William Booth in his letter had said that it would be good if the qualities needed for a General could be found in the 'direct heir ... the son or daughter of the General himself'. His father had also emphasised that a woman would be equally eligible with a man. Was William Booth dropping a hint about his first grand-daughter, Catherine, with whom he got on so well? When he wrote the letter she was 12 years of age. Did he already see in her the qualities of a future General?

Whatever Bramwell may have read into his father's comments, 29-year-old Adjutant Catherine, a brigade officer at the training college, would not in 1912 have met the tests of experience and acceptability to be his successor should he meet with an untimely death.

We shall never know what name Bramwell Booth placed in his first 'sealed envelope', but given the circumstances that faced him, it is not inconceivable that his choice 'in the first instance' was his wife, Florence Booth.

What we can be quite sure about is that within days of taking office, the new General instructed Dr Ranger to prepare a new appointment form, that he completed it privately with the name of his chosen successor, sealed it in an envelope, and then handed the envelope to his lawyer for safekeeping.

Commissioner Edward Higgins becomes Chief of the Staff

Within two years of Bramwell Booth becoming General, the First World War broke out. The new General not only held the Army together at that time, a remarkable feat considering that there were Salvationists on both sides of the conflict, but extended its work and influence even further during those years.

In 1919, when the Chief of the Staff, Commissioner T. Henry Howard, retired from active service, General Bramwell Booth appointed the British Commissioner, Commissioner Edward Higgins, to be his new Chief of the Staff. In a further and unprecedented move, a move which caused some eyebrows to be raised, he made his wife, Florence Booth, a commissioner in her own right and appointed her British Commissioner.

Commissioner Edward Higgins was to be the Chief of the Staff for the next 10 years, and was therefore to find himself centre stage in the build-up towards the drama of the constitutional crisis of 1929.

Edward Higgins was the son of officer parents. His father was also a commissioner and was usually referred to as 'Old Commissioner Higgins' to distinguish him from his son. Edward Higgins Jnr began his officer service as a corps officer and was then, with his wife Catherine, appointed to divisional work followed by appointments at the training garrison for cadets in London. In an era when short-term appointments were in fashion, Edward Higgins's service was characterised by lengthy appointments of increasing responsibility. He served nearly seven years at the training garrison, rising eventually as Colonel Higgins to become number two to the principal, Commissioner Evangeline Booth.

William Booth had spotted the potential in Colonel Edward Higgins, and in April 1896 summoned him to his home in Hadley Wood and appointed him second-in-command of the Army in the USA. He was then 31 years of age. The Army in America was in turmoil because of the resignation of Ballington and Maud Booth. Evangeline had applied much-needed first aid and was temporarily in charge. Commissioners Frederick and Emma Booth-Tucker were on their way to assume command and Edward Higgins was to be their chief executive officer. At that time the Army in the USA was still administered as a single unit, and the chief secretary was therefore truly the second-in-command of what was already a vast operation.

Edward Higgins held that appointment for the next nine and a half years, and became second-in-command yet again to Evangeline Booth for six months when she became the USA Commander in 1904. He was then appointed to International Headquarters as Assistant Foreign Secretary for six years. This appointment was providential in that it gave him an extensive knowledge of the international Army and made him a well-known figure on that scene. Then in 1911 William Booth summoned him again to his home, this time to promote him to the rank of commissioner and appoint him British Commissioner.

General Albert Orsborn was a young corps officer at the time and recalls how the advent of Commissioner Higgins as British

Commissioner 'came like a trumpet call to the whole of the Field'. He writes: 'I was in my third corps. This new leader ranged the whole territory at a cracking speed. He meant to establish contact as quickly as possible. He was in his mid-forties, tall, upstanding, handsome, with shining eyes and a delightful smile. His voice was resonant, and in a pleasant key. I thought the master-word in his speaking was 'opportunity'. He used it soon and often in his addresses. It was indicative of his outlook.'[5]

No one was surprised when eight years later, in 1919, General Bramwell Booth appointed Commissioner Edward Higgins to be his Chief of the Staff. In Edward Higgins the General had not only a multi-gifted second-in-command but also someone who was personally devoted to him.

'I consider the General has conferred a great honour upon me in selecting me as his Chief of the Staff,' he wrote to Mrs Booth as he prepared to take up his new responsibilities, 'and I shall lay myself out to try to meet his and your every expectation in the appointment. My real affection for you both will make all my service for you a pleasure, and I shall enter upon my work without a shadow or a reserve. I am all for the General, and while I have no doubt I shall make some mistakes, yet those mistakes will never be made through any effort to act contrary to his wishes. What the General desires will always be my main consideration.'[6]

Those sentiments were to be tested to near breaking point in 1929. In the end they were to snap.

Chapter Four

Warning Rumbles

COMMISSIONER Edward Higgins, Chief of the Staff, put his pen down and looked at the words he had just written.

'The General is our Fighting Champion!' he had penned. 'Next to the divine presence, his love to God, his vision and purpose, together with his manifold gifts and abilities, *are surely our most precious possession.*'

General Bramwell Booth's 70th birthday on 8 March 1926 was fast approaching. The General, visionary and energetic as always, had prepared a nine-point programme of expansion in England, Europe and Africa to cover his next 10 years. He was also launching a special capital projects fund – a 70th birthday thanksgiving scheme – to assist missionary work, his first love. The Chief of the Staff was writing the explanatory pamphlet about the scheme that would go out to all officers.

Was it too fulsome, he wondered, to say that next to God's presence, General Bramwell Booth was the Army's most precious possession? He thought for a moment. No, it was not, he concluded. The words expressed exactly what he genuinely felt and believed, and he knew that officers and Salvationists around the world would rise up and say a loud amen to what he had written. The words stayed.

On his 70th birthday Bramwell Booth had every reason to be an exceptionally happy man, blessed in his family, his immediate colleagues, his worldwide Salvationist family and his service for the Lord.

The birthday celebrations were held in the Royal Albert Hall, where a message of congratulations from the King was handed to him as he went on to the platform. The following day Mr David Lloyd George, former Prime Minister of Great Britain, presided over a lunch in his honour with 500 guests. In the evening he took tea with 1,000 women who had passed through the Army's homes. Two days later he presided over a Missionary Demonstration in the Royal Albert Hall, and on the following evening went to tea with 1,000 men from the London shelters.

He preached to great crowds as he toured Britain, and wherever he went was received with acclamation. His travelling commissioners returning from the far corners of the earth brought reports of the Army advancing on all fronts. It was an auspicious start to the decade ahead, a decade which surely would crown everything he had accomplished hitherto.

Nevertheless the Chief of the Staff knew there was an underside to the plaudits the General was receiving. All who worked closely with the General knew. Were the advancing years taking their toll? His pace was still such as would leave many a younger person trailing breathlessly behind, but there were question marks. This was not the Bramwell Booth of old. This was a man under stress.

Commissioner Higgins realised that for the upper echelons of the Army's leadership the tectonic plates had shifted. Warning rumbles had been heard. Yet despite the question marks he remained convinced that Bramwell Booth was still the Army's most precious possession.

However, Edward Higgins was concerned, and even Bramwell Booth's joy on his 70th birthday was mixed with apprehension.

A trumpet sounds

The first seismic movement had been felt exactly one year previously, March 1925, when headquarters officers around the world received an anonymous four-page manifesto 'The First Blast of a Trumpet' addressed 'To Staff Officers Only'.

It was an attack on the established order of things. Nothing like it had ever happened in the Army before. Staff officers around the world were disconcerted as they read:

The 1877 Annual Conference of the Christian Mission, which 'heartily endorsed' that William Booth should govern without it. William Booth is seated prominently in the centre, with Bramwell Booth (aged 21) seated on the ground next to him on the right. Catherine Booth stands between them on the second row. George Scott Railton is seated on William Booth's other side. The first three evangelists in the front row, seated left to right, are: William Ridsdel, William Pearson and Elijah Cadman. Emma Booth (aged 17), wearing a lighter-coloured dress and a distinctive hat, stands looking sideways four places to the right of her mother. Evangeline Booth (aged 11), also wearing a distinctive hat, is the last person on the right in the second row. None of the other members of the Booth family are in the photo.

London. September 29th 1879

In pursuance of the power entrusted to me by the Deed Poll of the Christian Mission now known as the Salvation Army, I hereby will and decree that in case of my death my son William Bramwell Booth shall take my place as General Superintendent of the said Christian Mission or Salvation Army and I wish him to possess all the power and influence now possessed by me in the said Army according to the Covenants and provisions of the said Deed Poll and I hope and desire that all my faithful people will receive him and love and follow him as they have received loved and followed his father in the name of the Almighty God so that they may be led on to further victory and blessing. Amen!

William Booth — General of the Salvation Army

Witness Thos H Whittington
Solicitor to the Christian Mission

The first document placed in a 'sealed envelope' by which William Booth appointed Bramwell Booth to be his successor. The statement, in his own hand, was written at a time when Bramwell was 23 years of age. It was replaced 11 years later by a more formal appointment document that was also placed in a 'sealed envelope'. This second 'sealed envelope' was opened in 1912 upon William Booth's promotion to Glory.

Left: William Booth in 1909 with Bramwell Booth, his Chief of the Staff.

Below: The Bramwell Booth family – late 1925. General Bramwell Booth is flanked by his wife Florence and eldest daughter Catherine. On the left stands son Bernard with his wife Jane seated in front of him holding their daughter Helen, the first of three children. On the right stands son Wycliffe holding Stuart, with his wife Renée seated holding Geneviève. Wycliffe and Renée had six children in all, four of whom became officers. Several of their grandchildren are officers today. Standing in the second row, left to right, are daughters Mary, Dora and Olive.

General Bramwell Booth, aged 70

Mrs General Bramwell Booth

Commissioner Catherine Booth

Commissioner Edward Higgins

Commander Evangeline Booth

This is the first blast of a trumpet, to be reiterated if necessary, against the assumption of infallibility and the exercise of arbitrary and despotic power by the present General of The Salvation Army …

Our Founder, so willing in all things to efface himself, was nevertheless wise in reserving in himself the concentration of power that could make possible a compact and efficient organisation … An organisation, destined to become so vast in extent and so complex in its operations, was at the beginning, and necessarily so, directed by one master mind …

The marvellous success vouchsafed of God under the plan followed by the Founder is not proof that continued concentration of power in a single individual could or would be of permanent blessing. The history of the movement, its worldwide ramification, its personnel, distinguished alike by keen intelligence and wide vision, prove without peradventure that the perpetuation of power in one man, or in one family, cannot continue without instigating a revolt that will end either in the dissolution of the Army or in a final paralysis of any initiative on the part of its soldiers. The system is thoroughly and unqualifiedly bad and it must be destroyed …

Leading officers, and some of the most promising men of the rank and file, resent with increasing indignation the disesteem and contumely to which they have been subject under the present regime. If there has been no open manifestation of the prevailing dissatisfaction, it is because such expression would inevitably result in an immediate expulsion from the Army or in a humiliating reduction in rank …

To the rule governing the appointment of a successor to the General we take unqualified exception. The present General has decreed the one to succeed himself. It is the common and widespread conviction that he has named his wife. Should this prove to be true there will ensue an insurrection that no human power can check …

The nepotism that characterises the present regime is particularly offensive. The favouritism shown by the General for his children, so conspicuously evident in all Army publications, is not only a violation of good taste, but is also absolutely ridiculous. Even their insignificant activities are bruited abroad as of those of a royal family. This perhaps would be of little moment were it not the warning presage of their future elevation to power.

The grievance of which we complain can be speedily and easily relieved. The leadership of the Army should no longer remain self-perpetuating but should be committed to a governing council to whose choice the staff officers and the rank and file would yield ready and loyal obedience ... To this council should be referred not only the appointment of succeeding Generals, by popular vote or otherwise, but also the supervision of our financial system, authority being vested in the council to fix all salaries including that of the General, and to supervise all other expenditures, and direct the management of all properties and vested funds now held by the Army ...[1]

The blast of the trumpet reverberated around the Army officer world. Any hope that it would be heard by staff officers only was soon dispelled. Mimeographed copies began to circulate widely among officers of all ranks, but it did not become general knowledge among the Army's rank and file. Commissioner Edward Higgins later commented:

Whilst every effort failed to trace the author of the memorandum, it soon became apparent that whilst perhaps only a few would *express* sympathy with the method adopted by the writer, yet a large number were sympathetic with the grievances mentioned and the reforms demanded. It was idle to close one's eyes to the ominous signs of a coming difficulty. The situation was discussed wherever groups of officers met. The policy adopted of treating the incident with some measure of contempt by making no reference to it in officers councils or in official documents, did not result in quietening the agitation. 'What does it mean?' 'What is going to be done about it?' were questions asked of each other.[2]

The blast of the trumpet was a two-fold attack. It attacked the principles underlying the governance of the Army and it attacked the personalities involved.

The trumpet objected in principle to the authority vested in the General. It was therefore a direct attack on the most fundamental principle enshrined in the 1878 constitution: 'The Christian Mission is and shall be hereafter for ever under the oversight, direction and control of some one person, called the General Superintendent.' What had been right and necessary in the time of William Booth, it argued, was no longer right for today. Power and authority should be shared with the capable leaders who had now arisen. The manifesto did not mince its words: 'The system is thoroughly and unqualifiedly bad and it must be destroyed.'

There was also a personal element. The trumpet objected to Bramwell Booth's leadership style. Bramwell Booth had always been a strong leader, but as his natural powers declined he had changed, and rather than mellowing with age he had developed what some felt to be an overbearing streak. His colleagues also noted with apprehension that his attention to minor details was often obsessive, that his decisions were increasingly arbitrary, and that he no longer handled dissent well. The word in the corridors of power was that it was best not to voice a contrary opinion – one risked being appointed to a lesser responsibility; being consigned to the 'freezer', it was called.

The trumpet also objected in principle to the General's constitutional power to appoint his own successor, adding the personal element that if Mrs Booth were appointed 'there will ensue an insurrection that no human power can check'.

The trumpet furthermore objected to the 'favouritism shown by the General for his children'. This objection loomed surprisingly large at the time, for in March 1925 none of the children held exceptionally large responsibilities.

Six children of Bramwell and Florence Booth remained as officers after the promotion to Glory in 1917 of Captain Miriam Booth, the third daughter, following a long illness. Catherine, the eldest, had by that time been off the scene for three years on sick leave, and no one knew whether she would ever be well enough to return to active duty. Mary, the second-born, was the divisional commander in Manchester. Bernard was the national youth secretary for the British Territory, and Olive and Dora held subsidiary appointments on divisional headquarters. Bramwell Booth had appointed his youngest son Wycliffe to be his ADC – and it was this appointment that seemed to attract special ire.

However, the prominence given to the children by disproportionate coverage in *The War Cry,* together with factors such as the General's quaint insistence on senior leaders 'consulting' his children, had led to the belief that Bramwell Booth looked upon his family as a 'royal family'. In his first address as General he had said: 'My wife and my children are yours in a sense that they are not my own,' and some feared that there was a dynastic dimension to his thinking.

The trumpet blast also objected to another feature of the 1878 constitution: the sole trusteeship of assets by the General. The Army had outgrown that, said the manifesto, and responsibility should now be shared. The trumpet sound furthermore criticised the lack of openness about the General's personal finances.

The blast of the trumpet, however, had a solution for all of these ills: 'the leadership of the Army should be committed to a *governing council'*, a council which in addition to governing the Army would also select successive Generals. This was in fact a call for the re-establishment under another guise of the Annual Conference of the 1875 constitution to provide a balancing 'authority' to that of the General.

It was heady stuff. It was also ironic. Bramwell Booth had always taken his father as his role model, and what William Booth had done Bramwell Booth now did. Yet what was applauded in the father was criticised in the son. What was perfectly acceptable in the founder of a fledgling movement was unacceptable in his heir. The movement had moved on.

William Booth was an absolute autocrat – and was lauded for it. Bramwell took his cue from his father – and was called a despot.

William Booth relied greatly on his wife – and was hailed for making Catherine Booth co-founder of The Salvation Army. Bramwell Booth looked to his wife Florence for counsel – and was criticised for it. 'Condemned over the eggs and bacon,' it was said when he reversed some decision the next day.

William Booth was applauded for appointing his son to be his Chief of the Staff. Bramwell Booth was berated for making Wycliffe his ADC.

William Booth appointed his other children straight to large commands and gave them extravagant titles such as *Maréchale,* Commander and Consul – and Salvationists were delighted. Bramwell Booth insisted that his seven children must begin as cadets and work their way up to larger responsibilities – and was accused of nepotism.

William Booth decreed he would be the sole trustee to expedite property and financial business, and the evangelists roared their approval. Bramwell Booth continued the system and was condemned for so doing.

William Booth was hailed for relying on a trust fund established by a benefactor so that he would not have to draw on Army funds for his personal needs. Bramwell Booth followed the same pattern through the Wisely Trust – and was censured for it.

William Booth, to universal approval, appointed his son to succeed him. When it was thought that Bramwell Booth might appoint a member of his family to follow him, he was accused of wanting to create a dynasty.

It was tough to be the son of a founder.

Constitutional reform

Though 'The First Blast of a Trumpet' was anonymously written it brought into the open what a number of leaders had been considering for some years. 'The recent events,' wrote Lieut-Commissioner William McIntyre (Territorial Commander, USA Southern Territory) following the 1929 High Council, 'have not come as the result of sudden action, but they have been the steady growth of perhaps a quarter of a century or more – a growing feeling that some day, somehow, a revision of our constitution must take place and be adjusted to the purposes, the conditions, and the needs of the present day.'[3]

To some of the Army's elder statesmen it had become clear that the Army had outgrown its constitution. When the 1878 constitution was drawn up, no one, not even William Booth, had foreseen that what was then a small and insignificant mission would one day be a vast world-encircling movement with hundreds of thousands of members and with immense financial and property resources. It was increasingly felt that in the light of these developments the constitution had to be re-visited.

Any revision would be about limiting the power of the General, and it was therefore not something about which one wrote papers or spoke openly. Some leaders had ventured to raise the matter with Bramwell Booth. They had found him unresponsive, and as he clearly did not appreciate dissent, the matter was not pressed.

In private conversations between the Army's senior leaders, ways in which the power of the General might be limited had been discussed. Thinking was at first tentative and unformed, but the conviction gradually grew that the limitation of power could be achieved by three constitutional changes:

First, that the General should no longer have the power to appoint his successor through the 'sealed envelope' method. Instead, Generals should be elected by an electoral college – perhaps by the commissioners.

Second, that the Generalship should no longer be for life. Instead, there should be a fixed retirement age for the General.

Third, that the General should no longer be sole trustee of the Army's property and funds. Instead, there should be a body of trustees. The concept of sole trusteeship had become the focus of special public criticism in 1891 when William Booth launched his appeal for funds in connection with the Darkest England Scheme.

The General's role as sole trustee related mainly to property and funds held in Great Britain or in the British Dominions. In other countries the sole trusteeship of a General resident in London had frequently proved incompatible with national legislation. Yet even then, the perception within the Army that all property belonged to the General was remarkably international. It was not unusual for officer parents anywhere in the world to admonish their children not to jump on 'the General's sofa'. In Britain that was literally so. As the Army's sole trustee, the General owned everything down to the last teaspoon.

On the radical fringes a fourth way of limiting the power of the General was sometimes mentioned, namely that the Army should no longer be under the exclusive oversight, direction and control of just one person. Instead there should be some other 'authority' which would act as a check and balance on the power of the General.

This is what 'The First Blast of a Trumpet' had called for with its proposal for a 'governing council'. However, in the higher reaches of leadership the idea had only limited support. It was feared that this might be a step too far. If the Army at the top was going to return to being run 'by committee' as the Christian Mission had once been, the pressure for it to be run by committee at territorial, divisional and corps level would be difficult to resist. Also if government by committee were to return, an essential dynamic that had made the Army what it was would be threatened. Such ideas therefore remained at the fringes of reformist thinking.

One thing, however, was very clear to the Army's senior leaders when the trumpet sounded its blast in March 1925: the burning issue was constitutional reform. The personal factors arising from Bramwell Booth's leadership style were real but they were secondary. What was in the firing line was the constitution of 1878.

After the blast

Bramwell Booth, always sensitive by nature but by this stage of his life hyper-sensitive, was deeply wounded by the attack in 'The First Blast of a Trumpet'. He could not bring himself to believe that it expressed the feelings of the majority, but the fear that it might, and that he was ignorant of the extent of the dissatisfaction, now began to gnaw at him. The memorandum had hit its intended target. 'From that time,' wrote Edward Higgins later, 'his decision, his courage, his confidence was shaken, and it was revealed in many ways during the years that followed.'[4]

It was still gnawing away inside him when he reached his 70th birthday a year later – in March 1926. How widespread was the desire for constitutional reform, especially in the USA where the agitation had been more open? In April 1926, accompanied by his wife, he crossed the Atlantic to find out.

Between meetings during the coast-to-coast tour he had lengthy conversations on the subject with his sister Evangeline. She had been pressing him for some years to consider constitutional reform and had become a focal figure for those wanting change. Already in her 23rd year of command in the USA, she had brought The Salvation Army in that country to hitherto unparalleled heights of effectiveness, influence and prominence. Her own prestige within and without the Army had never been higher. Her views were therefore important.

The Commander warned her brother not to ignore the pressure for reform that was building up, but when Bramwell and Florence sailed for home some weeks later, it was in greater peace of heart and mind than when they had arrived. With the many expressions of personal affection and loyalty to the office of the General that they had received from officers and soldiers, they felt sure that the reform movement could be contained.

Further good news awaited them on their return to London in May 1926. The doctors had declared their daughter Catherine, now aged 43, well enough to return to active duty. Bramwell Booth was delighted. He promoted her to the rank of full colonel and appointed her Leader of the Women's Social Work in Britain – the work that Florence had once pioneered. Six hundred officers would now be serving under Colonel Catherine Booth's direction.

The remainder of the year 1926 was taken up with the supervision of major projects and undertaking tours to Europe and the Far East. When in Korea, General Bramwell Booth was faced with demands by some officers and local officers for greater recognition of national officers. His response was to dismiss the officers involved. The officers were subsequently reaccepted, but when news of the incident reached the senior leaders at International Headquarters they sadly concluded that stress had yet again caused him to over-react. In his heyday Bramwell Booth would have handled such opposition with ease and turned it to his advantage. That aside, 'for the remainder of the year 1926 Bramwell Booth's health and happiness and energy were remarkable,' comments historian St John Ervine. 'As a septuagenarian he was busier than as a boy of sixteen.'[5]

An unexpected intervention

No sooner had the year 1927 got under way, Bramwell Booth was faced with another anonymous document circulating among senior officers. It was in the form of a satirical fable and was entitled 'The Two Wise Mice'. Its pithy wording, Latin epigrams and distinctive style pointed to Commissioner Frederick Booth-Tucker – Bramwell Booth's brother-in-law – as its author.

Commissioner Booth-Tucker was the Army's first and greatest missionary and was revered throughout the Army world. As a young man he had entered the Indian civil service and had reached a position of high rank before he threw in his lot with William Booth in London, returning to India as the leader of an invading 'army'. Adopting Indian dress, he gave his life to the Army's mission on that great sub-continent, where he was known to everyone as Commissioner Fakir Singh.

Towards the end of his days, William Booth had spoken to his son-in-law about Bramwell. 'Tucker,' he said, 'when I am gone, I want you to stand beside Bramwell. Don't be his ditto or echo. You have an independent mind and judgment, and I want you to express it freely. While he will have the deciding voice, I want you to express your own views frankly and fearlessly.'[6]

Following the death of his wife Emma in the USA, Commissioner Booth-Tucker returned to India and the work there expanded greatly under his leadership. However, when at the age of 66 he suffered a major health setback he was appointed to International Headquarters. When his health improved miraculously he wanted to return to India, but General Bramwell Booth would not consent. Booth-Tucker therefore chafed at being confined to literary duties at the international centre.

Frederick Booth-Tucker was among those who saw the need for constitutional reform and from time to time, as William Booth had bidden him do, he expressed his views 'frankly and fearlessly' to Bramwell Booth. The General listened, but nothing ever seemed to come of these conversations.

Booth-Tucker's sense of frustration was compounded when Bramwell Booth introduced mandatory retirement ages for officers. This had been discussed as far back as in William Booth's day, but had not been implemented. Officers prided themselves on literally giving a lifetime of service to God and the Army, and went on until they could no longer manage. The introduction of set retirement ages was a nettle that sooner or later had to be grasped. In 1919 Bramwell Booth did so.

The retirement ages that were decreed varied according to rank, appointment and gender. Field officers were to retire at 60, staff officers at 65, and commissioners at 70, with single women commissioners retiring at 65. Lieut-commissioners – a rank that Bramwell Booth introduced in 1920 and which continued until 1973 – also retired at 65.

The immediate effect of mandatory retirement ages was to cut a swathe through the ranks of senior leaders who had long adorned the London scene. Booth-Tucker's 70th birthday fell on 21 March 1923. He was granted a two-year extension and retired in May 1925. Yet he considered his enforced retirement at 72 an affront. He had come into the Army to give a lifetime of service, not to sit at home in a rocking chair.

The introduction of retirement ages had an unintended consequence – it put the spotlight on the General's own position. If everyone had to retire by a certain age, why should the General not have to do so as well? After all, it was said, no one bore a greater burden of leadership than the General.

It was taken for granted that Bramwell Booth, just like his father, would remain General until he was promoted to Glory, and it was generally assumed that this is what the Founder had intended for all succeeding Generals.

Curiously the 1878 Deed was less than crystal clear on that point. The constitution declared in its *Fourthly* that 'William Booth shall continue to be for the term of his natural life the General Superintendent of the Christian Mission unless he shall resign such office'. William Booth, by name, had the right to remain General 'for the term of his natural life', but the constitution did not *explicitly* grant this right to any of his successors.

Instead the constitution simply said in its *'Fifthly'* that the 'sealed envelope' would come into play 'at the decease of the General Superintendent or *upon his ceasing to perform the duties of the office'* – the phrase on which the 1904 Supplementary Deed hinged. There were those who argued that by the use of that phrase the Founder was indicating that future Generals might not serve for the term of their natural life.

The point was further reinforced in that in its *'Sixthly'* the constitution stated that the leadership succession would take place 'at the decease of the General Superintendent, *or at such other period as may be named in the document appointing him'*. This phrase implicitly granted the General the right to set a limit to his own term of service. William Booth had been very specific in the document he left in the 'sealed envelope': Bramwell Booth was to succeed him 'as from the time of my decease', but he *could* have written: 'as from the time of my resignation from office'.

Whatever might have been William Booth's intentions with regard to his successors, it is clear that the 1878 constitution permitted Bramwell Booth to remain in office until his death if he so chose, and also permitted him to resign from office if that was his wish.

Retirement was therefore an option open to Bramwell Booth, but it needs to be recalled that at that time in the Army's history the idea of a 'retired General' was as unthinkable as that of a 'retired Pope'.

The key point in all of this, however, is that the initiative about retirement lay entirely with the General. There was no other 'authority' within the Army that could force the General to retire at a certain age. Orders and regulations about retirement governed all officers – except the General. By making retirement mandatory for everyone except himself, Bramwell Booth had stirred up ill will from his most senior colleagues.

In the fable of 'The Two Wise Mice' – a document of 18 pages – the two wise mice, King and Queen of the underworld, are clearly William and Catherine Booth. The Queen dies first, and then later the King. 'Now when the new King came to the throne, for some time he followed the wise example of his father and mother', but then things begin to go wrong, for the new King is 'a Foolish King'. He stops listening to his experienced advisers, puts some of them in the 'freezer' and retires others. He censors the press and makes it clear that should he die, his wife – 'the Foolish Queen' – will succeed him until one of his children is ready to take over.

Through an angel, the Supreme Sovereign outlines a series of reforms the Foolish King must undertake. He must immediately restore to their former positions all of the courtiers he has sidelined or retired from service. He must cancel the plans to appoint a member of his family to succeed him. He must 'call the Privy Council his father had created', a clear reference to the High Council that William Booth had created by the 1904 Deed.

This Council must be summoned at regular intervals, and the King must acquiesce if the Council decides to remove him from office. The Council will always decide who will be the next King. Kings will not serve for life but for a fixed term as decided by the Council. An executive board must be appointed to represent the Council between its meetings. A trust must be formed to relieve the King of responsibility for funds and property, and the King's remuneration must be decided by the Council.

In Army terms it is clear that the fable calls the Annual Conference of the 1875 constitution back to duty – but with a vengeance, for now the General will be the servant of the Council.

Readers of the fable were as much amused by it as bemused by the strength of its tone. However, no one missed the point. Reform was in the air – and some of it was ultra-radical. The pressure was building up.

A voice from Texas

No sooner had the fable of 'The Two Wise Mice' gone the rounds in early 1927 than another bulletin came through the mail. Most officers in the USA received a copy. This time the document was not anonymous. It was 'Bulletin No. 1', dated 30 April 1927, from a W. L. Atwood, whose postal address was Post Office Box 1147, Wichita Falls, Texas.

The four-page mimeographed bulletin attacked Bramwell Booth for his 'imperial rule', criticised him for not delegating sufficient authority to leaders in the USA, and for continually appointing British officers to key positions in that country. 'The General should be divested of all his authority so far as it pertains to the United States,' wrote the author, 'and this authority should be invested with our Commander. Future Commanders should be elected from our own officers in the same manner that the President of our country is elected. A survey that I have made shows that a majority of the officers are in sympathy with this movement.'[7]

With its extensive dissemination, Atwood's bulletin caused a stir among officers in the USA. One who received a copy was the revered Commissioner Samuel Brengle, the saintly American officer whom Bramwell Booth had set aside as a 'spiritual campaigner' to the world. Commissioner Brengle was among the leaders who had approached Bramwell Booth about the need for constitutional reform. He had warned the General that 'the love of democracy and antagonism to autocracy, especially in America,' was 'as potent in action as the most powerful and explosive gas under pressure'.[8]

Not knowing that Atwood's bulletin had been widely circulated, Commissioner Samuel Brengle first set it aside with hardly more than a glance, but when he learnt that it had been put into the hands of cadets he was galvanised into action. Commissioner Brengle voiced his indignation in a letter sent to leading officers in the USA and abroad. He roundly condemned William Atwood's bulletin. 'If change must come to fit new times,' he wrote, 'let it come in a Christian spirit, let it come in open and frank counsel.'[9] However, in a private letter he warned General Bramwell Booth about the influence of 'the very small man in Texas'.[10]

W. L. Atwood followed up with a second bulletin later in 1927, and the next year launched the first edition of a mimeographed publication called *The International Salvationist* to which officers and soldiers could subscribe.

The first edition of this publication criticised the prominence given to the Booth family. The second edition in April 1928 quoted in full an important exchange of letters between Evangeline Booth and the General on constitutional reform. This exhausted the patience of the Commander who cabled William Atwood on 2 May 1928: 'I ask you not to circulate any of my recent correspondence with the General that may be in your possession for this would be particularly painful to me. Therefore if for no higher reason than for my sake, please refrain.'

William Atwood's response was to quote her cable in the third edition of *The International Salvationist* and yet reproduce in full her next 21-page letter to the General. With that *The International Salvationist* ceased publication.

Who exactly was this mysterious W. L. Atwood whose name became synonymous with the reform movement in the USA?

From contemporary diaries and correspondence we now know that he was a young Salvationist in his mid-twenties at the Wichita Falls Corps who at one time had offered for officership but who had not been accepted for training.[11] Atwood described himself as 'a Salvationist in poor standing with headquarters', saying: 'I criticised the present General in no measured words for failing to appoint the American officers recommended by our dear Commander ... I am therefore considered reactionary by my divisional commander, and for such he has cancelled my commission as corps secretary.'[12]

However, it is not clear how active he really was in the corps. In 1979 Salvation Army historian Edward H. McKinley noted that though the corps records of the Wichita Falls Corps were 'reasonably complete' back to 1928 there was no mention of a W. L. Atwood, and that 'two elderly soldiers remember that Atwood attended services at the corps occasionally in the 1920s, but was never a soldier'.[13]

What is clear is that W. L. Atwood was a determined and enterprising young man with strongly held views. What is also clear is that some who wished to fan the flames of controversy provided him with leaked material to serve their own purposes, and also provided financial help to cover printing and mailing costs. However, what remains surprising is that someone with so little standing in the Army became so influential in the build-up to the constitutional crisis. Even William Atwood himself must have been astonished when at the height of the constitutional crisis the London *Daily Chronicle* carried the banner headline 'General Booth blames "Man from Texas"'.[14]

A significant promotion

In November 1927 General Bramwell Booth promoted Colonel Catherine Booth to the rank of commissioner. It was a double promotion – Catherine went straight from being a colonel to being a full commissioner, bypassing the rank of lieut-commissioner. It was unusual, but not totally without precedent. Eighteen months previously the General had given Colonel Samuel Brengle a similar double promotion to full commissioner – and everyone had considered that to be a masterstroke.

The potential significance of the promotion was not lost on close observers of the Army scene – including W. L. Atwood and his informants. Most of the first edition of *The International Salvationist* was devoted to its implications. 'The universal indignation aroused throughout the Army world by the promotion of the General's eldest daughter, Catherine, to the rank of full commissioner is a significant sign that the pernicious system of recklessly advancing his own family by the General, irrespective of ability or fitness, is universally felt to be one of the biggest menaces at present existing to the best interest of the Army.'

Even more sober observers than W. L. Atwood did wonder whether this was a sign that Bramwell Booth was thinking in dynastic terms. Nobody could be sure. After all, the Leader of the Women's Social Work had always held the rank of commissioner. Catherine Booth had been Leader for a year and a half and no one disputed that she had risen efficiently to the challenge.

However, the tectonic plates had shifted yet again. From that moment on, when there was talk about Bramwell Booth appointing a member of his family as his successor, the focus was no longer so much on his wife as on his daughter Catherine.

Meanwhile another drama was reaching its climax.

A relationship breaks

General Bramwell Booth had a trusted confidant. He was Colonel George Carpenter, who together with his wife Minnie had arrived from Australia in 1911. George Carpenter was appointed Assistant Secretary to the General, and retained that position when he later was appointed to the key responsibility of Literary Secretary. In the years that followed, Bramwell Booth and George Carpenter grew close, and in their daily conferences the General would often take him into his confidence and confer with him on matters far beyond literature. George Carpenter became a sounding board for his General. Carpenter, whose warm, friendly and low-key personality endeared him to everyone at International Headquarters, was so devoted to Bramwell Booth that he made it a personal rule never to leave the building in the evening until he saw the General's light go out – in case he might be needed for anything.

George Carpenter was always open with the General. 'Upon entering his confidential service he told me always to express my own opinions concerning matters that were before him. This I did. He was not always pleased with my frank expressions, but never resented them.'[15] That is, until 'The First Blast of a Trumpet' sounded in March 1925.

At their conference the next day the General asked him if he had received a copy. Yes, he had. The General asked: 'Who wrote it?' George Carpenter said he had no idea who the writer was and expressed his deep distaste for the attack on his leader. 'Who wrote it?' asked the General again. George Carpenter said quietly: 'General, it is not so much who wrote it, but is there any truth in it?'[16]

They discussed aspects of the document, the General seeking Carpenter's views. 'General, your policy is causing unrest,' he said. As the discussion continued it became clear that Carpenter's assessment of the situation – especially relative to the influence of the family – was unacceptable to the General, who at one point asserted: 'But my children expect to be heard.'

The interview closed, but a bond had been broken. From that time on their meetings became less frequent until in the end they became rare occasions. In time Colonel George Carpenter discovered how truly out of court he was when even matters directly related to literature were decided without reference to him.

Colonel Carpenter never breathed a word to others at International Headquarters about the breakdown of the relationship, but it was evident to all. Attempts at restoring the previous bond were made but quickly petered out. Occasional notes were exchanged, occasional conversations held. In one of them the General said that he felt that Carpenter was showing a disloyal spirit. This prompted George Carpenter on 8 January 1927 – nearly two years after 'The First Blast of the Trumpet' had opened a rift in their relationship – to write a long letter to his General. It was to bring matters to a head:

Your remark that my letter of 5th inst. evidenced a disloyal spirit touched me deeply. Far from being disloyal either in word or practice I have carried my loyalty to a degree that would outside Army circles be considered ridiculous. *I* do not feel so. I have served you as unto the Lord.

In Salvationists, as I know them, whether Staff, Field, or rank and file, I see a general and unshaken loyalty to the Army and its principles. The same for yourself in the main, but not all that I could desire, for there is a widespread feeling that you show unseemly preference for your family in the life and affairs of the Army ...

The Army is perhaps the last great public body to remain under autocratic government. In most civilised lands a man may speak openly as he feels concerning public affairs and rulers ... Within the Army there is a settled belief that one may be a Salvationist of unimpeachable devotion, of ability and godliness, but should he or she express views out of accord with the General and in particular in regard to arrangements for his family, he or she is accounted disloyal and is in consequence discredited ...

I see people fair to your face and to your family speaking otherwise away from your presence. This I feel to be the *real* disloyalty, and is poisoning the truth and honour of the Army ... It is a mixture of cowardice, sycophancy and self-interest. I have reproved this kind of thing both in public and in private.[17]

In a brief acknowledgment, Bramwell Booth described the letter as 'a bomb', adding that 'your difficulties are really moonshine. I will see you as soon as I can.' The letter, however, was regarded as a sign of insubordination and Colonel Carpenter was informed that he must either divulge the names of the people who were fair to the General's face but otherwise behind his back or withdraw the letter. This George Carpenter refused to do.

A difficult interview with the General, at which the Chief of the Staff was also present, followed.

'I have been wounded in the house of my friends,' began the General. 'I have always had such affection for you and confidence in you.'

'But, General,' replied Colonel Carpenter, 'with all that affection and confidence, if I cannot speak to you out of my heart concerning things I feel to be injurious to the Army, who in the name of heaven can speak to you?'

Bramwell Booth leaned back in his chair and then after a moment sighed.

'I would rather you had not told me.'[18]

Great efforts were made to persuade Colonel Carpenter to withdraw the letter. Catherine Booth spoke to him for two hours. Even so, George Carpenter would not disclose any names, neither would he withdraw the letter.

Shortly afterwards Colonel George Carpenter was appointed editor of the Sydney *War Cry*, an appointment he had held 22 years previously when that publication covered the whole of Australia and not just part as now. The move caused shock waves to reverberate around International Headquarters and beyond. Even some who previously had refused to believe that officers could be sidelined for disagreeing with the General began to wonder.

On 15 March 1927 when Colonel and Mrs Carpenter left for Botany Bay, virtually every officer and employee of International Headquarters went to St Pancras Station to see the boat train off. The well-wishers were headed by no fewer than 14 commissioners. The demonstration spoke volumes. It must have been affirming for the Carpenters, but for General Bramwell Booth it was another warning rumble.

Twelve years later, when George Carpenter walked through the doors of International Headquarters again, it was as General George L. Carpenter, the fifth General of The Salvation Army.

Chapter Five

Confrontation

WHEN on a crisp autumnal day in October 1927 Commander Evangeline Booth arrived at the cathedral of Notre Dame in Paris she was drawn aside by officials. Thousands of American veterans of the war had crossed the ocean to participate in the 10th anniversary of the entrance of the United States into the First World War, and they had carried with them Evangeline Booth as their orator and their emblem. The service in Notre Dame was the culmination of a week of celebrations arranged by the American Legion.

As Evangeline Booth was ushered into a side room, she was informed that General Pershing, commander of the American forces in the war, and Marshall Foch, Marshall of France and Supreme Allied Commander, had specifically requested that she march between them at the head of the procession into the cathedral.

Every eye was on the Commander as the solemn procession reached the altar. No one was surprised to see her there. The exploits of The Salvation Army's 'doughnut girls' in serving the troops in France during the war had made her a household name throughout the USA. In 1919 she had received the Distinguished Service Medal from President Wilson honouring the Army's work with the troops and citing 'the great executive abilities of its Commander'. Standing by the altar, clad in the Expeditionary Force Salvation Army uniform that she herself had designed, she dominated the proceedings of that day.

However, Commander Evangeline Booth was not in Europe just for the anniversary celebrations of the American Legion. Ahead of her lay an important interview with her brother, General Bramwell Booth, at International Headquarters in London.

A factor in the strained relationship between Bramwell and Evangeline was her role as National Commander and long-term plans – dating back to the time of William Booth – for changing the command structure in the USA. The main point of contention, however, was constitutional reform. Their many conversations on the subject had never led to Bramwell Booth taking any action. Unrest on the subject was increasing among senior officers. Evangeline Booth was therefore on the way to London to force the issue. As the daughter of the Founder, sister of the General and National Commander of the Army in the USA, she was in a uniquely strong position to do so.

The interview took place at International Headquarters on 11 October 1927. The meeting was brief, tense – and momentous.

The Commander's Fifteen Points – October 1927

Evangeline Booth presented a paper with 15 numbered paragraphs. 'The conviction is growing everywhere,' she began, 'that the time has arrived when some change must take place in the constitution of the Army, particularly with respect to the appointment of the General. It could never have been in the minds of the few evangelists who consented to the proposal to invest the Founder as sole trustee for all temporalities of the Army, and give him such absolute power, that it would grow to such proportions. While officers were content during the Founder's life to entrust him with all authority, including the appointment of his successor, it must be apparent that with the changing conditions some alteration in the Deed Poll of 1878 must be brought about.' She continued:

> It is almost universally hoped that the present General will be the last one to be appointed by his predecessor ... To have the High Council, or some such body within the Army, select the succeeding Generals would provide a safeguard for the future.
>
> There may be certain legal difficulties in the way of changing the deed poll in this particular, but beyond all reasonable doubt those

difficulties can be overcome. 'Where there's a will there's a way.' ... If other religious bodies can change their constitution it must be clear that The Salvation Army can.

A change is inevitable, and the only question is whether you will bring it about in your lifetime, which is the most desirable, or risk the Army splitting upon this issue.

If strong representations have not been made to you by officers of rank and experience along this line, it has not been for the lack of conviction, but because of fear lest they should be penalised for stating their views, and perhaps there can be no greater indictment than this of the system as it is.

If you would like to know the convictions of your leading officers upon this point, including commissioners, why do you not give them an opportunity to express themselves, making it clear at the same time that their present positions and future appointments would not in any way be affected by the views they held?

A brief discussion ensued during which the Commander emphasised that many commissioners shared her opinions – including the Chief of the Staff, Commissioner Edward Higgins. She then handed the General a copy of her paper. General Bramwell Booth assured his sister that he would carefully consider the points she had made and that he would respond to them in due course. There was not much more to say. They rose and when they reached the door they paused and then, as was their custom, they hugged and kissed.

It was the last time they were to meet on earth.

The Chief of the Staff

General Bramwell Booth had been surprised to hear the Commander say that the Chief of the Staff, Commissioner Edward Higgins, his trusted right-hand man, shared her views on the need for reform, for the Chief had never expressed any thoughts on the subject to him. When Bramwell Booth mentioned to the Chief what the Commander had said, it was the Chief's turn to be surprised, for he had never spoken of his views on constitutional reform to her or to any other person.

As the subject had now been broached, Commissioner Higgins took the opportunity to acknowledge that he too believed there ought to be a change in the method of appointing the General. He made it clear, however, that in his view this was a matter for the General alone to decide, and that he was against any agitation on the subject.[1]

That the Chief of the Staff shared the Commander's views 'was doubtless a shock to the General,' writes Edward Higgins's biographer, 'for he preferred to think that in this matter as in others he and his Chief were in full accord, although there had never been any discussion of this particular subject between them ... Realising the delicacy of the position, Higgins urged the General to relieve him of his position as Chief of the Staff and to select someone in entire harmony with his views, at the same time promising to accept any other position in the Army entrusted to him.

'General Bramwell Booth was unable to grant this request, urging that the Chief should stand by him. This the latter promised to do if it was understood that he would express no views contrary to his convictions. At the same time, he was willing to pass on the General's views, provided it was stated they were the General's.

'On two occasions when the position between the two men was at a stalemate, the Chief of the Staff reiterated his plea for relief, but his requests were not granted.'[2]

There was a deep and mutual bond of affection between Bramwell Booth and Edward Higgins even though they disagreed on the matter of reform. 'As long as I am entrusted with the position I occupy,' wrote the Chief to the General some weeks after the Commander's visit to International Headquarters, 'I could do no other but stand by you *whatever you decide*. Whether it entirely accorded with my views or not, it would be dishonourable for me not to do so, and my influence wherever I am will all be exerted for you, and to uphold your authority.'[3]

Bramwell Booth had already agreed a request by Edward Higgins that he be allowed to retire early, on his 65th birthday rather than on his 70th, and this date – 26 November 1929 – was fast approaching.[4]

Such was their relationship that Bramwell Booth already viewed with dismay the loss of his Chief of the Staff on that day.

During the next months Edward Higgins was to find himself at the very epicentre of a constitutional hurricane. As General Albert Orsborn comments: 'He did not know that he was cast for a part in Army history very like that of a sea captain who appeared in one of his favourite platform illustrations: an extremely stormy Channel crossing, with the boat thrown about alarmingly. Many passengers were terrified. Higgins, who was a good sailor, moving along the deck, lifted his eyes to the bridge. There stood the Captain, completely in command, serious but not alarmed, confidently steering his ship through the storm.'[5] *Storm Pilot,* the title of Edward Higgins's biography, sums up his role perfectly.

Other voices

Following the visit of the Commander, Bramwell Booth spoke privately with a few of his closest colleagues at International Headquarters about her demand for constitutional reform. Though there was little sympathy for the fact that the Commander was agitating on the subject, some took the opportunity to state that they too agreed with much of what she had said.

Commissioner Henry Mapp, the International Secretary for the United States, the British Dominions and the Missionary West Territories, was one of the commissioners who at that time told the General that he supported constitutional reform. He was the son of English parents living in Bombay, had become an officer in India, and by the age of 29 was already the territorial commander for Ceylon. Following appointments in Britain he became chief secretary for Canada, and then territorial commander for South America, for Japan and for Russia, before returning to International Headquarters.

Having now made his position clear to the General, Commissioner Mapp felt free to share his convictions about reform with others, and as the international secretary for virtually the entire English-speaking world, he was in a key position to do so.

Another leader who at that time made his position on reform clear to Bramwell Booth was Lieut-Commissioner Isaac Unsworth, a travelling commissioner at International Headquarters. Isaac Unsworth was one of the Army's most experienced international officers, having served not only in Britain but also in South Africa, the Caribbean, Ceylon and Australia, and was personally close to Bramwell Booth. In a revealing note to a colleague in the USA he wrote:

After the big row led by the Commander and followed by several commissioners of high standing ... I have at last spoken out my full mind to the General on the matter of the Army's future, and am now considered to be a rebel to the family arrangement.

I merely put the question to him, whether the time had not arrived when he should call to his side some of his old and trusted commissioners and discuss with them the question of succession and other matters vital to the Army's future, and see if some way could not be found to settle the whole affair without breaking up the unity of the movement. To my great surprise he rose to his feet and said I had joined the enemy against him, that he 'would not yield an inch for anyone let the consequences be what they might'; that he had received his orders from his father regarding the succession, and that it was a principle of the constitution which he intended to uphold and carry out.

I asked him then whether he could really hand over to a successor all the powers and responsibilities of Army trade, finance, appointments, direction, banking, yes, all the weighty matters of government, and feel that one person could really carry out successfully these great duties. I told him I personally could not see anyone in view and doubted if anyone else could ... I asked him if he thought Mrs Booth, should she survive him, would be able to keep the Army together. He angrily asked me, 'Why not?'

He later wrote me a letter in which he hinted that he may be compelled to effect some change, that I must pray for him, etc. But I am persuaded that the home influence will be too strong for him, and he will pursue his old course and one of his family will be nominated to fill his place, let the consequences be what they may.

Just think of it, my dear friend, the Army has to be blindfolded re the matter of succession until the fatal day when some little lawyer man will fish out of his safe a piece of paper and call out a name. And from that moment the person whose name is found thereon has to be accepted by the whole Army as General, and will be vested with all the tremendous powers of that office. And it may be Wycliffe, Bernard or Mary. Catherine is out of the running as her health could not stand the strain.[6]

The reference to the health of Catherine Bramwell Booth is of special interest as by that time she was a commissioner and had been in charge of the Women's Social Work for a year and a half.

Yet another leader who spoke up for reform was retired Commissioner John Carleton. Commissioner Carleton was 79 years of age, but was still lithe, upright and vigorous, with a razor-sharp mind. He could easily pass as a 50-year-old. Though a retired officer, he remained the Joint Managing Director of The Salvation Army Assurance Society. He was known to all Salvationists because as a young officer he had offered to go without his daily 'pudding' for a year in order to raise funds for the Army – an offer which had led William Booth to institute the annual Self-Denial Week. He was one of the most respected of the Army's elder statesmen and was to become a pivotal figure in the crisis of 1929.

Disagreeable discoveries

The Commander's visit had intensified the pressure for reform. General Bramwell Booth was anxious to give convincing replies to each of the 15 points that she had raised so that the debate about reform would be closed down once and for all. He therefore consulted extensively with Mr William Frost and his personal legal adviser Mr Frederick Sneath before replying. In this process he made what to him were some disagreeable discoveries about the 1904 Supplementary Deed.

His close colleagues had warned him about what might happen upon his decease if he insisted on nominating a member of his own family as his successor through the 'sealed envelope'. Writes Lieut-Commissioner Isaac Unsworth to the Commander: 'The General has had his lawyers at the office and has gone over the matter with them, and finds to his own chagrin that the contention of the commissioners is right. Should he nominate anyone to succeed him who is unsuitable, they can refuse to accept him or her. This has thoroughly alarmed the General and Mrs Booth.'[7]

Then there was that fateful catch-all phrase in the 1904 Deed in the list of grounds on which a General could be removed from office. Writes Commissioner Carleton to the Commander: 'It was a bombshell for him to learn that a General could be removed from office for "other circumstances" which rendered him unfit for office besides those things specifically mentioned in Clause 2. He was very emphatic that the High Council could only act for such things as lunacy, insolvency, misconduct and such like. His legal advisers have put him right on that point and he will now move heaven and earth to get that altered.'[8]

'Other circumstances', he learnt, could include impairment of natural powers or of judgment – in fact *anything* the commissioners considered relevant to the situation. Mr William Frost indicated privately to Commissioner Carleton that in his opinion the words gave 'ample scope to the commissioners'.[9]

Following these discussions with his legal advisers Bramwell Booth decided he must seek independent legal counsel on how the 1904 Supplementary Deed might be amended and 'strengthened'. The catch-all phrase needed to be removed or changed – it left a General dangerously exposed. Furthermore, the High Council could too easily be called – it only needed seven commissioners to trigger it. There were also other points that needed attention. Bramwell Booth therefore asked a top constitutional expert to undertake a full review of the text of the 1904 Supplementary Deed.

In the meantime the Commander's Fifteen Points had to be responded to.

The General's response to the Fifteen Points – November 1927
In his response, dated 24 November 1927, Bramwell Booth set out his convictions on the subject of reform – convictions which he held as strongly as his sister held hers. Each paragraph was drafted with

the utmost care, but one paragraph in particular was to ignite an explosion as the movement towards reform began to accelerate.

The General began his reply by meeting head-on the Commander's assertion that if other religious bodies can change their constitution then the Army can: 'Let me say at the outset that neither I as an individual nor the Army as an organisation have any such power.'

He then reiterated that whereas the Supplementary Deed of 1904 could be varied with the consent of two thirds of the commissioners, this did not mean that the Foundation Deed of 1878 could be varied. 'In reality neither I nor any other General, either with or without the consent of any officers, can have the power to alter that Constitutional Deed ... upon which The Salvation Army has been built.' He continued – and this is the explosive paragraph:

> And, indeed, if I felt it desirable to exercise, with the consent of the commissioners, the powers of alteration of the [1904] Supplementary Deed given to the General by that Deed, it would rather be with the aim of protecting the essential features of the Foundation Deed of 1878 than otherwise.

As for altering the original 1878 constitution itself, 'I have not the legal power that has been attributed to me. But if I had, I should greatly fear, nay I should be even unwilling, to exercise it. I should feel that to do so should be wrong.' The 1878 and 1904 Deeds 'are both gifts which were left us by our Founder ... When I am asked to tinker with his foundation and to alter in a material part his conception of our system ... I cannot take upon myself so grave a responsibility.'

> As to the appointment of a succeeding General, your suggestion aims at cancelling the General's most urgent duty – his duty to discern and name his successor; and it aims at this for no useful purpose, for if the named successor be a person whom the commissioners generally consider to be fit for the office, why interfere? If, on the other hand, after due consideration and trial he be found to be unfit by the

commissioners, they already have the power of deposing him and of electing a fit person in his place.

The suggested alternative 'would entail delay and uncertainty, and an appreciable if not serious break and stoppage in the control and administration of the Work, and possibly engender personal seekings and rivalries which might break up the unity and spoil the teamwork of the higher command, and even spread downwards, weakening the whole organisation.'

> Nothing in the whole range of Salvation Army life and growth appeared more important to the Founder than providing – as far as human foresight and wisdom could provide – for the appointment of future Leaders who should be free from the danger of having to rely upon favour, either national or international, in order to obtain or retain their positions. It would be idle to say he did not realise that certain risks must attach to any method of appointment, but after long consideration ... he concluded that the method of appointment on which he decided in 1878 ... was, on the whole, the safest and best.

'You will see, therefore,' he concludes, 'that I am opposed to the suggestion which has been made ... It misconceives the fundamental character of the office of the General.' Bramwell Booth then ends with a ringing declaration of his credo:

> The General is not the maker or unmaker or alterer of the original Trust. He is the Trustee, the servant of the Trust. His great duty is to conform to its terms, preserve its integrity and spirit, to guard and fulfil it, and to hand it on in complete and unimpaired efficiency to his successor. That has been and is my aim.

Opposite views

Brother and sister held diametrically opposite views of what was best for the Army. The son and the daughter of William Booth both claimed that their different views were those of their father. For Bramwell the 1878 constitution was holy writ. He was utterly convinced that his father would want him to protect it at all cost and to 'hand it on in complete and unimpaired efficiency to his successor'. For Evangeline the 1878 constitution was a document which William Booth had himself already 'supplemented'. Even though William Booth had set the 1878 constitution in stone, to her it was crystal clear that her father, ever the pragmatist, would want the Army's constitution to evolve to match changing circumstances.

With both Bramwell and Evangeline having inherited the iron wills of William and Catherine Booth, they were not easily to be diverted from their views, and were in fact prepared to go to the very edge of the precipice – and beyond – to remain true to their convictions. The Army was about to discover what happens when an irresistible force meets an immovable object.

It was an argument about principles, but there was also a human dimension. If Bramwell's conviction prevailed, his daughter could be the next General. If Evangeline's conviction carried the day, she herself was likely to be the next General. To what degree that human factor influenced events even the protagonists themselves probably never knew.

The Commander ponders

Commander Evangeline Booth was disappointed with the reply that she received to her Fifteen Points, but an action plan had begun to form in her mind. She knew that the next step had to be the preparation of a point-by-point rebuttal of the arguments that General Bramwell Booth had advanced.

She consulted with her territorial commanders in the USA and with like-minded colleagues in London. No single leader dominated the reform movement in Britain as she herself did in the USA and she therefore kept in touch with several of them.

Commissioner John Carleton sent her an analysis of the reply Bramwell Booth had made together with suggested lines of response. He advised her to draw attention to the paragraph in which the General had mentioned the possibility that the 1904

Supplementary Deed might be amended. By so doing, he said, she would also warn any commissioners who might see the correspondence that they could be asked to give their consent to such changes. When the Commander's next letter appeared it contained verbatim a number of the paragraphs and sentences suggested by Commissioner Carleton.

The Commander also discussed her proposed reply in detail with her distinguished legal adviser, Mr George W. Wickersham, who had been the USA Attorney General under President Theodore Roosevelt.

It was not until 9 February 1928 that the Commander's response was ready to be mailed. If Bramwell Booth hoped that his letter of 24 November 1927 had settled the matter of reform once and for all, his hopes were dashed when he read her response. It was a letter of 21 pages and immediately became known as her Long Letter.

The Commander's Long Letter – February 1928

In her Long Letter, Evangeline Booth began by challenging Bramwell Booth's contention that it was not legally possible to modify the 1878 constitution, arguing that the way it had been 'supplemented' and 'amplified' in 1904 was nothing less than 'sweeping modifications of that sacredly unalterable instrument' – and that what had been done once could be done again. She wrote in strong terms:

> The implication so pervading your memorandum that the Foundation Deed of 1878 is complete, final, and unalterable, and that it must remain untouchable as the Alpha and Omega of our constitution, for ever defiant of every amendment that development, progress or future generations may demand, fails to accord with our experience as an organisation, and is utterly repugnant to the responsibilities that attach themselves inalienably to God-guided and Christ-following men and women.

She then, very significantly, narrowed her request for reform to one point only: 'The chief and only change that is of immediately pressing importance is that which has to do with the method of appointing or choosing the General's successor', adding that this particular reform could be legally achieved even without altering the 1878 constitution. She reminded her brother that the deed poll offered two alternatives when it came to the General exercising 'his most urgent duty'. In the 'sealed envelope' he could either name his successor or indicate 'the means which are to be taken for the appointment of a successor'.

> Adopting either you would be in perfect legal order. Your legal responsibility to direct the High Council, at your decease or upon the cessation of the duties of your office, to proceed to the election of your successor is no less obligatory than is your responsibility to discern and name your successor.

The Commander then upbraided her brother over his fears that electing a General might 'engender personal seekings and rivalries'. She argued that with the 'sealed envelope' system 'the tendency is surely and almost unavoidably towards dynasty', and that the power invested in the office of the General 'constitutes most serious temptation when conjoined to paternal affection and family influence'. Personal seeking would therefore be less likely if the General were to be elected by a group of leaders.

> Since you cite the possibility of 'personal seekings and rivalries' being associated with this reform, may I not reasonably ask whether the possibility of that very thing is not the greatest blight that attaches to the present system?
> You are a father with sons and daughters whose rapid advancement in both rank and position has been and is the subject of worldwide criticism. Should one of the children be appointed as your successor it would be strongly resented, especially by those very officers whose hearty cooperation is so essential if your successor is to have the strong confidence in all lands.
> A body of 50 commissioners would be less susceptible to corruption than is one man. The High Council would be far less exposed to the

temptation of personal seeking or personal favouritism than is positively inherent in the present system.

Evangeline Booth then quoted and challenged the 'explosive' paragraph in Bramwell Booth's memorandum in which he mentioned that he might wish to amend the 1904 Supplementary Deed:

> Am I to accept this as an intimation that you have in mind the withdrawal of those too meagre protective powers conferred upon the High Council that provide for the removal of a General who may be mentally or morally unfit, or who may be deemed unsuitable through 'other circumstances' for the great command?
>
> I cannot help but say that it would indeed be an unjustifiable and most flagrant action on the part of the Chief Executive of our international peoples to answer a prayer for fuller liberty with a course of further oppression and deprivation. It is unthinkable. I really think some reassuring word should be forthcoming immediately upon this issue.

With all the dramatic eloquence at her command, the Commander moved to her climax by pleading with the General to remove 'the enslaving provision of the 1878 Deed Poll', this Deed Poll which is 'a millstone about our neck, a stumbling-stone in our path, and impediment to our progress', this 'impossible 1878 Deed Poll' with its 'obsolete and entirely unreasonable restrictions', whose 'weakness, imperfection and incompleteness ... was definitely acknowledged nearly 20 years ago, when our Founder laboured with you and others to provide some corrective for those self-evident weaknesses'. She ended with a call for action:

> The time for much argument is passed – deeds alone will meet the demand ... I am convinced that you could not close your remarkable career with any single act that would bring to it a greater crowning than this piece of fundamental defensive and constructive work which is the supreme need of our glorious movement.

A fateful step

Two weeks after writing this letter, Evangeline Booth took the next step in the implementation of her own action plan. On 24 February 1928 she wrote to all commissioners and territorial commanders, including with her letter the three pieces of correspondence she had had with the General on the matter of reform. They each received a copy of her Fifteen Points as Exhibit A, Bramwell Booth's reply as Exhibit B, and her Long Letter as Exhibit C. In her covering letter she mentioned that she already had the support of 21 commissioners and added: 'I do not want you to feel under any obligation to commit yourself to me. All the same, if you care to write me, I shall be glad indeed to hear from you.'

Sharing private correspondence in this way was unheard of. It was no longer a matter of a sister pleading privately with her brother. It was now the Commander taking all her fellow leaders around the world behind the scenes and asking them to take sides in the dispute. She was in effect setting herself up as the leader of the opposition. It was a fateful step.

Some leaders had become aware of rumblings on the constitutional reform front, but for many of them, especially those working in isolation in distant commands, the content of the package from New York came as a complete surprise.

It is clear that the Commander hoped that the circulation of the correspondence would result in irresistible pressure being brought to bear on Bramwell Booth to initiate reform. However, hers was not the Army way. By her letter the Commander was hoisting the flag of defiance and calling her fellow leaders to arms.

Chapter Six

Pressure

SATURDAY morning was part of the working week in the 1920s, and it was on a Saturday morning – 3 March 1928 – that the Commander's letter with its three 'exhibits' reached the commissioners based in London. General Bramwell Booth had received his copy some days before. It had come as a bitter blow – the first of a long series of blows he was about to receive.

As the commissioners at International Headquarters and the other London headquarters read the correspondence the alarm bells began to sound. Their attention focused on the paragraph dealing with the possibility that Bramwell Booth might seek to secure the necessary approval to alter the 1904 Supplementary Deed 'with the aim of protecting the essential features of the [1878] Foundation Deed'. What did that mean? The 1904 Supplementary Deed was their defence against an all-powerful General. Were those provisions about to be weakened?

They had more reason to be concerned than they realised, for they did not know that Bramwell Booth had already sought independent legal counsel on how the 1904 Supplementary Deed might be modified. On exactly the same Saturday morning that the London commissioners received their copies of the circulated correspondence, General Bramwell Booth sat in his office and read the leading counsel's opinion:

The real point is that a small, but eager and determined minority ought not to be at liberty to cause the expense, dislocation of work, and inevitable scandal incidental to an advertised formal discussion of the fitness of a General of The Salvation Army for his work. The very fact that the High Council has been summoned to sit in judgment upon him would in the minds of many be enough to condemn him, on the principle that Caesar's wife must be above suspicion.[1]

The implication was clear: the number of requisitioners needed to set in motion the calling of a High Council – which according to the 1904 Deed was either 'the Chief of the Staff and four other commissioners' or 'seven commissioners without the Chief of the Staff' – should be increased in order to make it more difficult for a High Council to be summoned.

Legal counsel had also reiterated how vulnerable the General's position was through the inclusion of the catch-all words 'other circumstances' in the 1904 Deed. If nine out of ten commissioners agreed that 'in consequence of ... *other circumstances*' he was unfit to continue as General, they could remove him from office through a 'write-in' without even calling the High Council. He was also warned – as he had been by his own legal adviser – that if the High Council was called, the Council itself might use those words as a basis for removing him. Legal counsel recommended that the catch-all phrase be deleted or be rewritten so as to indicate clearly that it referred only to wrongdoing on the part of the General, not to circumstances in general.

Even without the benefit of this background knowledge, the London commissioners were disturbed that Saturday morning as they read the exchange of correspondence between the General and the Commander. Discreet telephone calls and conversations established that the feeling of alarm was widespread. The arrival of the correspondence had acted as a catalyst. It was time for the London-based commissioners who favoured reform to nail their colours to the mast. Word was quietly passed from one to the other that an unofficial meeting would be held on Monday evening to discuss the situation. The venue would be 35a Gloucester Road, Kensington – the home of Mrs Carton, Commissioner David Lamb's married daughter – and the time would be 7pm. Attendees were asked to come in civilian clothes so as not to draw attention to themselves.

If the circulation of correspondence by the Commander was unprecedented, a secret 'out of office hours' meeting of commissioners in 'civvies' at a 'non-Army' location was totally unparalleled. Was it a conspiracy in the making?

Gloucester Road

First to arrive for the meeting on Monday 5 March 1928 was Commissioner Henry Mapp, followed by Commissioner Samuel Hurren – the British Commissioner whom Bramwell Booth had mentored from his boyhood – and then Commissioner David Lamb. These three were the prime movers towards reform among the London commissioners in active service.

Commissioner David Lamb was the International Social Secretary and Director of Migration. He was the most outstanding Army statesman and constitutional expert of his day. Already chief secretary in South Africa at the age of 23, he had been recalled to Britain a year later to help launch the Darkest England scheme. Through his work in establishing workshops and farm colonies, and subsequently the migration service, Commissioner Lamb worked closely with governments at home and abroad and became a much respected figure in the highest of circles.

The next to arrive were the two retired commissioners who were active in the cause of reform, Commissioner Frederick Booth-Tucker and Commissioner John Carleton.

Within a short space of time four more commissioners followed: Commissioner Charles Jeffries, Principal of the International Training Garrison, who before his conversion had been second-in-command of the 'Skeleton Army' that attacked early-day Salvationists, and had since been one of the pioneer officers in Australia and territorial commander in Scotland and North China. Commissioner Robert Hoggard, International Travelling Commissioner, who had pioneered the work in Korea and had been territorial commander in Scotland, South Africa and New Zealand.

Commissioner Arthur Blowers, International Secretary for India, Ceylon and the Eastern Missionary Section, who had given 37 of his years of service to the Indian sub-continent. Finally Commissioner Richard Wilson, Secretary for Trade at Salvationist Publishing and Supplies Ltd, whose service had been centred on Britain but who in his earlier years had been in charge of the Army's work in Denmark and later in Norway.

The appointed hour of 7pm was fast approaching. The meeting had been mentioned to other London commissioners, but it was known that some of them were not happy with the stirrings about reform and therefore no one else was really expected. Then just before 7pm the door bell rang again. In walked Commissioner Edward Higgins, the Chief of the Staff – also in civilian clothes.

There were suppressed murmurs of surprise. As Chief of the Staff, Commissioner Edward Higgins was the General's eyes and ears, his spokesperson – in every respect his alter ego. What was he doing here?

His presence was controversial and was later to be criticised by members of the Booth family. He himself probably hesitated before deciding to attend, but the 'storm pilot' must have felt that he was more likely to bring the ship safely to port by staying on the bridge than by abandoning it at a critical juncture.

As we know, Edward Higgins was sympathetic to reform, and as Chief of the Staff he had probably seen the disturbing legal opinion received two days earlier as to how the 1904 Supplementary Deed might be modified. His aim was to seek to persuade Bramwell Booth to take the initiative in bringing about reform, and he no doubt felt it important that the General should be made aware of the strength of feeling in favour of reform and against any modification of the 1904 Deed. At the same time he wanted to avoid agitation that might get out of control. By keeping his hand on the helm he could influence the course of events. Bramwell Booth never learnt that his Chief had attended this meeting.

After initial discussion, Commissioner Samuel Hurren produced the draft of a letter addressed to the General that he had prepared.

Various amendments were suggested. It was vital to get all the nuances right. The General's ultimate authority in constitutional affairs had to be recognised, but it was important that the General should know that they as a group supported the Commander's views on reform and were adamantly opposed to any change being made to the 1904 Supplementary Deed.

One senses Edward Higgins's steadying hand in the drafting. Some were later to feel that the letter was almost too deferential in its tone. Eventually an agreed text was arrived at. Commissioner Hurren undertook to have the letter typed up clean overnight. First thing the next morning, 6 March 1928, Commissioner Hurren signed the letter and then went from office to office at headquarters until all had signed. As agreed at the meeting, he did not ask the Chief of the Staff to sign because of his unique relationship with the General.

When General Bramwell Booth later entered his office that morning he found the letter lying on his desk. He opened it and read:

Dear General,

We have, as you will know, received a communication from Commander E. C. Booth with certain enclosures, and whilst feeling sympathy with her representations upon the question of the method of the appointment of future Generals of The Salvation Army, also consider that it would be wise to contemplate the advisability of some change at this point before greater demands are more widely made or public controversy aroused.

We nevertheless realise that this question is largely if not entirely one of your own decision and that it is possible that we have no power to influence you upon the matter, as will be realised by both present and future Salvationists or other persons interested in the subject.

We nevertheless most earnestly hope that the suggestions put forward may receive most serious consideration as we believe the question to be one of vital importance to the future stability and usefulness of the Army.

We are bound in any case to solemnly declare that we view the statement that it may be intended to alter the Supplementary Deed of

1904 with the gravest alarm and misgiving, considering that however simple your proposals may or may not be, the proceeding will be attended with consequences of a most serious character.

We regard the Deed of 1904 as the complement of the original [1878] Deed, but more particularly of the method of the appointment of future Generals, and as a sacred trust and responsibility bequeathed to and imposed upon not only yourself, but all the commissioners of The Salvation Army.

We therefore most seriously and respectfully beg you to reconsider your intention to proceed with the amendment of this deed for which we can see no useful reason to the organisation. And we think it only proper to inform you with the greatest and most respectful submission that we can in no manner be parties to the action proposed, and that, should the matter most unfortunately be proceeded with, we would to our infinite sorrow and regret feel compelled to jointly advise our comrades to also withhold the consent required under the provisions of the deed in question.

We most earnestly pray that you may receive this communication, conceived as it is in a spirit of deep affection and loyalty to yourself as well as to the principles of the Army, in such a manner as to enable you to give the assurances upon the subject mentioned which the present circumstances require.

The letter was signed by the seven active commissioners and the two retired commissioners who had been present at the meeting the night before.

A thunderbolt

The letter came as a thunderbolt for the General. As Mrs General Bramwell Booth was later to say to the High Council: 'There was not the slightest preparation of his mind for this shock ... This was a blow not only to the General as General, but to his heart.'[2]

Let Catherine Booth, with the protectiveness of a daughter, take up the story: 'Sitting alone in his room at Headquarters, Bramwell Booth bowed his heart in grief. He was stricken in that hour after such a fashion that, when presently he went into his wife's office, she started in alarm at his aspect, and knew before he spoke that calamity was at hand. He said, quietly, as was his wont, "My darling, here is trouble," and handing her the letter added, "Unless I had seen it with my own eyes I should never have believed Hurren's name was there."

'The force of this blow was twofold,' continues Catherine Booth. 'First, that these commissioners were in agreement with Commander Eva Booth, and secondly, that they should decide among themselves upon this method of informing him of their view. Apart from the two retired, all the commissioners who signed the letter were in close contact with him. Any one of them could see him easily at the shortest notice, he constantly conferred with them, had been on familiar terms with them all their lives; none was without tokens of his friendship, and it was inconceivable to him that they should choose to address him formally in writing, and as a group, before having previously expressed an opinion to him individually, or sought his view of the matters concerned. Further, each held a position of highest trust and was fully aware that the use of combined signatures was not in accord with the Army's military form of government, and would, in fact, be regarded by them as reprehensible in their subordinates.

'By that letter Bramwell Booth received a hurt from which he did not recover. Months afterwards, when he was trying to rest mind and body, his heart was still tasting the bitterness of that hour. Again and again he would suddenly break into the occupation of the moment to ask "Why didn't they speak to me?" or "I must have been very mistaken in A—— or B——, he has always come to me before."

'These men knew him, he and they shared numberless recollections of happy intimacies, journeyings together, discussions of their work. He had counted on a personal tie between them and him, between them and his father, and now, at the first breath of schism, they ranged themselves against him. Had they not been so fully established in his confidence they would not have had power to wound him so deeply.'[3]

It came as an immense shock to Bramwell Booth to learn that so many of the London commissioners were in sympathy with the reformist views of Evangeline Booth. He had always looked upon her views as something of an aberration – a personal agenda of hers – but it was clear that the desire for reform spanned the Atlantic. There were now two bodies pressing for reform – one in the USA headed by the Commander, and one in Britain headed by the signatories of the letter. The manner in which the news was conveyed also hurt him deeply – but he seems to have been strangely unaware of the atmosphere of fear that he himself had engendered among his closest associates.

General Bramwell Booth interviewed each of the signatories individually, with the exception of Commissioner Booth-Tucker, and drew some comfort from their assurances of personal loyalty. The encounter with Commissioner Samuel Hurren must have been especially painful.

On 10 March 1928, in the midst of working on a full reply to Evangeline Booth's Long Letter of 9 February 1928, Bramwell broke off to pen a personal note to her: 'We seem to be drifting apart and it wounds me to the quick. Is it inevitable?' He continues with words that Evangeline must have read with some surprise: 'I had no idea till I received yours that you attached so much importance to the method of appointing succeeding Generals or I would certainly have put before you some important views – especially the dear General's thoughts and experiences in dealing with this matter.' He then appeals to her as brother to sister:

But even though we do not agree on this, can we not differ without bringing in personal bitterness? You and I have been very near together … Can we not love on to the end …? Life cannot be so very long now for either of us.

You will, I am sure, realise that a great responsibility rests upon me. I received it from the dear General – nay, I received it from God – and if it should be that, as I conceive it, I am not at liberty to alter its conditions, do not condemn me or feel to me as a kind of enemy. Rather pray for me that grace and courage may be given me to do what God wants, and hold up my hands in every endeavour to keep the idea and plan of the Army what the dear father wished them to be.

There was to be no respite from jolts. On 13 March 1928 Bramwell Booth learnt that copies of the London commissioners' letter had been circulated to leading staff officers around the world. Even Commissioner Edward Higgins was disturbed by this unexpected turn of events which threatened the stability of the ship. *'This is too bad,'* he wrote to the General. 'Who else, I wonder, has the London commissioners' letter? I cannot understand this. Somebody is being used for propaganda. *I am sorry.'*[4] It seemed that forces had been unleashed that could no longer be controlled.

A crunch day

The blows kept hammering down on him. The next day – 14 March 1928 – was to be a crunch day. Early on that day Bramwell Booth received a cable signed by six commissioners (of which two were retired) and two colonels in the USA:

> In the opinion of leading officers, there is not the slightest question as to the desirability of constitutional change. Hope you will be able to make effective. We fully agree with Commander's proposal. We entreat you to crown your long successful career triumphantly by granting what ultimately is inevitable.[5]

Nevertheless, during the morning of that day – 14 March – Bramwell Booth reaffirmed his position in a brief holding letter addressed to all commissioners and territorial commanders:

> In view of the letters which have been sent to you ... I think it best to write to you very briefly. I received from the Founder, my beloved father, my position as General, making me guardian of Salvation Army interests everywhere, and the upholder of its principles and government. I neither can nor do I desire to make any change in the constitution of the Army ... I shall be writing to you more fully later.

During the afternoon of 14 March 1928 Bramwell Booth took the momentous step of changing the name of his appointed successor in the 'sealed envelope'.

Some days previously Bramwell Booth had given instructions to Mr William Frost that with the utmost secrecy a new appointment form was to be prepared for him to complete and sign. William Frost tells the story:

'Not only was the document prepared with this great secrecy, but the signing of it was also kept as secret as possible. It was in fact signed in a London Turkish bath, and elaborate precautions were taken to ensure that no one (except one of the General's sons) should know what was being done.

'With one of our managing clerks as a second witness, I attended at the Turkish baths with the form of nomination in my pocket. The General (who was actually in the course of taking a Turkish bath and was in a dressing gown) filled in a name, a piece of blotting paper was placed over this (so that we, as witnesses, could not see it), the General then signed the document, and we two witnesses signed it.

'The date was inserted (it was March 14, 1928), I placed the document in the envelope and sealed it down immediately and brought it away with me.'[6]

Bramwell Booth had first nominated a successor through the 'sealed envelope' method when he became General in 1912. As previously noted, that might well have been his wife, Florence Booth. Whether he had made subsequent changes we cannot know. Neither will we know exactly what prompted him to place a new name in the 'sealed envelope' on 14 March 1928, but it is likely that Bramwell Booth recognised that a constitutional storm was brewing and that it was now timely to bring to fruition his long-term plan for the succession.

Catherine Booth's health, against the expectation of many, had held up well and she was making her mark as Leader of the Women's Social Work. Now, surely, was the moment for her name to be placed in the 'sealed envelope' as the next General of The Salvation Army.

It is inconceivable that it could have been the name of anyone else. We know that Bramwell Booth was thinking long-term; he had plans for the next decade. Mrs Booth at 67 years of age was already two years over the retirement age for women commissioners, and opposition to the possibility of her being appointed had been openly voiced. The Commander was *persona non grata* and would anyway reach retirement age in less than three years. The Chief of the Staff was due to retire within 18 months.

Furthermore no rational sense can be made of events past and yet to come unless the 'sealed envelope' contained the name of a member of the General's immediate family. Complete certainty on the matter is not possible, but what is certain is that by this time every leader around the world took it for a fact that the name in the 'sealed envelope' was that of Catherine Booth. Had they known that the name had been inserted as late as 14 March 1928 any remaining doubt would have been dispelled.

As seen from his perspective, Bramwell Booth was right to get the matter of the succession settled, for the march of events was to be remorseless. He did not know it, neither did anyone else, but he had only eight weeks left during which the Army was effectively to be under his oversight, direction and control.

Chapter Seven

Breakdown

ON 15 March 1928 – the day after Bramwell Booth had changed the name in the 'sealed envelope' – he left for Germany and France, where for the next two weeks he conducted campaigns.

While he was in Paris he told the territorial commander for France, Commissioner Albin Peyron – to whom he was related through the marriage of his son Wycliffe to the Peyrons' daughter Renée – that he would probably call a meeting of all the commissioners to discuss the constitutional issue.[1]

The General returned to London on 27 March and was reassured by a note from the Chief of the Staff which awaited him: 'Everything is all right here. There are, of course, business matters awaiting your return, but I do not think there is any increase of anxiety on the special difficulty.'[2]

Even so, the General *was* anxious, and was beset on all sides and under increasing strain as he resumed his work at International Headquarters. Added to the usual incessant volume of business were the many letters and telegrams arriving from territories around the world about the material that the Commander had circulated. 'Wires from almost all territories expressed loyalty to the General, and determination to stand by the constitution,' reported Mrs Bramwell Booth,[3] but some leaders took the opportunity to urge the General to consult with his top leaders on the matter of the constitution. Commissioner Samuel Brengle wrote:

May I earnestly suggest that you lift the whole subject out of the realm of controversy by taking immediate counsel with representative leaders who are in touch with all ranks of officers throughout the world, inviting the fullest and frankest discussion and expression of opinion and conviction, facing all facts and fears, weighing impartially all dangers, canvassing the subject from every possible angle, and then arriving at your final decision, based, as it will be, upon accepted conclusions gathered from a survey so exhaustive that it will enlist the sympathy and heart support of your representative leaders.[4]

Weighing continually on Bramwell Booth's mind was how best to respond to the Commander's Long Letter of 9 February – the letter that she had circulated as Exhibit C. He was acutely conscious of the fact that all commissioners and territorial commanders had received a copy of her letter and that they had also received a copy of the communication from the nine London commissioners supporting her position on reform and opposing any change to the 1904 Deed. In his brief holding letter of 14 March he had reiterated: 'I neither can nor do I desire to make any change in the constitution of the Army.' However, he had also said that he would write more fully, and he knew that everyone was waiting to see how he would respond. It was vital to get it right.

The stress became almost unbearable. He could not sleep at night. As Mrs Booth later shared with the High Council: 'From March 1928, night after night he would talk to me for hours during the night and in the early hours of the morning as to what could be done to meet the situation wisely, without making scandal, without stirring antagonism.'[5]

What were some of the options for meeting the situation wisely that must have churned in Bramwell Booth's mind during those long night hours?

The General's options

One option was to pursue the plan to modify the 1904 Deed in order to make it more difficult for the High Council to be called. However, any proposed change to the 1904 Deed would need the consent of two thirds of the commissioners. In the light of the letter from the

London commissioners in which they had said that they themselves would withhold such consent and would actively urge their colleagues around the world to do the same, Bramwell Booth must have wondered whether this option was still viable.

A second option – at the other extreme – was for him to take the initiative and propose that changes should be made to the 1878 constitution. 'Where there's a will there's a way,' the Commander had said. There was a way, but it meant making the Army subject to Parliament. This possibility was so abhorrent to Bramwell Booth, so utterly unthinkable to him, that when he said he had no power to change the constitution he really believed it to be the case. Furthermore, even if there was a way there was no will. Bramwell Booth did not wish to change the 1878 Deed. To him the 1878 constitution was the Founder's special gift to the Army, and as his father's successor he felt it was his supreme duty 'to conform to its terms, preserve its integrity and spirit, to guard and fulfil it, and to hand it on in complete unimpaired efficiency to his successor'. It was therefore unlikely that Bramwell Booth would pursue this option.

A third option that Bramwell Booth must have seriously considered was to bring about reform *within the terms of the 1878 Deed*. The Commander had rightly reminded him that on the matter of selecting a General 'the 1878 Deed Poll provides the choice of two distinct procedures – adopting either you would be in perfect legal order'. Bramwell Booth could simply announce that he was going to avail himself of the second procedure, and that the 'sealed envelope' would contain not the name of his successor but 'the means' to be taken 'for the appointment of a successor' – say, that the commissioners would elect the next General.

Had Bramwell Booth adopted this course of action it is unlikely that there would have been a 1929 crisis. The ground would have been taken from under the feet of the reformers. Even though the General would not have met *all* of their demands, he would have acceded to their principal request, and would thus have made it difficult for the reformist movement to maintain its momentum.

However, there would have been a price to be paid. Bramwell Booth would have had to forego the right to name his successor. The next General would therefore probably not be his daughter Catherine but his sister Evangeline. For Bramwell Booth that would have been a high price to pay.

A fourth option that we know Bramwell Booth mulled over was whether to call a commissioners conference to discuss constitutional reform. In the history of the Army no commissioners conference had yet been held on that or any other subject. Leaders had met for staff councils in connection with international congresses but such gatherings were of an informative, inspirational and spiritual nature. A commissioners *conference* as such would be a very different matter.

Bramwell Booth would have had hesitations about calling such a conference. Even though it would be 'advisory' only and the commissioners would not be able to outvote the General, there was a real danger that Bramwell Booth could find himself isolated on the issue of reform and that the moral pressure would in the end prove irresistible. Why then call a conference, he must have asked himself, to be pressurised into doing something he did not wish to do and genuinely believed he had no power to do?

A fifth option that we also know Bramwell Booth seriously contemplated was to appoint a commission to study all aspects of constitutional reform and to make recommendations about the way forward. This would have the advantage of providing the kind of in-depth research that a commissioners conference could not undertake, but it would have the same disadvantage as calling a conference in that the commission might recommend changes that Bramwell Booth did not wish to make. This would leave him in a vulnerable position.

A sixth option Bramwell Booth considered was to evaluate all the advice he had received, decide the matter himself, and then bring the full authority of his office to bear on the announcement of his decision. This to him was the Army way. As he had responded to the American commissioners who had cabled him:

There always has been and ever will be the possibility in questions of government and administration upon which there may be room for two opinions, both based upon a sincere desire for the best. But those who find they hold opinions diverging from those of the General, having once wisely and properly expressed them, must subordinate their opinions to his with whom after all there must rest that final responsibility which is at the very root of our constitution, and only he can be truly loyal who accepts and acts in harmony with that fact.[6]

As Bramwell Booth tossed and turned during the night hours it was this sixth option to which he most inclined.

The family factor

Bramwell Booth discussed these matters with his wife during the dark night hours, and consulted with other members of the family during the day. The family advice was consistent and clear: he must on no account yield to the pressures to which he was being subjected. He owed it to the Army, to his father and to himself to remain true to the 1878 constitution. However, Bramwell still pondered his options.

'It is thought by those who are best able to judge that the General is weakening,' writes the Commander to one of her commissioners, 'and that it is possible he would give in, but Mrs Booth maintains a desperate, insistent fight against it. I understand that after the General had some serious interviews with leading commissioners a week or two ago there was a great to do.'[7]

The family factor was to be very influential at this time and in succeeding months. In fact Colonel Gerald Freeman, who was on the General's personal staff for 20 years and was present at the 1929 High Council as the assistant recorder, reckoned that 'the basic cause which called the High Council into being was that, as time passed, the General was more and more influenced by his wife and children. There were of course other factors at work, but the foregoing was the genesis of the trouble.'[8]

The reformers' options

The London commissioners had sought the opinion of leading counsel Gilbert H. Hurst of Lincoln's Inn regarding their options. On the key question as to whether they – even if 'unanimous' in their desire for reform – were 'helpless' to effect constitutional revision if the General did not wish to take the initiative, his sobering opinion was: 'I do not think that revision must be *initiated* by the General but his consent must be obtained, and the result is therefore the same, and accordingly the commissioners even if unanimous are helpless without that consent.'[9]

Therefore the only option open at this time to the reformers was to keep up the pressure on the General. Constitutionally only the General could take the initiative. There was no Conference, no second 'authority' or assembly as there had been under the 1875 constitution, to which they could appeal. Even if the High Council were called, it was not a body authorised to discuss or legislate on constitutional reform. Its only purpose was to adjudicate whether the General was unfit for office, and if so to depose him and elect a successor. So other than concerted pressure the commissioners were 'helpless'. There was also the danger that if the General gave a definite 'no' to the idea of reform in his reply to the Commander's Long Letter, it could well spell the end of the quest for reform.

As part of the pressure, the reformers quietly encouraged senior officers around the world to appeal to the General to consider constitutional reform. 'I learn that nothing could hold Canada back,' writes the Commander about an initiative by senior Canadian officers, 'and also that the effect of their appeal to the General through Commissioner Mapp has made a tremendous impression, not only upon the General himself, but upon all leading commissioners.'[10] Commissioner Henry Mapp left for a tour of Australia and New Zealand, and it was probably not coincidental that soon afterwards the General received 43 letters from senior Australian officers and 31 letters from their counterparts in New Zealand appealing to him to yield to the Commander's requests.[11]

Typical of such pleas for the General to look favourably on constitutional reform was the note that he received from his friend and colleague of old, Commissioner Hugh Whatmore, territorial commander of the Australia Southern Territory: 'One word from yourself would set the minds of our trusted officers at rest, and secure for you in the closing years of your great life an increase of love, loyalty and confidence, which would be a crowning glory to your wonderful work.'[12]

Increasing pressure

On 12 April 1928 – two weeks after returning from Paris – Bramwell Booth left International Headquarters late one evening in order to prepare for a weekend of evangelistic meetings in Sheffield. It was to be the last time he crossed the threshold of what had been his 'home' for five decades.

The next day Bramwell Booth came down with influenza, but insisted on fulfilling the Sheffield engagement. On 14 April he conducted there three meetings in the Empire Theatre. 'Snow, driven by bitter blasts,' reports *The War Cry*, 'had been harrying the waiting queues surrounding the great building, and with every seat occupied there yet remained hundreds more, patiently waiting for two hours when accommodation might be expected to become vacant.' On the return journey he was subjected to further misery when the heating in the train failed.

Bramwell Booth was by now seriously ill. He kept going, but was not well enough to conduct the 'Two Days Before God' meetings in Westminster Central Hall on 23 and 24 April, nor share in the Men's Social officers councils on 29 April, nor speak to the cadets at their Covenant Day on 1 May. He was able, however, to attend the 21st anniversary celebrations of the Home League at the Crystal Palace on 8 May. 'Though not speaking at any length (reported *The War Cry*) the General for a moment stood beside Mrs Booth and expressed in two or three words his great pleasure in being at the gathering.'

The Commander's Letter of April 1928

Shortly after his return from Sheffield Bramwell Booth had received a further lengthy letter from his sister Evangeline in which she once more urged him to take the initiative on constitutional reform. She hoped this would reach him before he took any final decision on the matter and announced it. Her letter of 9 April 1928 is a personal and passionate plea from sister to brother:

> We have conversed on the subject many times. You will remember on the occasions of your visits to this country and my own to England, how seriously we have talked together, and how earnestly I have entreated you to consider the effecting of a change in the constitution that would ensure the future stability of the Army.
>
> Do you not remember, dear Bramwell, when we journeyed together from San Francisco to Seattle, I knelt by your side and spoke of growing unrest among our people upon the question of the successorship of the General? And how I felt that the fact of the General's deciding his successor – precluding even his closest advisers having a voice in the matter – and the result of this decision being in a 'sealed envelope', would after your reign work an injustice to the Army?
>
> With all sisterly affection I implored you to think seriously of the evil consequences which, unless faced and remedied, I feared would ensue, releasing disruptive forces of incalculable injury to the Army.
>
> And do you not call to mind how in reply you said: 'Well, Eva, perhaps the time is soon at hand we must do so – when there must be a change of government of the Army'?
>
> Since that day the discontent has become so alarmingly prevalent that I could not, either in justice to you or to the organisation, do other than express to you as I did in my long letter the conviction I carry – a conviction shared by many others – that there is nothing in the terms of the Deed Poll to preclude your instituting the governmental change that would allay this growing unrest and be of priceless advantage to our international Army.

Evangeline Booth pleads with her brother to institute reform in order to 'defend our father's memory'. She reminds him that William Booth was accused by people outside of the Army of having dynastic intentions. 'Do not we, his children, know how foreign was such a concept to him? I hear his voice now as he addressed us, his children – saying: "The Army is not mine! It is not yours! The Army is God's and the world's." In loyalty to his memory it is for us, his own children, to do what beyond all peradventure our father would have done to allay the present discontent and to introduce a reform of such undeniable worth to the Army's growth and prosperity.'

Evangeline then urges Bramwell to do what their father would have done in his day – take counsel from his leading officers:

> Often he said to me (as for example when he sent for me, one o'clock in the morning, at Columbus, Ohio, and we talked together until break of day) that he never for a single moment intended that the destiny of the Army should be left entirely to the discretion, and under the sole control, of any one individual, and that you knew well his mind as to taking myself and one or two others in your private counsel.
>
> He repeatedly impressed upon us the advantage of boards, of councils, and the value of the judgment and opinions of our leading staff. He never failed to make himself strong in council and in conference, and in his trusted men he reposed unbounded confidence. Why have you not done this? And upon such a question as we now discuss, why do you not do it?

Evangeline Booth continues by recalling William Booth's speech at the 1877 Annual Conference. 'I was very much impressed with the assurances our father gave to the Conference that, should anything of a life and death character arise, he would certainly take the Conference into his confidence by calling first the principal officers in order that he might "receive information" and avail himself of their counsel. And "if any great question involving the happiness of us all were to arise, the only plan would be, it seems to me, to call together the most experienced of our brethren, and if need be, all the others."' She then skilfully argues that the Founder made a moral commitment to the missioners, one that Bramwell must now honour:

These references seem to me to be of great importance at the present moment. They not only give a clear indication of the Founder's mind, but might well be regarded as one of the conditions upon which the members of the Conference accepted the provisions of the Deed Poll of 1878.

She continues:

There is no objection to the plan of a General. An army must have a general. But our objection is that our voice is not heard; that the leaders in our ranks are not consulted; are not taken into counsel, or even their views sought. This we cannot help but feel – I feel – to be contrary to the Founder's most positive method and intention, and strongly savours of despotism. Surely, in a question of such vast importance as the one now before you, it is wisdom not only to seek the views of the High Council, but to give those views the utmost weight!

She ends on a personal note:

In conclusion, and with all the intensity of a pure soul, let me say that if ever in your mind, or that of any other, there rests the shadow of a thought that I aspire to your position, let it be known to you, and to all the world, that such an ambition has never for one moment been entertained by me.

Having poured out her soul to her brother in a private letter, the Commander then circulated the letter to selected commissioners and territorial commanders.

Denmark Hill

On 10 May 1928 Bramwell Booth by a supreme effort gathered his strength for the stone-laying at the William Booth Memorial Training College at Denmark Hill. No project lay closer to his heart than this fulfilment of his father's dream for a University of Humanity. However, he was far from well. As Mrs Booth later told the High Council: 'I think all who saw him on that occasion realised that he was then in a serious state of health. The next day the doctor said that immediate treatment was essential, and that all strenuous work and public engagements must cease for a time.

'The doctor gave his diagnosis,' recalled Mrs Booth, 'but cheered us by a splendid report as to the General's condition. He was absolutely sound; there was no organic trouble, his blood pressure and the condition of his arteries were those of a much younger person, indeed were excellent. The report of a blood test was also good. The specialist said that in order to begin completely to rest, it would be wise to go right away for three weeks or a month. He thought that rest with complete freedom from worry would bring the General back to work more fit than he had been for some years, and probably with 10 years' full work ahead.'[13]

A brief respite would do wonders. The Chief of the Staff wrote to him: 'I shall do my best in co-operation with Mrs Booth to carry on. A month or two of quiet and absolute rest will be a wonderfully good investment if, as I believe, it will give to the Army and the world its General for another 10 years. I will consult with Mrs Booth freely and fully. I think we understand each other and shall pull together, moved by a common impulse to take care of everything for you. We will strive with all our powers to be *good* stewards, and not be afraid of your return.'[14]

That return was fully expected to be by the end of July 1928 at the latest. All his engagements were cancelled until then; but Bramwell Booth was never to return. The stone-laying at Denmark Hill was the last time he was seen in public.

The decisive response

There could be no departure for the needed respite until the decisive response to the Commander's Long Letter of 9 February 1928 had been written.

Bramwell Booth had read and re-read the letter many times since its arrival and had also studied carefully the Commander's further April letter. He had reviewed the welter of contradictory advice and appeals he was receiving. He had come to the conclusion that, given his strong inner convictions, to engage in further consultation would be pointless. What was needed was a clear enunciation of his position, a decisive response backed by the full weight of his office that would once and for all end the debate.

Bramwell Booth had written to the Chief that he felt 'an expansion' of his original reply of 24 November 1927 to the Commander, 'especially bearing on the legal aspects of the matter would be useful'.[15] Following discussion with Mr William Frost, the lawyer had drawn up a statement on the legal position, which Bramwell Booth now proposed to send out as an attachment to his own detailed and comprehensive letter.

The Chief of the Staff, understanding and reluctantly accepting that the General's bottom line was 'no change', feared that the lengthy draft letter complete with attachment would only keep the debate going. 'To illustrate what I mean,' he wrote to Mrs Booth, 'I have no doubt some will reply and say they do not want the constitution altered, but think the General should take advantage of the alternative provided in the constitution for the method of appointing the future General. I would *anticipate* this, and thus do away with necessity for further argument about it.'[16]

The Chief of the Staff had therefore sent the General a rough draft of a letter he had prepared giving 'a more *emphatic* decision', which was 'more likely to settle the minds of our people'. The General had accepted the Chief's argument and was now focused on preparing a much shorter response.

The matter was now urgent. More than two and a half months had passed since the Commander's Long Letter had arrived. With the stone-laying now over, and the doctors having recommended that he should take a break from all activity, it was important to get the response finalised and despatched.

The critical letter addressed to all commissioners and territorial commanders was dated 15 May 1928. General Bramwell Booth began it by regretting 'that the Commander should have sent her communication to you and others without waiting for a reply from me or giving me time to reply to her'. He then gave his final decision on the matter – couched in language that he hoped would close the issue for ever:

> I feel that I should now definitely say, as a result of further consideration of the whole subject, that any change in what we term our original [1878] Deed Poll cannot be entertained by me. I have neither the power nor the desire to make any such change. I received our 'system' from the Founder's hands as a sacred trust, and I cannot abandon that trust. I do not believe that you would ask me to do so.

Having considered the matter for the seven months that had elapsed since the Commander's visit to International Headquarters, his position remained exactly the same as it had been in his November 1927 response to her. He would *not* initiate constitutional reform.

In his letter he then turned to the 1904 Deed. 'The Commander has, I fear, inspired in some quarters the idea that I had decided to alter the Deed of 1904 which we call the Supplementary Deed. I had made no such decision, and what I wrote gave no ground for the fear.' His words were intended to allay any remaining fears, but his choice of the pluperfect verb tense, '*I had made* no such decision', left some of his readers wondering whether he was leaving himself room to make such a decision in the future, and in fact increased their fears.

Having announced his decision and thereby hopefully ended the debate, Bramwell Booth sought to strike a positive note as he moved the attention of his leaders to the future – a future to be built on the 'splendid' legacy left by William Booth:

> I think I should say to you that one good result appears likely to spring from this. It has brought out amongst our leading officers a body of thoughtful opinion in favour of our constitution and which puts the work before every other consideration. This is, of course, a real source of strength, and helps me … It only remains for me to express my strong desire that any further discussions on these matters so splendidly provided for by our first General will be avoided, and that

our whole time, thought, and energy will be devoted to the work entrusted to us.

Bramwell Booth felt sure that his letter would elicit a groundswell of support. He envisaged that his authority as General and his personal bond with each of his leaders would carry the day. He knew that his leaders well understood the Army way – once the leader has taken the decision the debate is over, and you get on with the work. That is how they themselves operated in their own commands, and there was no doubting the personal affection with which he was regarded by his team of leaders around the world. Nobody, but nobody, wanted the General to be hurt.

So it was with quiet confidence that on 17 May 1928, two days after despatching the letter, Bramwell Booth left London together with Florence to seek refreshment and healing in the beauty of the countryside.

Chapter Eight

The Gathering Storm

THE Booths were into hydropathy in a big way. Catherine Booth, the Army Mother, had unbounded faith in the treatment of illness by water, externally and internally. It was a faith she sought to share not only with her family but also with the Army as a whole. Arrangements were made at the first training garrison for the teaching and practice of the treatment to cadets, and instructions were published in *Orders and Regulations for Officers* with careful descriptions of the various methods. Bramwell Booth had ensured that plans for the new training college at Denmark Hill included a separate building for the teaching and practice of hydropathy. The building is now a childcare centre, but for many decades after hydropathy ceased to be practised there it was still known as the 'hydro'.

It was therefore only natural that when the doctors prescribed complete rest for three weeks to a month, Bramwell and Florence Booth headed for Smedley's Hydropathic Establishment in Matlock, a place they had often visited before.

Bramwell Booth was suffering from what the doctors diagnosed as nervous prostration. Organically sound, it was his nervous system that was his Achilles heel – as it had always been. In 1878, when Bramwell was 22, he had been so overwrought by the incessant pressure that, following the War Congress of that year, his parents had arranged for their young Chief of the Staff to rest in the south of Sweden. Bramwell Booth's idea of a rest was to conduct twice-daily spiritual meetings for 10 days at the farmhouse where he was staying! These resulted in the conversion of Hannah

Ouchterlony, who shortly afterwards pioneered the Army in Sweden.

After two months of rest in that country Bramwell Booth returned to his post at headquarters, and for the next 50 years never left it. In her biography of her father, Catherine Bramwell-Booth reflects on the years between 1878 and 1928: 'Fifty years of continuous work intervened. He had furloughs, so called. *They never again included one whole work-free day.*'[1]

During all of these years Bramwell Booth had striven courageously – and successfully – to overcome the effects of the bouts of acute nervous stress that would sometimes smite him. At times the symptoms were serious. Mrs Bramwell Booth records in her diary for 16 June 1909: 'Anxious re Chief of Staff. Serious nervous breakdown.'[2] Only family and close colleagues were aware of the lonely fight.

Commissioner Samuel Hurren was later to tell the High Council that when he was private secretary to Commissioner T. Henry Howard, Chief of the Staff, his diary for the years 1913/14 contained 'more or less frequent references to the General's increasingly nervous state', and that he had observed how Bramwell Booth during his Generalship had 'maintained a fairly even and level state of general and nervous health lasting for some months, perhaps even a year or two, but on each recurrence of the nervous troubles the level of subsequent restoration had been a little lower than that previously attained'.[3]

No escape

With the reticence that is seen in all walks of life about ascribing health breakdowns of public figures to nervous problems, *The War Cry* on 26 May 1928 simply informed the Army world that 'doctors have most emphatically insisted upon the absolute necessity for our beloved Leader taking a complete rest from all public engagements and business affairs for a time'. To the leadership of the Army around the world, the Chief of the Staff was more informative and wrote on 22 May 1928 that whilst 'the doctors pronounced the

General to be organically sound, they considered that he was in a very overwrought condition nervously'.

The sudden disappearance of the General from public view and the lack of specific information about his medical condition had resulted in rumours beginning to circulate, and the Chief of the Staff felt it necessary to add in his letter to leaders: 'I do not think for a moment there is any need for great anxiety, and you may brush aside groundless rumours which may reach you of a character contrary to what I have herein stated. I mention this as I understand already some extraordinary statements are being circulated.'

Bramwell Booth's condition did not improve as quickly as the doctors had hoped. At the end of June the specialists examined him again. Their verdict continued to be that there was no reason why he should not fully recover, but that it was imperative that he should have rest of mind. 'What an irony it seemed to me,' Mrs Booth was later to tell the High Council. 'I could not explain that "freedom from worry" was the one thing which love and care could not give him.'[4]

July and August were spent in Surrey. He walked in the heather-clad countryside and was taken for drives, but rest of mind eluded him. Writes Catherine Bramwell-Booth of those days: 'Now is revealed the full extent of the lack of his resources. Was anyone to blame? His upbringing? His circumstances? Himself? This man of wide outlook, versatile of thought, of unflagging enthusiasm, has no hobby! He has learned no end of things, but he has not learned to play! It has never been essential to him before; now unless he can distract his thoughts by some interest apart from his work, it will fare ill with him. His dear ones rack their ingenuity. A game of chess may occupy an hour, but he is more likely to break off in the middle and begin to discuss the forbidden subjects. The fact is that all his own flesh and blood are part and parcel of the Army and associated with the worry.'[5]

His friends were 'Army' too. Commissioner Theodore Kitching was a frequent visitor. Theodore Kitching had been Bramwell Booth's private secretary when he was the Chief of the Staff. He had become private secretary to the General in the Founder's later years, and when Bramwell Booth became General had continued in that role until he became Editor-in-Chief. Theodore Kitching had remained personally close to Bramwell Booth, and the General looked forward to his visits – but the talk inevitably became 'Army'.

Occasionally colleagues of old from further afield, like Commissioner Hugh Whatmore on leave from Australia, were permitted to call, but even then 'the subject' was never far below the horizon. Commissioner Whatmore wrote a tender follow-up letter to Mrs Booth about the private conversation he had with her during his visit, when 'I felt it most difficult to say what I felt':

> I have for so many years loved the General and yourself, and at a certain period was so close up to the General, that I ought to be able to express myself without any danger of either causing offence or of being misunderstood. And yet the impression has unfortunately gone round the world that if your most loyal and faithful officers express a view contrary to your own, however respectfully, they are made to suffer by a manifest loss of your confidence or are penalised in some other manner. That is what a great number of officers believe, and if I may say so, is, I am sure, the answer to the very moving question you put to me last Friday, as to why certain officers had not spoken to the General personally, rather than having joined together in signing a letter to him.
>
> Bear with me, Mrs Booth, when I tell you frankly and with no small measure of diffidence, that there is a widespread fear that the General may appoint a member of your family as his successor, and it is this fear that has caused officers, who the General has trusted for a lifetime, to express their hope and the hope of those they represent, that he may be saved from following such a course, and instead adopt the plan which has been laid before him, and which will still be in keeping with the constitution. Will you not, Mrs Booth, advise the General in this direction?

While seeking to rest, Bramwell Booth fretted about his absence from headquarters. Mrs Booth recalled that 'during the autumn the General expressed great anxiety lest advantage should be taken of his illness to further the views of those who desired a change in the constitution'.[6]

In September Bramwell and Florence moved to their beloved hideaway villa in Southwold, hoping that the seaside would refresh his body and mind as it had so often done before. Neighbours noted that 'Captain and Mrs Bernard' were back among them.

'Bramwell Booth's condition fluctuated,' records Catherine Bramwell-Booth. 'Periods of great depression became frequent. He was discouraged. His anxiety about the Army increased, and he talked of it with anguish of spirit, painful to witness.' In October he was afflicted with almost complete insomnia. 'Neuritis attacked him and his right arm became seriously affected. He suffered much pain. It seemed impossible to allay his fears that his absence would facilitate agitation in favour of changing the constitution, and that the High Council might be called to precipitate a crisis.'[7]

The family was fiercely protective of Bramwell Booth. Nothing must be allowed to hinder his recovery of health. His whereabouts were kept secret and the occasional bulletins in *The War Cry* contained little specific information. June 23: 'With sustained quiet and freedom from the anxiety of affairs, he will win back his strength.' July 21: 'The improvement in the General's health is being maintained.' August 25: 'There are indications that progress, though slow, is being made towards normal health.' In the September issue of *The Deliverer* Commissioner Catherine Booth writes: 'There is every evidence that he is climbing steadily towards a complete restoration of health.' Then, after a gap of six weeks, *The War Cry* reports on October 6: 'The General has not been quite so well as it had been hoped that he would be from the previous improvements that had taken place in his condition.'

Though well-intentioned, the lack of specific information added a sense of mystery to the uncertainty. Where was the General? How ill was he really? The family kept spreading the word that the General would soon be back, but no one knew for sure.

The Chief of the Staff kept in touch and would occasionally call to discuss important items. These visits always cheered the General.

The flow of legal documents requiring the General's signature was incessant. When William Booth had been ill he had been able to delegate the signing of legal documents to others, but in 1925 a new Trustee Act had limited the power of a sole trustee to delegate authority. A sole trustee could now only delegate the signing of documents to others if he was out of the country. There was therefore no respite for the General.

Clouds on the horizon

The General's health breakdown faced the reformers with a predicament. It was a totally unexpected turn of events. What were they now to do? Their one option had been to increase the pressure on the General to initiate constitutional reform, or at least to meet with his commissioners to talk about the subject. For as legal counsel had underlined, without the General taking the initiative the commissioners were 'helpless'.

By his decisive letter of 15 May 1928 Bramwell Booth had made it clear that he would not be taking any initiative towards reform. However, his quiet confidence that his leaders, in the 'good old Army' way, would salute and get on with the job looked increasingly misplaced. The responses as they arrived were not encouraging. It was impossible to keep this information from Bramwell Booth, and when it was gently filtered through to him it added to his sense of impending doom.

Putting pressure on a person who was sick was out of the question, but the reformers assumed with everyone else that the General would soon be back – at which time renewed pressure could be brought to bear.

However, as Bramwell Booth's absence became longer, the weeks turning into months, the very absence of the General for such a length of time became in itself a new and unanticipated factor in the equation.

The Booth family feared that his absence might become a reason for the High Council being called. As Mrs Booth later recorded: 'Commissioner Catherine twice saw the Chief and reported fully to him certain information she had received indicating that definite steps were being taken to persuade commissioners to call the High Council. On each occasion the Chief promised to enquire carefully and satisfied the commissioner there was no truth in what she had heard.'[8]

The 'storm pilot' was in fact making sure that the hatches were battened down. He reported to Mrs Booth: 'I have now seen all the *nine* excepting Booth-Tucker and Jeffries [who was absent abroad], and I have their utmost assurance that they will be no party to any further action. They did not contemplate any, but I am glad I saw them as they could not do anything now after making such a declaration to me.'[9]

The Chief of the Staff did not forget the American scene. 'Two weeks ago,' he told Mrs Booth, 'I wrote a very strong private letter to Commander Evangeline, telling her what I felt about the propaganda going on and of Atwood's performance, intimating to her that if there was a continuance of it she would discover a strong body of opinion in England, if not in America, that would rise up and denounce the whole thing. I pleaded with her to stop everything. I had a cable from her on Friday acknowledging the letter and promising me she would do nothing further *for the present.*'

In the same letter Commissioner Higgins sought to reassure Mrs Booth about rumours that the High Council might be called from across the Atlantic. 'It cannot be called, I am *sure*, for they could not get the necessary seven commissioners. [Only full commissioners, not lieutenant-commissioners, could requisition the High Council.] In the USA there are three – Evangeline Booth, Gifford and Brengle. The latter, I am sure, would not join in anything of the sort. So five names would have to be got off the American continent ... They are not available. *I am confident.*'[10]

Transatlantic planning

Though restrained by the changed circumstances from taking further direct action, Commander Evangeline Booth continued to discuss plans for reform with the four American territorial commanders who worked under her direction. They were a team of veteran giants, and they were solidly behind her in the quest for change. Heading the USA Western Territory was Commissioner Adam Gifford, who, after migrating from Scotland as an 18-year-old lad, had met the Army in the USA, and had risen to become the first territorial commander of the Western Territory when it was created in 1920.

Leading the USA Southern Territory was another 'pioneer' territorial commander – Lieut-Commissioner William McIntyre. Commissioned as an officer in Canada when 17 years old, he had commanded seven corps – including the largest in the country – before being appointed a divisional commander at 19. Transferred to the USA in 1893 he had, 34 years later, become the first territorial commander of the Southern Territory when it was formed in 1927.

Commanding the USA Central Territory was an internationalist – Lieut-Commissioner John McMillan, a Scot by birth who had entered training in Canada and had given 20 years of service in Australia before returning to the UK. He was later to become Chief of the Staff to Evangeline Booth when she was the General.

Lieut-Commissioner Richard Holz, who led the Eastern Territory, was the very embodiment of Army history. Of German descent, Richard Holz became an officer at the time Major Thomas Moore commanded the Army's forces in the USA. In 1884, when Major Moore seceded and became 'General' of the 'Salvation Army of America', Richard Holz was one of a number of officers who followed him out of the international Salvation Army. When 'General' Moore was deposed by his followers four year later, 'Colonel' Richard Holz reluctantly accepted the leadership of the 'Salvation Army of America' in the hope of realising reconciliation with the parent movement. For this reason he did not adopt the title of 'General'. In 1889 'Colonel' Richard Holz marched a contingent of 30 officers back to the international Salvation Army, and was himself appointed in command of the New York Division with the rank of major.

Even with such a heavyweight team around her there was little that Commander Evangeline could do 'for the present' to bring about reform. However, learning in July 1928 that the London commissioners had engaged Mr Percival Wright as their own legal adviser – whose office in 19 Godliman Street was just round the corner from International Headquarters – and knowing that her attorney, Mr George W. Wickersham, was planning to visit Europe in August, she asked him to meet with Mr Wright and Commissioner Henry Mapp. The three met in Paris.[11]

At this meeting Mr Percival Wright briefed his American counterpart on his discussions with the London commissioners, and it was also decided to launch a public awareness campaign by commissioning an article for *The Law Journal* about sole trusteeship and The Salvation Army, to be followed by a wider newspaper campaign later. On his return Mr Percival Wright duly engaged a barrister journalist to write the article.

As the London commissioners could not charge up Mr Wright's fees as official International Headquarters expenditure, it was agreed that the Commander would reimburse any expenses through her attorney. This unusual arrangement increased the Commander's hold on the developing situation.

Mr Percival Wright had been robust in his advice to the London commissioners. He was of the opinion that, whatever the legal position, the commissioners had 'a moral obligation to the rank and file of The Salvation Army and the members of the charitable public who give it financial support' to take action if the General was unable 'to carry out the duties of his office'. As early as 29 August 1928 he wrote: 'It seems to me that next to the General, the highest authority in the Army is the High Council, and I am of the opinion that steps should be taken to call this Council together for the purpose of determining whether the General is, in fact, unfit for office.'[12]

For seven commissioners to requisition the calling of the High Council on the ground of the General's health was full of risk for them personally. It would take at least six weeks for the members of the High Council to assemble in London from the ends of the earth. During that time General Bramwell Booth might return to duty fit and well – and that would leave the seven requisitioners in a difficult position. The prognosis from the members of the Booth family continued to be upbeat. The General would be back soon – at the latest by Christmas. The family was not unaware of the fact that this optimistic note afforded a protection against the High Council being called.

In early September 1928 Commissioner Mapp called together the London commissioners sympathetic to reform to consider possible options open to them. As a result they met with the Chief of the Staff to put out 'a feeler to ascertain as to whether he would receive a request from the London commissioners to call the High Council, if a situation arose in the agitation that made it necessary'. The ground for calling the High Council would be that unrest had reached crisis level. The Chief did 'not favour it'.[13] The pilot was still proving adept at battening down hatches.

The Commander, anxious to retain control of the reform movement, gently chided Commissioner Mapp: 'I am a little sorry I was not approached and my views obtained' before the Chief was consulted. She counselled restraint:

> I have conferred with my advisers here and the more we consider the matter, the more we lean to the desirability of giving the General an opportunity to meet or refuse to meet the commissioners. There can be no doubt there is a good deal of sympathy for the General in his condition, and anything that is done which could be interpreted to mean that 'the commissioners were hitting the General when he was down' would only tend to thwart our purposes. I am strongly of the opinion that it is wisdom on our part to give the General an opportunity to talk the issue over with his leading men ... In the event of the General refusing to meet with his commissioners then serious consideration could be given for the next move.[14]

For the Commander it was the lack of knowledge about the General's true condition that was the main hindrance to action. 'Consideration should be given,' she wrote to Commissioner Mapp, 'as to whether the General is in physical condition to meet his commissioners, and if not, is it wise to precipitate matters? Should not the General be given a little further time to see if there is a possibility of him recuperating or otherwise? One of the difficulties is that we do not seem to be able to get any authentic information about the General's health.'[15]

In a letter to Commissioner Charles Jeffries a week later she reiterated that she favoured 'the General being asked to assemble his commissioners to discuss with them every aspect of the reform proposals before making a more pronounced move', as this would provide 'more justification for calling the High Council were the General to refuse this reasonable approach'.[16]

The reformers on both sides of the Atlantic were feeling their way towards a new strategy. Once the General was back the pressure for him to call a constitutional conference – perhaps in connection with the centenary celebrations of William Booth's birth in April 1929 – would be resumed, and if he refused such a 'reasonable approach' his very refusal could in itself constitute a reason for calling the High Council to adjudicate him unfit to hold office.

On 30 October 1928 Commissioner Jeffries updated the Commander on developments in London. The General's health had suffered a setback, and he quoted from a letter he had received from the Chief of the Staff in which the Chief wrote: 'I found the General no better yesterday, indeed if there was a change, it was for the worse. The specialist called says he is *very ill*, but thinks he can pull him around, so hope is rekindled and we must wait believingly.'

On the matter of the succession, Commissioner Jeffries confided: 'The rumour is insistent that Catherine is to be the new General, and I believe her name is down ... There is a suggestion that is being stressed here, that it is the General's intention to resign his position, and that Catherine will step immediately into his place. That would be a very awkward situation, and once that is done it may be very difficult to alter it.'[17]

Mr William Frost is briefed

When the General's health worsened towards the end of October 1928, the Chief of the Staff met with Mr William Frost to brief him on developments. He told him that in his opinion 'serious difficulty was practically certain to rise'. Mr Frost went away greatly perturbed by what he had heard. He decided to take action, and he later put on record in a letter to the Chief of the Staff what happened following that interview:

> I gave the position the gravest consideration, and formed the judgment that, in the circumstances that had arisen, the General's highest duty to his Trust was to vacate office and himself instruct you to convene the High Council, for the purpose of receiving his resignation and electing his successor.
>
> But at the same time I realised that so momentous a decision ought not to be based upon my unaided judgment, and so, on 25th October 1928, I had a long conference with Mr J. H. Stamp, the counsel who has advised the General for many years past, and laid the whole position before him as fully as it was known to me, but without informing him of the conclusion at which I had arrived.
>
> The judgment he unhesitatingly and strongly expressed was the same as my own, and he based this upon grounds which subsequent developments have shown to be only too well-founded.
>
> I thereupon – the same evening – prepared documents for giving effect to this advice if the General decided to act upon it.[18]

The draft letter of resignation prepared by Mr Frost for the General's signature was addressed to the Chief of the Staff. It was never used, but the draft remains of historical importance. William Frost had been advising Bramwell Booth since the Army's earliest days. He knew Bramwell Booth better than some of his commissioners did, and understood how his mind worked. Here he was putting into words what he felt Bramwell Booth not only ought to write but perhaps, in his heart of hearts, wanted to write:

> DRAFT ONLY
>
> There does not appear to be any reliable prospect of my recovery being very complete or very rapid. So far as I am personally concerned I am content to let things take their course, but so far as the Work is concerned, I am advised that I ought now to take immediate action for its efficient leadership and continuity ...

As you know, a feeling exists that it would be better if future Generals were elected by our High Council instead of being nominated by the General for the time being. My own views on this question are known and I do not discuss them now.

What I think it right to do in the present circumstances is to ask you to convene our first High Council for the purposes of electing my successor. I may possibly feel able to make some recommendation to the Council, but as to this I shall make up my mind further on, before its meeting is held.

My resignation is therefore to be considered as tendered to the High Council, to become effective as from the date of the due election of my successor.

'The tragedy is that the General was never afterwards well enough to be approached on such a grave matter,' continued William Frost in his letter to the Chief of the Staff, 'and it cannot therefore be too clearly understood, in justice to the General, that although the facts are as I have stated, they never came to his knowledge, and that accordingly he never had the opportunity of either accepting or rejecting the legal advice that would have been tendered to him had the state of his health permitted him to receive it.'

The advice that Bramwell Booth's legal advisers would have offered in October 1928 had they had opportunity was breathtakingly radical. They were not recommending that the General should resign and that the successor nominated in the 'sealed envelope' should take up office. They were recommending that the General should resign and at the same time cancel the 'sealed envelope' lying in the safe. In its place, they in effect recommended, he should avail himself of the alternative option in the constitution, namely to indicate 'the means which are to be taken for the appointment of a successor'. That the General might himself call the High Council to receive his resignation and to elect his successor was an eventuality that even the 1904 Deed had not anticipated, but constitutionally it was perfectly possible.

One can only conclude that the two lawyers had themselves become convinced that the tide towards reform was irresistible, and that it was in the best interests of the Army – especially as a trust – for Bramwell Booth as the sole trustee to take the initiative. They may also have feared that if Bramwell Booth died and the 'sealed envelope' contained the name of a member of the General's family, the commissioners would call the High Council anyway to challenge the appointment.

The letter in which Mr Frost records what happened following his October briefing by the Chief of the Staff is dated 4 January 1929, just four days before the opening of the High Council. In the letter Mr Frost explains that he is writing in order that the Chief might 'let members of the High Council know, as they are entitled to know, what the legal advisers of The Salvation Army did in discharge of their duty when the present crisis became imminent'.

Events move to a climax

As the end of October 1928 approached, events began to move relentlessly towards their climax. On 29 October International Headquarters issued a bulletin to the press by Dr (later Sir) John Weir – the foremost homeopathic doctor in London whose patients included the Prince of Wales and the Duke of York – and Dr E. Wardlaw Milne, stating that 'General Booth is suffering from nervous prostration and his condition gives rise to some anxiety. It is essential that he has complete rest from all work for several months and this, we hope, will ensure his complete recovery.' This was followed some days later by the announcement that 'the General's condition is less satisfactory during the past twenty-four hours'. A message of sympathy from the King was telephoned to him.

On Saturday 3 November a number of newspapers in the USA reported that Bramwell Booth had died. The next day *The Sunday News* carried a banner headline: 'Woman Head of the Army? – Daughter May Succeed Aged General Booth'.

On Tuesday 5 November Mr Percival Wright reminded Commissioner Henry Mapp that if the General was unable to 'carry out the duties of his office', then, in his view, 'the High Council should be called together to deal with any emergency that might suddenly arise'. He added: 'It seems to me that such an emergency has now arisen.'

Mr Percival Wright also raised the unwelcome prospect that Bramwell Booth, or his family on his behalf, might apply to the court for relief from his duties as sole trustee of the Army's assets because of his incapacity. 'You will realise, from what I have told you at various times,' he wrote, 'that the General himself is unable to appoint anyone to act as his deputy so far as his position as trustee is concerned, but there is no reason why he, or Mrs Booth on his behalf, should not now take advantage of the opportunity to go to the court and ask for his nominee to be appointed in his place. This would create a still more difficult position than the one at present existing.'[19]

At this point Bramwell Booth needed only to have resigned from office for his nominee to automatically become his successor as sole trustee through the 'sealed envelope' system. However, should the High Council be summoned, the General would, from the moment of its summoning, lose the power to appoint his successor even if he resigned or retired from office. The prospect that he might even then seize the initiative and seek to circumvent the provisions of the Supplementary Deed Poll of 1904 by appealing to the court for it to appoint the person named in the 'sealed envelope' as the sole trustee – whether temporarily or permanently – was to lurk in the background throughout the coming weeks.

On Saturday 10 November the article commissioned by Mr Percival Wright appeared in the influential *The Law Journal* under the eye-catching title *'One Man' Charities*. Taking as its starting point a case *Re Booth and Southend-on-Sea Estate Company's Contract* – a case the Army had won in March 1927 – the article discussed the 'possibilities of evil' arising from sole trusteeship. 'The powers of a sole trustee can easily be so wide-flung and untrammelled as to leave him in the most complete and autocratic control of very large trust funds ... By its Foundation Deeds the General alone has power to expend on behalf of the Army all moneys contributed for its purposes ... Moreover the Deeds provide that the General may appoint his successor and so perpetuate any policy of which he himself approves ... The present unfortunate and somewhat prolonged illness of General Bramwell Booth might easily jeopardise the whole future of the great work founded by his illustrious father.'

The article clearly labelled the Army as a 'one man' charity, and because of it some sections of the press interpreted the brewing crisis as being mainly about sole trusteeship and about the control of money and property.

On Sunday 11 November, following an unauthorised and ill-advised briefing by the press officer at International Headquarters, several British Sunday papers printed speculations about the future leadership of the Army – some suggesting that Commissioner Edward Higgins or Commissioner Catherine Booth might succeed to the Generalship. *The Sunday News* announced that there was a strong feeling in the Army in favour of more democratic government, and an overwhelming desire that Commander Evangeline Booth should be the new General.

With Salvationists reading the reports in the press, the crisis could no longer be concealed from them. On Monday 12 November the Chief of the Staff issued a press release: 'All the statements made in the press as to the names of possible successors to General Booth have been entirely without knowledge, responsibility or authority. All discussion as to the possible successor to the present General of The Salvation Army is premature, if not improper, seeing that General Bramwell Booth remains the head of the Army, and hopes are still entertained as to his relatively early recovery.'

Tuesday 13 November 1928

On Tuesday 13 November, Mr Wright reported to Mr Wickersham in the USA: 'I understand that *The Times* is now in possession of information, which it intends to publish very shortly, setting out the whole of the facts regarding the matter, including the requests which have been made to the General for a revision of the constitution. It was intended that this matter should be published on Monday (yesterday) but at the urgent request of Commissioner Higgins, the Chief of the Staff, publication was withheld.' This was on the understanding that there were developments on the way. The pilot was still busy battening down hatches.

Mr Wright also informed his counterpart in the USA: 'With regard to convening the High Council, there is still one commissioner in London who is averse to signing the required requisition, but who may shortly be prevailed upon to see the wisdom of having the High Council in London ready to deal with the position. It is believed that the General is much worse and may not recover.'[20]

The *Daily News* informed its readers that 'an important announcement may be made in the next few days concerning General Booth and the future of The Salvation Army'.

On this same day – Tuesday 13 November – the Chief of the Staff travelled to Southwold to tell Mrs Booth that the High Council would probably be summoned. The historian St John Ervine gives a moment-by-moment account of the next crucial hours based on interviews with the key participants:[21]

'The Chief of the Staff reached Southwold about 3.30pm, and was told that the General was asleep under a narcotic. The household was in distress, for it was thought that Bramwell Booth was dying. Commissioner Higgins turned to Mrs Booth and said that he had intended to speak to her about the prospect of the High Council being called, a prospect which, he feared, was very close, but that in the circumstances in which he found her and the family, he thought that perhaps he had better defer his communication.

'She begged him to tell her his news immediately, and he then suggested that Commissioner Catherine Booth should hear it too. The stricken women were told that, as far as the Chief could gather, it was unlikely that the calling of the Council could be deferred, as he had hoped, until the end of the year. He was daily expecting to receive the requisition, although he would continue to do his best to dissuade the commissioners from presenting it.

'He then expressed his sympathy with Mrs Booth, and showed her the clause in the Deed Poll of 1904 which stipulates that if the General should die after the High Council has been summoned, but before it meets, his nomination of his successor shall be null and void, and asked if he might see the General.

'Brigadier Bertha Smith, an Army nurse, accompanied him to the sick room where a natural emotion filled the Chief at the sight of his unconscious General, who seemed to be in a state of coma. Death, he thought, was imminent. As he prepared to leave the house, Mrs Booth begged him to summon the commissioners to pray for her husband, and he readily agreed to this request.

'He caught a train to London about 5pm and arrived there late in the evening. He was greatly agitated, pale and panting with anxiety. The General, whom he had left in what he supposed to be a state of coma, might even now be dead. If he were already dead, his nominee would now be General.

'He learnt that Commissioner Samuel Hurren, the officer commanding the British troops, was still on the premises, and sent for him. Commissioner Hurren came into the Chief's room and found him pacing up and down, uttering fervent wishes that he himself were dead so that he might be free of all this distress. He was told of the dangerous state of the General's health and warned to be ready for any and every emergency.

'What was said at this encounter was not officially recorded, and the recollection of the two parties are not in agreement, but it *is* agreed that a reference to the calling of the High Council may have been made before Commissioner Hurren, bewildered by the Chief's agitation, went away. But Commissioner Hurren, according to Commissioner Higgins, gave no hint or indication as he left that he would sign a requisition on the following morning or that he was about to take any steps whatsoever to have the High Council called.

'After Hurren had departed, Commissioner Mapp telephoned to the Chief to enquire about the General's health, but no mention of the High Council was made by either of them.

'At about 10pm on Tuesday night, the Chief of the Staff, in great distress, went home. He had not even a presentiment that the next day the High Council would be called.

'Commissioner Hurren, after he had left Commissioner Higgins, telephoned to Commissioner Mapp and said that the Chief's agitation gravely perturbed him.'

In a formal account of the events of that evening written four years later and addressed to Edward Higgins, Commissioner Hurren recalls:

Your condition so alarmed me that I at once informed Commissioner Mapp by 'phone that from what I could see we should soon be without General or Chief of the Staff, and that you had expressed yourself as wishing you were dead. Commissioner Mapp in the meantime had heard from you and was of the same opinion, and we agreed that he should get in touch with the men and arrange for a meeting early next morning. The possible requisitioners met at about 9am on the fourteenth, and I reported to them our conversation.[22]

'The historian,' writes St John Ervine about himself, 'has discussed the matter with several of the officers who played principal parts in it, and he is as certain as he can be of anything that up till a late hour on Tuesday night, November 13, the idea of calling the High Council on the following day had not presented itself to a single mind.'

However, overnight the phones were busy, and opinion hardened. The commissioners feared the consequences of calling the High Council to declare the General unfit for office. It could badly rebound on them. Yet, as Mr Percival Wright had kept insisting, they also had a moral duty to act.

What they most feared was that Bramwell Booth might die during the night. They knew what would happen if he did. It would be an action replay of what had happened when William Booth died. They would be summoned next morning to the office of the Chief of the Staff. Mr William Frost would pass the 'sealed envelope' round for their inspection. He would then open it and read out its contents. Almost certainly it would be Catherine Booth who there and then, legally and in fact, would become the next General of The Salvation Army. The new General would address her commissioners. They would respond politely. How could they do otherwise?

Immediately after the meeting the news about the Army having a new General would be communicated to the worldwide Army and to the media. General Catherine Booth would instantly take control and issue her first orders. By the afternoon she would receive her gold trimmings from the trade department. Congratulations, good wishes and promises of allegiance would begin to pour in from leaders in the four corners of the globe, and arrangements would be set in hand for public welcomes at home and abroad. The Salvationists of the world, trained for generations to welcome with open arms whichever officer headquarters sent them, would welcome the new General with genuine joy – to most of them she would seem a perfectly obvious successor to the Generalship, and even more so because she was General Bramwell Booth's 'chosen one'.

In such a scenario would seven commissioners be found who would dare to requisition the High Council to have her declared 'unfit' for office? It was not even remotely possible.

If action was to be taken, it had to be taken before Bramwell Booth died.

Wednesday 14 November 1928

Early the next morning, Wednesday 14 November, seven London commissioners on active service met in the office of Mr Percival Wright in Godliman Street. It was the same group that had signed the letter to the General in March of that year with one exception. Commissioner Arthur Blowers was unwilling to sign the requisition and his place was taken by Commissioner Wilfred Simpson, International Travelling Commissioner and, poignantly, a first cousin to Mrs General Bramwell Booth. They read the text of the requisitioning letter and then appended their signatures:

Commissioner E. J. Higgins
The Chief of the Staff of The Salvation Army
101, Queen Victoria Street, London, E.C.4

We, the undersigned, being seven commissioners for the time being of The Salvation Army, hereby request you to approve a meeting of the High Council in accordance with provision of the Deed Poll of the 26th day of July, 1904, for the purpose of adjudicating whether the General for the time being is unfit for office.

Signed by:

Samuel Hurren   David Lamb
Robert Hoggard   Henry Mapp
Charles Jeffries   Wilfred Simpson
Richard Wilson

International Headquarters
14th November 1928

Meanwhile the Chief of the Staff, unrefreshed by his night's rest, entered his office in Queen Victoria Street. His attention was immediately drawn to the headline in the *Daily News* of that day: 'Eva Booth Coming to London – Claim to 'Army' Leadership to be Pressed – General's Eldest Daughter Chosen?' The paper's New York correspondent wrote: 'Commander Evangeline Booth has every intention of pressing her claims to the succession as head of the Army in place of her brother, General Bramwell Booth.' The correspondent had got it wrong, but the article did nothing to soothe nerves that morning.

The Chief of the Staff then began to attend to his mail. It was going to be a full day, but not an unusual one. He planned to call for prayer for the General at the daily prayer meeting at 12.30pm. However, he had hardly begun his work when Commissioners Lamb and Hurren telephoned him from the office of Mr Wright to tell him that the requisition was signed and that they would bring it to him immediately.

139

The news was unexpected. The Chief of the Staff immediately telephoned Mr Frost, requesting him to come to his office at once. Commissioners Lamb and Hurren reached International Headquarters before the solicitor and handed the requisition to the Chief.

History was being written in that moment. Very little was said. For the Chief of the Staff it was a moment of mixed emotions. Commissioner Hurren later reminded Edward Higgins that when he and Commissioner Lamb 'waited upon you with the requisition … your relief appeared to be as great as your previous distress'.[23] What was not said – there was no need, for it was understood – was that it was the Chief of the Staff's word to Commissioners Hurren and Mapp the previous evening about Bramwell Booth being on the point of death that had unintentionally triggered the calling of the High Council. Yet the 'storm pilot' must have been relieved that the time for being blown around by the winds was over. Now was the time to get the ship safely into harbour.

'As Commissioners Lamb and Hurren withdrew, Mr Frost arrived,' continues St John Ervine in his account of those hours. 'The solicitor had only a few minutes to spare for the Chief at that hour, as he was on his way to Southwold to see Mrs Bramwell Booth and had an early train to catch, but he was able to give Commissioner Higgins a summary opinion on the position and to tell him that it was his duty, under clause four of the schedule to the Supplementary Deed Poll of 1904, to call the High Council.'

Commissioner Higgins quickly dictated a brief letter to Mrs Booth, which Mr Frost took with him to Southwold:

Mr Frost will have told you that I had a requisition this morning first thing from the necessary number of commissioners to call the High Council. I have had a strenuous fight, carried on now for several months, and can look everyone in the face and say I did my best to prevent this.

It has been months of mental and I was going to say spiritual agony, done because I thought the General would wish me so to act. After all

140

this time it has proved ineffective, and we are faced with whatever the calling of the High Council may involve ...

I saw Mr Frost immediately as he will have told you, and shall see him again tonight when he returns from Southwold. It is now rather a legal position, and I must be guided by what he says. I do not think there is any alternative course open to me, unless I am prepared to leave it all to others, which in the interests of all I am not willing to do.

According to the 1904 Deed, Commissioner Edward Higgins as Chief of the Staff could have refused to be party to the calling of the High Council – and the Booth family were to hold it against him that he did not avail himself of that opt-out clause. Had the Chief refused to call the High Council, then after 14 days the duty would have fallen to the 'Secretary for Foreign Affairs' – a position that had been discontinued. If this non-existent person did not act, then after 21 days summonses could be despatched and 'the High Council convened by any three commissioners of the Army'.

The Booth family felt that the onus for calling and organising the High Council should have fallen on the seven requisitioning commissioners. However, Mr Frost's advice had been clear. It was the Chief's *duty* to summon the High Council, and 'in the interests of all' Commissioner Higgins was not 'prepared to leave it all to others'. The pilot was not going to let the crew take over the running of the ship.

'A point of doubt arose in the minds of the requisitioning commissioners,' records St John Ervine. 'Would the delivery of the requisition be sufficient to prevent the accession of the General's nominee if the General were to die before the summonses to the High Council were issued? It was subsequently ascertained that it would, but on Wednesday morning [14th] the requisitioning commissioners were dubious about this, and to secure their position they requested the Chief of the Staff to issue one summons immediately. In terms drafted by Mr Frost, it was delivered to Commissioner Mapp by Commissioner Higgins before noon on that day.' It was in the form of a cable as would be sent to all eligible members in the next few days:

On joint requisition of seven commissioners the High Council of The Salvation Army is hereby convened and you are summoned to attend. Purpose of meeting is to adjudicate on question whether General for the time being is unfit for office and should be removed therefrom under Clause 2 Subclause 3 of Deed Poll 26th July 1904. Place Sunbury Court date of meeting Tuesday January 8th next 10.30 morning. Your highest duty to attend. Leave everything to do so. In the meantime am advised to ask you to bear in mind you are member of an adjudicating tribunal and would be acting properly in refusing public discussion and reserving judgment until you have heard what is submitted to the tribunal. Signed Edward Higgins Chief of the Staff

Commander Evangeline Booth in America was convinced that her brother lay dying, and on that same Wednesday cabled Commissioner Higgins, beginning 'as Chief of Staff I hold you responsible to read the following to the General':

In these suffering hours my heart is close to yours. May the peace of our Lord be your comfort. If you are leaving us, my dear brother, you will have an abundant entrance into the City of God and, in the presence of our beloved father and mother in the land where all mysteries find their meaning, you will learn that although I have disagreed with many of your policies, I have always held in my heart for you a sincere and deep affection, serving you both in word and deed with the utmost loyalty, and have without fault ever put first the highest interests of the Army with which by God and our father we were entrusted. My prayers are momently with you and my heart's love enfolds you. Eva.[24]

Bramwell Booth was too ill to receive the message. He was even too ill to be told that the High Council had been called.

Chapter Nine
Battle for Hearts and Minds

'SALVATION ARMY Calls High Council' blared the press headlines as Salvationists woke up the next morning, Thursday 16 November. 'Sharp Crisis Over the Issue of Future Leadership.'

The Salvation Army was still big news in Britain in the 1920s. Special tables for journalists were provided at all major public meetings with the proceedings being reported the next day in the leading national dailies. Now that there was a whiff of a crisis the press was hot on the scent. From now on the internal debate about the need for reform, which had rumbled for years in the upper echelons of Army leadership, was to be conducted in the full glare of publicity.

The previous evening International Headquarters' press office had issued a brief statement from the Chief of the Staff: 'The High Council of The Salvation Army has been summoned to meet in London early in January next. All discussions as to supposed claimants to the Generalship of the Army are premature, if not absurd. There are neither claimants nor candidates for the position. The matter, by the very nature of Salvation Army polity, is one which can only be decided when a vacancy occurs.'

Mr Percival Wright had also been busy on behalf of the seven requisitioning commissioners: 'I went last evening to the *Daily Mail*, *Daily Express* and *Daily News*,' he informed Mr George W. Wickersham, 'and all of these three leading papers have published articles today.'[1] Through these articles, and others that followed, the requisitioning commissioners were able to provide background information about the High Council and its calling – and get their own case across early both to the public and to the Army world. Mr Wright followed up with a cable to his USA colleague the same day: 'Everything decided at Paris now accomplished. Position safe. Nothing to do till the Commander arrives.'[2]

The press had another source of information – retired Commissioner Frederick Booth-Tucker – who considered that to keep the dailies briefed was a contribution he could make to the cause of reform. This he did openly – and often controversially. He had already informed the press that Commander Evangeline Booth was overwhelmingly wanted by the rank and file as the next General, adding his own slant (which the reformers must have read with surprise) that during the last 12 months the Army's leaders had been 'making representations to the General, saying with one voice, "By all means nominate your successor, but make the appointment subject to the approval of the commissioners".' Now he ventured to add: 'If the General's nominee as his successor should prove to be any member of his family, the High Council will challenge the nomination.'

Within a few days the press would have yet another source of information – the supporters of the Booth family. With copies of past and present correspondence being leaked to the press by supporters on both sides, the media was not short of material about which to speculate.

The reaction of Salvationists

The War Cry, published only weekly, found itself at a disadvantage as a communicator of news. It was not until the issue dated 24 November 1928 that it was able to quote the press statement made by the Chief of the Staff nine days earlier. *The War Cry* was not noted for an understated approach to news, but the announcement that the High Council had been called was almost laconic in its brevity. All it said was: 'The High Council of The Salvation Army has been summoned to meet in London early in January next.' It did not explain what the High Council was, who its members were, or why it had been summoned.

144

Most Salvationists had never heard of the provision for a High Council. Its existence was one of the Army's best-kept secrets. Even General Albert Orsborn recalls that 'until 1928, in my 23rd year of officership, I knew nothing of the High Council'.[3] *The War Cry* in all its long history had never mentioned the High Council by name before. Well-informed officers and soldiers knew from reading their respective orders and regulations that there were 'means' for removing a General from office. Bramwell Booth in *Echoes and Memories* had referred to 'machinery' for that purpose. The machinery, however, was kept well under wraps. For an actual published mention of the High Council by name Salvationists would have had to go as far back as 1914 when *The Salvation Army Year Book* had stated that 'a High Council of the Army is constituted, providing a means for removing from his position as General of The Salvation Army any General committing a breach of trust', but that had long since been forgotten.

The calling of the High Council therefore came as a thunderclap out of a clear blue sky and the reaction of officers and soldiers was one of shocked bewilderment. When they discovered that its purpose was to provide a means of removing a General who had committed 'a breach of trust' they were even more perplexed and dismayed. They knew that their beloved General was ill, but was being ill a 'breach of trust'?

The War Cry of 24 November had informed them that 'although the General has rallied since a week ago, he is not yet out of danger. We are sorry that the condition of the General remains such that he cannot be informed of the calling of the High Council.' This was troubling. Had not the doctors just days previously expressed their hope for his 'relatively early recovery'?

Dismay turned to anger. The seven requisitioning commissioners had to bear the brunt of the reaction. 'We did not anticipate we should be subjected to the abuse and misrepresentation that was heaped upon us,' recalls Commissioner Charles Jeffries. 'To say that we "waited until the General was ill in order to strike" was a malignant slander, unworthy of those who first uttered it and caused it to be circulated. *We had rather waited for the General to get better,* and only when we felt that to delay any longer might imperil the future unity and safety of the Army did we act.'[4]

However, a battle had begun. It was a battle for the hearts and minds of the members of the High Council, and beyond them for the hearts and minds of the Salvationist family and of the public.

The chances of the requisitioning commissioners getting the necessary support at the High Council looked slim as three in four members would have to agree that Bramwell Booth was unfit for office. Sixty-four members had been summoned, but Commissioner Elwin Oliphant who was on sick leave had replied that he was too unwell to come. With 63 members present, Bramwell Booth needed only 16 votes in his favour to retain office. With the presence of members of the Booth family and other commissioners who had openly declared their support for the General, 11 votes out of these 16 seemed assured. Also, given the close personal links that Bramwell Booth had forged with his leaders it seemed not only possible but highly likely that five more leaders could be found who would stand with their General.

Nobody of course knew how the bulk of the 63 members would vote. Everything was therefore at stake for both the Booth family and for the reformers – and especially for the requisitioning commissioners.

Mrs Booth takes the lead

All of Mrs Florence Booth's leadership qualities of resolution in adversity came to the fore as she sought to persuade the members of the High Council to her view. 'I rely upon you to stand by the principles of The Salvation Army as laid down by our revered Founder William Booth,' she cabled them even before the last summonses had been despatched.

On 21 November – five days after sending the cable – Mrs Booth reiterated her appeal with a letter to the members of the High Council and to staff officers generally around the world:

I write this letter in the General's sick room. He is so ill that I cannot be long away from him. In view of the various mis-statements which have appeared in the press in this country and elsewhere I feel that it is very important that the staff officers of the Army should clearly understand that the High Council has been called expressly for the purpose of deciding 'whether the General is unfit for office and should be removed therefrom'.

It is heartrending to all those who love him that such a thing should happen at what may prove to be the close of a long life of self-sacrificing toil and devotion to God and the Army. For over 50 years my dear husband has given himself without stint – first as his father's right hand in the formation and consolidation of the movement, and again, during the last 16 years, as our General and Leader.

Do you realise that seven commissioners have called the High Council for the purpose named at a moment when he lies seriously ill, unable to defend himself, and indeed at a time when he cannot even be made aware of their action, as the doctors declare that any shock might prove fatal?

As therefore he cannot speak for himself, I must make my poor efforts to do so for him. If the General goes to Heaven before the High Council can meet it may be that there will be no opportunity of removing the stigma which has been cast upon him by the requisitioning of the Council.

In order that you may more fully understand the position, I hope to have available copies of the Foundation Deed 1878 and the Supplementary Deed 1904 which will be sent to you, post free, if you will make application to Commissioner Catherine Booth, 101 Queen Victoria Street, E.C. 4.

This letter is confidential and not for publication. In the interests of the Army I have carefully avoided making reference in the public press to recent Salvation Army affairs. At this crisis you can all help the Army, to which for service and sacrifice we have all given our lives, by thinking clearly, acting courageously, and praying ceaselessly that God will restore the General to health for further service, and over-rule all for the Glory of his name.

The letter went to staff officers around the world, and in Britain supporters of the Booth family arranged for all officers to receive a copy. The letter was also leaked to the press by well-meaning friends and within days most Salvationists in Britain knew of its content. Requests for copies of the constitutional documents poured into the office of Commissioner Catherine Booth at '101'.

On 1 December Mrs Booth wrote a further letter to the members of the High Council alerting them that some might try to widen the agenda of the High Council:

> Personally I am persuaded that some are under the impression that the High Council could be used for some additional purpose than that of deposing the General and electing another General, and that it is because of this that they are willing to contemplate a course of action which would certainly cast a shadow over what may be the close of a singularly devoted life. If you will read it carefully, you will see that the 1904 Deed Poll makes no provision for the discussion by the High Council of any matters others than those named ... I have no knowledge of the charges which will be brought in the effort to prove the present General unfit, and I therefore cannot prepare his defence until the Council meets and these are made known.

Mrs Booth was not alone in her spirited defence of her husband. Commissioner Henry Mapp reported to the Commander that 'Catherine, Laurie, Kitching and Cunningham have combined to work against us. They are sending out cables, letters, etc. Their main line of operation is that we have attacked the General – his reputation – an old man lying ill, dying. Also, as in Mrs Booth's letter, that there is a departure from SA principles, dissension, controversy, agitation, General ill, and indicating we are the cause.'[5]

In addition to Commissioners Catherine Booth and Theodore Kitching, Bramwell Booth had a threesome of 'Scots Guards' among the commissioners at International Headquarters who now rose to his defence. Commissioner John Laurie, who hailed from Dumfries, was the Chancellor of the Exchequer. His officer service had been given in the British Territory and at International Headquarters. Commissioner John Cunningham, out of Perth, was the

International Secretary for Europe. He had served for 20 years in South Africa and had also worked in The Netherlands and in Indonesia. Commissioner Allister Smith, who will appear later in this account, was a son of Elgin and was now an International Travelling Commissioner. He had given 32 years of service on the mission field, pioneering the Army's work in Zululand and later in Kenya. Often referred to as The Salvation Army's David Livingstone, he had been admitted to the Order of the Founder in 1923. Together they were a highly influential group.

As the battle for hearts and minds continued, officers and soldiers in Britain and beyond began to study the constitutional documents for the first time. Discussion soon centred on the meaning of the word 'unfit' – with its two senses of 'unwell' and 'unworthy'. In the context of the 1904 Deed the word carried the sinister connotation of 'unworthy'. How far were the requisitioning commissioners justified in using it in its other sense of 'unwell'? There were also whispers of a hidden agenda.

On 3 December Lieut-Colonel W. W. Muirhead brought these questions to the surface with a letter addressed to Commissioner Wilfred Simpson, one of the requisitioning commissioners. In seven closely argued pages he homed in on what for the requisitioning commissioners was a sensitive point – their motive for calling the High Council. Was it called because the General was ill and therefore unfit to lead the Army, or was it called to block the succession in the 'sealed envelope' and to bring about constitutional reform?

The author argued that if illness was the motive, then the 1904 Deed made provision in Clause 2, Subclause 1 for the General to be removed from office by a 'write-in' of the commissioners without them even needing to assemble – with the nomination in the 'sealed envelope' remaining valid. The author accused the requisitioning commissioners of calling the High Council on a 'false issue' – the blocking of the General's nominee. He wrote: 'This appears to me to be a deliberate attempt to evade the spirit and purpose of the 1904 Supplementary Deed Poll. It savours of the sacrifice of principle in order to indulge personal dislike against some person

whom the General is supposed to have named as his successor ...
Shall we do evil that good may come?'

It was strong meat. Though purportedly a private letter, it was
extensively circulated by supporters of the family and its content
became widely known. Robust rebuttals followed – the judgment
and integrity of the requisitioning commissioners surely spoke for
themselves – but the letter left its mark.

Another officer who put pen to paper in support of the General's
position was Lieut-Colonel Albert Orsborn, who was responsible for
the men cadets at the International Training Garrison, and was later
to become General himself. He took up Bramwell Booth's cause in
an 'open' letter to Commissioner Charles Jeffries, his immediate
leader as the Training Principal. Among his points, Albert Orsborn
lamented that the High Council might close the General's service
'by force' and 'do violence' to the General and his family, and that
if this were to happen he as a young officer would be placed in a
'spiritual dilemma'. Commissioner Jeffries in his equally 'open' reply
was critical of Albert Orsborn's apparent acceptance of the idea that
the General could 'pass the Army on to his children as a family
heirloom' and thus create 'an unbroken succession of the Booths'.[6]

The requisitioning commissioners put their case

The seven requisitioning commissioners realised that they were
faced with a potential public relations disaster which could have
serious consequences for the voting at the High Council. As a group
they had to justify the extreme action they had taken, and in the
process counteract the information flowing from and on behalf of
the Booth family. They did so in three communications addressed to
the members of the High Council and in a pamphlet for general
distribution to Salvationists and friends.[7] In the pamphlet *The Why
and Wherefore of the High Council of The Salvation Army 1928-29*
they summarised the points they had made privately to members
of the Council.

Ten thousand copies of this pamphlet were issued on 8
December. It is a frank document in the way that it describes the

build-up to the crisis. The ill-health of the General is given as the main reason for the summoning of the High Council, but for those with eyes to see there are hints of an additional agenda. Some extracts will give the flavour of the document:

Why has the High Council been summoned?

It has been summoned because for many months the General has been unfit for the discharge of the public and administrative duties of his office. He has been seriously ill for a long time. The only course open to a sole trustee who finds himself unable to carry out his duties is to resign or apply to the courts to be relieved from his responsibilities, unless there are some provisions in the Trust Deeds which will provide for another course to be taken. Our Founder, foreseeing such an emergency as has now arisen, wisely provided for it in the Supplementary Deed of 1904.

What is the High Council's business?

The Council's business will be to decide whether or not the General is fit and able to continue to discharge the heavy duties of his office as General of the Army and sole trustee of its vast funds and holdings ...

What is meant by 'unfit'?

The word is used as in our orders and regulations and its dictionary meaning, that is to say – 'loss of competence, strength, skill or qualities required for any task or purpose: to be disabled or disqualified – as for instance, sickness unfitting a man for labour'.

Why did the commissioners submit their request to the Chief of the Staff in November?

Because there is no authority other than the High Council, within the Army or outside it, competent to deal with the present situation. In the crisis which had become acute by reason of the General's protracted illness (the issue of which might seem a little more hopeful had there not been many evidences during recent years of steady failure and approaching breakdown) they were led to conclude that the time had come when the issue of a requisition for the calling of the High Council was clearly their obligation.

Their action (perhaps unduly delayed out of personal regard for the General) was dictated solely by their concern for the Army to which they have given all their lives. They have since learnt, by cables and letters from all parts of the world, that some such action was expected, and they have reason to believe that, if they had failed to act, others would have taken the initiative.

Is the Generalship of the Army a 'life appointment'?

Contrary to what is commonly supposed, there is no ground in our constitution for the idea that every General shall hold office for life. The Founder alone, and by name, was given that privilege in the Deed of 1878, and it is a privilege which does *not* necessarily descend to his successors. This was a most wise precaution on the part of the Founder, for it restrains for all time any disposition upon the part of any General to regard the Army as peculiarly his own, and its officers and soldiers merely as his servants or employees. The Founder, moreover, had no intention of establishing – nor did he establish – anything in the nature of a dynasty. He frequently declared the Army was 'not a family affair'.

Were any representations made to the General before the High Council was summoned?

Yes! Affection and anxiety for the General in the heavy burdens he was compelled to carry caused several commissioners to approach him in March last, when it came to their knowledge he had taken steps towards altering the 1904 Deed in ways which, it was believed, would be seriously detrimental to the best interest of the Army.

What was the reason for the earlier representations made to the General?

The serious unrest existing in many parts of the world upon the question of appointing the General. A desire that he should meet his leading officers in conference on this and other questions affecting his own onerous position, the future of the Army and welfare of its officers. These and other representations made prior to March were not entertained, and the crisis became seriously emphasised through the breakdown of the General.

Above: General and Mrs Bramwell Booth enjoy tea in the garden on the General's 70th birthday.

Left: General Bramwell Booth (right) in conversation with his Chief of the Staff, Commissioner Edward Higgins.

Below: General Bramwell Booth at the stone-laying for the William Booth Memorial College on 10 May 1928, his last appearance in public. Mrs Booth stands between Lords Elgin and Glanely.

THE 1929 HIGH COUNCIL

Top Row – left to right: Lieut-Commissioners William Palmer and Bouwe Vlas. Lieut-Colonels Charles Mackenzie, Robert Steven and Edward Coles. Colonel George Souter. Brigadiers William Ebbs and Karl Johanson.

Middle Row – left to right: Commissioners Arthur Blowers and George Mitchell. Lieut-Commissioners Barnard Turner and Isaac Unsworth. Commissioner Samuel Brengle. Lieut-Commissioners Reinert Gundersen, John McMillan and William McIntyre. Commissioners Adam Gifford and Karl Larsson. Lieut-Commissioner William McKenzie.

Bottom Row. The first seven are the requisitioning commissioners. Left to right: Commissioners David Lamb, Richard Wilson, Charles Jeffries, Samuel Hurren, Robert Hoggard, Wilfred Simpson, Henry Mapp, John Carleton (Recorder), Edward Higgins (Chief of the Staff).

Top row – left to right: Lieut-Colonels William Hancock, Albert Marpurg and Thomas Wilson. Colonel Thomas Stroud. Lieut-Colonel Wilfred Twilley. Brigadier Alfred Lindvall. Colonel Joseph Barr. Lieut-Commissioners Stanley Ewens and Gunpei Yamamuro. Colonel Gerald Freeman (Assistant Recorder). Mr William Frost (Legal Adviser).

Middle row – left to right: Commissioner William Howard. Colonel Narayana Muthiah. Lieut-Commissioners William Maxwell, Charles Rich and George Jolliffe. Colonel Charles Baugh. Lieut-Commissioner Wiebe Palstra. Commissioners Theodore Kitching, Albin Peyron, John Cunningham and Allister Smith.

Bottom row – left to right: Commissioner James Hay (President). Lieut-Commissioner William Haines (Vice-President). Commander Evangeline Booth. Commissioner Johanna van de Werken. Colonel Mrs Annie Trounce. Commissioners Hugh Whatmore, Johannes de Groot and George Sowton. Lieut-Commissioners Richard Holz and Julius Horskins. Commissioner John Laurie.

Absent from the photo: Mrs Booth, Commissioner Mrs Lucy Booth-Hellberg, Commissioner Catherine Booth and Colonel Mary Booth.

Left: The seven requisitioning commissioners. Left to right: Commissioners Robert Hoggard, Richard Wilson, Charles Jeffries, David Lamb, Henry Mapp, Samuel Hurren and Wilfred Simpson.

Left: Commissioner James Hay, President of the High Council.

Below: Commander Evangeline Booth and Colonel Narayana Muthiah greet each other as they meet at the High Council. Looking on are Commissioner Adam Gifford (centre) and Lieut-Colonel Albert Marpurg (behind Colonel Muthiah).

Above: Commissioners John Laurie and Catherine Booth arrive for the High Council. Commissioner Theodore Kitching walks behind them.

The position of the requisitioning commissioners had been greatly strengthened when on 30 November eight retired London commissioners issued a statement in which they expressed their approval of the action taken by the requisitioners in calling for the High Council to be convened. 'Under the present sorrowful circumstances we consider that they could have done no other.' The signatories were heavyweights, every one of them an early Army pioneer. They were known and respected by all Salvationists, and their message did more than anything else to steady the Salvationist family at that time. The signatories were Commissioners John Carleton, William Ridsdel, Mildred Duff, Adelaide Cox, Frederick Booth-Tucker, William Stevens, Clara Case and William Iliffe. Their endorsement was included in the informative pamphlet reviewed above.

In their private communications to the members of the High Council the requisitioning commissioners were even blunter than in the pamphlet, and on the constitutional issue they trod new ground. In an unprecedented way they referred back to the original constitution of 1875 – the constitution that William Booth had annulled after three years – and clearly implied that the way forward to reform lay in a return to some of the provisions in that constitution:

It is not generally realised that the original Foundation Deed of our movement was executed by our Founder in 1875. The Deed provided that William Booth should be the General Superintendent, unless he should resign or be by disease or some other cause disqualified from discharging the duties of such office.

In a schedule to the same document it was provided that the nomination of a successor to the office of General Superintendent might be made by the one who held that office, and also by any 12 members of the Conference, and that the election of the General Superintendent should be by ballot, the candidate receiving the highest number of votes to be elected, and to hold office for a term of five years when he might be re-elected.

There were also provisions for the General Superintendent being removed from office by a vote of three fourths of the members of the

153

Conference, which was given power to manage all matters connected with the organisation during the intervals between its annual sittings.

The Conference also had power to over-ride and nullify any veto which the General Superintendent might have exercised in a way which did not meet with the approval of the Conference.

About this time (i.e. 1875 onwards) our movement began to extend, and the members of the Conference were scattered in various parts of the country. For this, and for other reasons not now apparent, it was decided in 1878 that the first Foundation Deed should be wholly annulled, and this was done at the annual meeting of the Conference on 7 August 1878, and on the same day our second Deed was executed.

With the provision of this document most officers are fully conversant. But they should bear in mind the clause which provides that it is the duty of the General to make a statement in writing as to his successor or *as to the means which are to be taken for the appointment of a successor at the decease of the General Superintendent or upon his ceasing to perform the duties of the office'*. This latter phrase apparently has in mind the provision of the 1875 Deed as to the election of a General by the Conference.

The whole control of the movement was left in the hands of the General Superintendent by this 1878 Deed and at that stage of our development this was undoubtedly the best thing for the progress of the work.

After several years of careful consideration and many conferences with his leading officers and the most eminent King's Counsel of that period, the Founder executed in 1904 the Supplementary Deed, by which provision was made for the High Council to function in the circumstances therein set out. In this Deed it is obvious that some attempt was made to get back to the original form of government by a Conference or Council as it was then called. This is very clear when one remembers that the Deed of 1875 specifically provided for the possibility of the General Superintendent being by disease or some other cause disqualified from discharging the duties of his office, although the phrase used in the 1904 Deed is 'adjudicated unfitness'. The same idea of the three-fourths majority is retained in order to ensure that such a serious step should only be taken with the consent of a substantial majority of those concerned.

The requisitioning commissioners also informed the members of the High Council that Mrs Booth's use of words like 'charges' and 'defence' were 'evidently based upon a misunderstanding of the situation'. The High Council was not an 'attack' on the General, nor was it a trial.

They also dealt with her assertion that the General was being deprived of 'his *right* to appoint his successor'. They reminded members that the 1878 Deed spoke not of a *right* but of a *duty,* and that this duty could be simply to make a statement as to how his successor was to be appointed. 'This erroneous idea of the possession of a "right" to appoint his successor is due to a fundamental misunderstanding of the position, and has been so often repeated that it has come to be regarded by many as a sort of perquisite attaching to the office of General.'

The requisitioning commissioners ended with the hope that the General might still decide to retire from office – and pointedly referred to family influence as the root of the present problems: 'We believe that if our General could think and speak for himself he would show such a high conception of his Trust that he would embrace the opportunity of being relieved of his office, and retire with full honours, dignities and emoluments, thus emphasising the high ideals he has so eloquently preached to all of us.'

The tide changes

The Chief of the Staff did not allow the pages of *The War Cry* to be used in the campaign of persuasion, and, acting on legal advice, refused to permit Army trust funds to be used by either side. The Booth family therefore had to draw on personal funds to pay for the sending of cables and letters and the printing of constitutional documents. The expenses of the requisitioning commissioners for the same purposes and for the printing of the pamphlet continued to be met by Commander Evangeline Booth in the USA through their respective attorneys.

So many were joining in the war of words that in the end the Chief of the Staff had to put his foot down. 'I feel compelled to insist,' he wrote in a circular letter dated 10 December 1928, 'that there shall be no more dissemination of correspondence amongst officers and others upon matters pertaining to the calling to the High Council.'

After the initial hostile reaction within and without the Army to the calling of the High Council the tide turned. Informed opinion in the media recognised the need for reform and urged the abandonment of autocratic rule, dynastic succession and sole trusteeship. Salvationists found themselves inwardly divided – with their heads they understood what the reformers were saying, but with their hearts they were with the General and did not want him to be hurt. The proverbial man in the street proved the most persistent. He had got it into his head that the Army was 'getting rid of old General Booth' – and he would not be moved.

Brother and sister

An extraordinary twist was given to the battle for hearts and minds by the fact that from the moment the High Council was called Bramwell Booth began to recover. By 26 November he was again signing legal documents, something he had had to discontinue for the first time 15 days before. However, he was still deemed by the doctors to be too ill to be told that the High Council had been called.

The War Cry dated 1 December headlined 'A Definite Improvement' and informed readers that the 'doctors declare the General to be out of danger, and go so far as to state that they are now hopeful of his complete recovery'. The headlines in succeeding weeks stressed the continuing improvement in the General's health.

When Commander Evangeline Booth sent her deathbed message to her brother on Wednesday 14 November it was with every intention of sailing for London three days later on the *Majestic* in order to see him for the last time, or failing that, to be present at his funeral. It was a whiff of this intention that the *Daily News* had caught – and had misinterpreted – when on 14 November it announced that she was coming to London to press 'her claims to the succession'.

In the light of the change in Bramwell Booth's condition the Chief of the Staff urged her to wait, promising to alert her if there was a relapse, but the Commander fretted. In her anxiety to see her brother she cabled Mrs Booth on 22 November: 'My heart yearns to see Bramwell, if only for a short time. Would you like me to come at once? What is present condition of Bramwell?'

Mrs Booth cabled back: 'We must give the General every chance of recovery. The doctors are hopeful it can be done but on no account may he be distressed. In view of the past how could your presence do anything but grieve him deeply?' Mrs Booth also knew that if the Commander visited her brother it would be impossible to continue to keep from him the news that the High Council had been called.

The Commander was further burdened by the possibility that the High Council might fail in its intent and result in action being taken against the reformers. She wrote to her attorney, Mr Wickersham: 'The fact of my having been the one to take the initiative in the reform movement gives me a sense of tremendous responsibility. For to have led so large a number of our best and noblest in a course that, apart from reaching the desired culmination would under our present system so definitely be to their hurt, would almost kill me. I feel at every cost of nerve and brain and energy *we must cross the Rubicon*.'[8]

This Rubicon was not in New York – it was in London. After various changes of plans, in the end it was not until 22 December that the Commander sailed for London, via Cherbourg, on board the *Olympia*. The build-up grew apace in the USA press about the American Commander setting out for London in order to return as General unless thwarted by her niece. Such was the publicity, reported *The Times* of London, that in the end she 'sailed secretly', appearing 'on the passenger list under a different name – Miss E. Cory – and both she and her companions wore ordinary clothes instead of Salvation Army uniform'.[9]

Chapter Ten

Countdown

'THE rank and file of the Army feel that the time has come when they can no longer accept a worldwide leader as a sort of Santa Claus gift, sent with an air of mystery like an unopened parcel.' Commander Evangeline Booth was speaking on board the *Olympia* to the enterprising correspondent of the *Daily News* who had boarded the ship in Cherbourg for the final stage of its journey to England. She was in full uniform for the first time. The Commander continued: 'If I am elected to succeed my brother, General Bramwell Booth, I will not object. But you must remember that I am not putting myself forward as a candidate. I will take it as the will of Providence.'[1]

The *Olympia* docked in Southampton on Friday 28 December. When the boat train arrived at London's Waterloo Station, Commissioner Henry Mapp and several other members of the High Council together with hundreds of Salvationists were there to give her an enthusiastic welcome.

After greeting them, the Commander was driven to the London hotel where she was to be based for the duration of the High Council. She immediately got in touch with the Chief of the Staff, Commissioner Edward Higgins.

At the hotel a letter from her niece, Commissioner Catherine Booth, awaited her asking that they might meet as soon as possible. 'Of course I shall be happy to see you,' she replied, 'but I feel that before anything else I should see my brother, and that as far as possible I should keep my heart and mind clear from all else until I have done so.'[2] When the Commander visited International

Headquarters some days later it was Catherine Booth who seemed the reluctant one. 'Niece Avoids Her Aunt', headlined the press. They did not meet until at the High Council.

On the day the Commander arrived in London, she followed up with a further message to Mrs Booth requesting that she might see her brother. Bramwell Booth still did not know about the calling of the High Council, and even after he was told, Mrs Booth denied the request for a meeting on the ground that the General was not in a fit state to receive his sister.

It was clear that the leader of the reform movement had arrived, and the Commander's hotel room became her headquarters. Streams of visitors called, hundreds of letters had to be written and responded to. Under the heading of 'Commander Eva Booth's Sunday Conferences at London Hotel' the *Daily News* of Monday 31 December reported that she had conferred 'with a number of high officers of the Army, including several members of the High Council'. She wrote about those pre-High Council days to Colonel W. F. Jenkins, her National Chief Secretary in New York:

> As you may imagine, the situation here is very difficult and perplexing. There are so many cross currents that it is difficult to discern the way the stream is flowing ... I am kept hard at it from early morning till early the next morning, getting very few hours sleep. The Chief of the Staff wants me to see every member of the High Council personally, and of course it is very important that I should do so. Some of them do not know the first thing about the situation ... All the members arriving from abroad make a bee-line to my hotel, so you have some slight idea of how I spend my days.[3]

The Chief of the Staff was not a neutral observer standing aloof from what was happening. As we know, he had informed Bramwell Booth that he was in favour of reform and that he hoped the General would take the initiative. Now that those hopes had been dashed and the High Council had been called, Edward Higgins knew what a catastrophic setback it would be to the cause of constitutional reform if the High Council simply confirmed the General in office without raising the matter of reform. He therefore wanted every member of the Council to understand what was at stake.

At these pre-Council briefings members were shown photographs of the General's signature – one on a document dated 17 September 1926 and the other on a document dated 21 December 1928. The first was bold and dominant, the second an almost embarrassingly frail and shaky scribble. The family shouted 'unfair' – the second signature, they said, had been penned when the General was suffering from neuritis in his right arm – but members could not help noticing the recent date of the second signature. It had been penned at a time when, according to the family, the General was well on the way to full recovery.

'Discussions preliminary to the calling of the High Council were continued at The Salvation Army Headquarters yesterday,' reported the *Daily News* on Tuesday 1 January 1929, 'when the various commissioners and territorial commanders arriving from abroad met Commander Eva Booth and the London commissioners.'

However, the continuing battle for hearts and minds was not one-sided. Many arriving members were invited to see Mrs Booth on one of her visits to London, or were asked to meet Commissioner Catherine Booth in her office at 101 Queen Victoria Street to hear the other side of the story – and many did. Commissioner Samuel Brengle wrote to a colleague back home:

> We arrived on Friday, and on Saturday the Commander had me to private lunch with her. Catherine asked to see me and also the Chief, and then I got into a meeting of delegates where the requisitioning commissioners under the chairmanship of Carleton were threshing out plans of procedure. And as it unfolded I saw what serious and complex business was before us.[4]

Pre-briefings were handled with care by both sides – anything resembling pressure would be counterproductive in a gathering of such experienced Army leaders. Lieut-Commissioner Gunpei Yamamuro (Territorial Commander, Japan) had even chosen to travel to London via Canada rather than the USA in order to keep his mind open on the matter of reformist thinking.[5] Not all members of the High Council were reached after their arrival in London. Commissioner Johanna van de Werken, one of four Dutch commissioners at the High Council, who was 'on furlough' at the time, wrote later of those days:

> I did not meet any of the requisitioning commissioners before the High Council met, nor did I attend any meeting. Anything told me by way of explanation before the first gathering was without any pressure whatever, and of course *no pledges were ever asked, or given, as to votes*. I do not think anyone would have had either the desire or the courage to approach any member of the High Council with such a degrading proposal. The advice of the then Chief of the Staff was simply: 'Keep an open mind and when all has been laid before you, follow the dictates of your conscience.'[6]

Naturally, the press kept the pot on the boil. The *Daily Express* informed its readers that 'immediately the High Council of The Salvation Army meets next week its authority will be challenged on the ground that is has been summoned under the wrong clause of the deed poll by which it was appointed'.

Seven days to go

As already recorded, when General Bramwell Booth saw his wife and daughter approach his bedside at their Southwold home in the evening of the first day of January 1929, he could tell by the look on their faces that they were the bearers of bad tidings. He had in fact long suspected that the High Council had been called. There had been just too many times when newspapers and *The War Cry* had been kept from him, or when the conversation had deliberately been steered away from the subject. So strong was this inner conviction that he had pre-empted their announcement.

The Chief of the Staff informed the press that the General had been told. On Friday 4 January the *Daily News* quoted his statement under the banner headline 'Mrs Booth Tells the General'. In his statement the Chief of the Staff reported:

The General's first thought was for The Salvation Army. He realised the grave import of this action. He said: 'I have loved the Army; I have done my best for our people.' And after some questions and reflection, added: 'Whatever other people may think about the government of the Army, they must feel that this is rather rough on me.' Naturally the news came as a great shock, and the General passed a somewhat restless night, although his general condition remains hopeful.

As Mrs Booth and Catherine tried to update Bramwell Booth on everything that had happened in the six weeks since the High Council had been called, it was as if he had woken from hibernation to discover that his world had changed out of all recognition – and there were only seven days to go before the High Council was to meet.

A further blow

A bad blow for him was to learn that he could no longer turn to Mr William Frost for advice. William Frost had represented both the Army as a trust and Bramwell Booth personally as its sole trustee. The interests of the trust and its trustee were indivisible. Now with the calling of the High Council there was a distinction between the trust and the trustee, and Mr Frost had come to the conclusion that his first duty was to the trust – the Army – and not to the trustee. He had therefore advised Mrs Booth that she would need to seek alternative legal counsel for the General and for herself.

Though upset by Mr Frost's decision, Mrs Booth had already before the end of November engaged Messrs Waterhouse and Co as new legal advisers. Mr Frost had himself spent many hours briefing the new team. He followed up with a letter to them dated 3 December in which, 'with the greatest possible diffidence', he ventured to enclose a revised draft letter of resignation for General Bramwell Booth that he hoped Mrs Booth might bring to the attention of her husband. Addressed to the Chief of the Staff it read:

I have been very ill, as you know, for months past, and am still quite unfit for work of any kind. They tell me that this has rendered it necessary to convene our High Council. Quite so.

Please tell the Council, when it meets, that had I been able to do so I would have spared them all this trouble; but my dear wife and the doctors didn't think I was well enough to be told.

I have signed the necessary legal resignation, and all you will have to do is to elect someone who is strong enough to lead you on as I should have tried to do if my health had been spared.

God bless you all, and give you wisdom in your choice.

In her biography of her father, Catherine Bramwell-Booth regrets that her father no longer had the legal advice of Dr – now Sir – Washington Ranger when the agitation for constitutional reform began. 'How differently things might have turned out had the advice and help of this able, sympathetic spirit been available when Bramwell Booth stood practically alone in his endeavour to preserve the Army's constitution,' she writes.[7] Sir Washington was by then old and infirm, and he died during the High Council.

Now even Bramwell Booth's trusted adviser William Frost would no longer be there at his side. 'I gather that you have not felt able to help me personally,' Bramwell Booth writes sorrowfully to him. 'I count on you to stand by me as the trustee and by the constitution … I should like to hear from you.'[8] However, it would now be to his new legal advisers that he would have to turn for advice. Their legal expertise was of the highest, but they suffered from a major handicap. They had not lived with the Army for 40 years as Sir Washington Ranger and Mr William Frost had.

A battle to fight

We do not know whether Mrs Booth ever showed her husband the draft letter of resignation prepared by Mr Frost. What we do know is that when on 1 January 1929 Bramwell Booth was informed that the High Council had been called, resignation was far from his mind. 'The hope of preserving the Army's constitution unchanged now engrossed him,' remembers Catherine Bramwell-Booth. 'His strength rallied unexpectedly to the call. He had a battle to fight.'[9] Even at this late stage the battle to win hearts and minds took on new vigour.

As the countdown began towards the opening of the High Council on Tuesday 8 January 1929, each day seemed to strengthen the General's position.

On Friday 4 January – four days before the High Council – a letter to *The Times* by Commissioner John Laurie, Chancellor of the Exchequer, supported the General's stance – and indirectly undermined that of the requisitioning commissioners:

> The suggestion that a state of 'chaos' has supervened as the result of delays in the execution of legal documents is unfounded, as the General, despite his illness, is at the present time up-to-date with the signing of all legal, banking and other documents. Except during the period in November when he was in a critical state of health, there has been no serious delay in the securing of his signature to any documents necessary to the discharge of Salvation Army business.[10]

The next day, Saturday 5 January – three days before the High Council – a number of papers reported that 'General Bramwell Booth is planning to make a dramatic appearance in person at Sunbury Court, health permitting'. The *Daily Express* informed its readers:

> The General's decision to go to Sunbury created a sensation in the opposing camps of the Army. The Booth party, led by Mrs Booth and her daughter, Commissioner Catherine Booth, were electrified by the possibility ... They felt that the General's presence in the historic house would sway the balance in his favour. If he were summoned to the conference room the effect of any message would be heightened by the fact that he spoke with the eyes of his famous father upon him. Leaders of the reform party were frankly dismayed by the astute move of the General.

The following day, Sunday 6 January – two days before the Council – General Bramwell Booth prepared a letter addressed to the members of the High Council. He had it taken by messenger to the Chief of the Staff for him to convey to the High Council when its deliberations got under way.

The Chief of the Staff had last seen the General when he was lying in a coma six weeks previously, and as he read the letter that Sunday afternoon he was impressed by the intellectual vigour it revealed. If the General had written the letter himself, he mused, here back again was Bramwell Booth the astute statesman, the skilled advocate, the creative leader, whose arguments might well wrong-foot the requisitioning commissioners and carry the judgment of sufficient members of the Council for him to win the day.

The next day, Monday 7 January – the day before the High Council was due to open – the Booth family released the latest health bulletin on the General, and ensured it was circulated to High Council members, reported in the press, and published in full in *The War Cry*:

After having carefully examined General Booth on December 30, 1928, we are of the opinion that the General is making satisfactory progress towards recovery. His physical condition, though still poor, is gradually improving.

His illness has followed the expected course, and there is every reason to believe that the General should be able to resume work within six months.

As there have been rumours that the General's mental powers have been affected, we take this opportunity of stating that there never has been any question of mental incapacity. His intellect remains unimpaired.

He is now well able to give decisions and advice on important matters, but it is advisable that he should have as much quiet as possible and not be burdened with unnecessary anxieties, as this will tend to retard his recovery.

(Signed) John Weir
Ernest Wardlaw Milne[11]

166

By the Monday evening all members of the Council had arrived in London. Most were already in residence at Sunbury Court. All knew that the outlook seemed to be changing by the hour. That night 63 Army leaders went to bed wondering what the morning would bring.

Chapter Eleven
The Council Meets

IN good time for the 10.30am opening of the High Council on Tuesday 8 January 1929, Lieut-Colonel Albert Marpurg, chief secretary of the Denmark Territory, entered the council chamber at Sunbury Court and found his assigned seat. He placed his papers on the table in front of him and looked round as other members arrived. The feeling that he had lived with for the last seven weeks flooded over him once again, and he quietly murmured to himself: 'I should not be here.'

When on Saturday 17 November 1928 the telegram boy had called at territorial headquarters in Copenhagen just before noon with the cable from International Headquarters he had opened it himself. It was a summons to attend the High Council in London on 8 January 1929 – and it was addressed to him.

A mistake, surely, he had thought to himself. True, he was temporarily in command of the territory – and had been appointed 'Chief Secretary in-charge' – but that was just because there was an interval of some weeks between one territorial commander leaving and the next arriving. Colonel David Wickberg had now been appointed as the new territorial commander and he and Mrs Wickberg – parents of Erik, who would one day be the Army's ninth General – were due to arrive within three weeks to take charge of the territory. In fact that very morning Lieut-Colonel Marpurg had put the finishing touches to the programme for the welcome meeting. On reading the telegram he knew he must get in touch with International Headquarters.

When he did it was to discover that there had been no mistake. The 'storm pilot' steering his ship through uncharted waters knew how vital it was to get the membership of the first High Council exactly right according to the 1904 Supplementary Deed. Every vote was going to count, and any omissions or unwarranted inclusions in the membership of the Council were bound to be challenged.

In the 1904 Deed the membership was defined as 'the persons holding *at the qualifying date* the following offices: the Chief of the Staff, the Secretary for Foreign Affairs, all the commissioners of the Army not being commissioners on the retired list, all the officers holding territorial commands in the Army in any part of the world whatever their rank in the Army'. The qualifying date was the date when the first summons had been sent – 14th November 1928. On that day it was as if a snapshot was taken of the Army's senior leadership – and whoever held the qualifying rank or appointment on that day was summoned.

Nevertheless there were difficult judgments to make in some cases. Was Mrs Booth – a commissioner in her own right – to be invited? She herself did not think she would be because as the wife of the General she would have a conflict of interest. What about lieut-commissioners who were not territorial commanders? It had been established that lieut-commissioners could not requisition a High Council, but could they attend? What about the officers in charge of smaller commands that were not 'territories' as such. The distinction between 'commands' and 'territories' was not as clear-cut then as it is today, and the phrase 'officers holding territorial commands' was open to varying interpretations.

Mr William Frost's advice was that a policy of inclusion rather than exclusion should be adopted. If there were going to be challenges about membership it would be better to have everyone present in London rather than having to adjourn the High Council once it had started to await the arrival of any missing members.

So all commissioners and 'officers holding territorial commands' on the qualifying date had been summoned from around the world. The inclusion of what today would be called 'officers commanding' meant that a number of relatively junior officers – seven lieut-colonels and three brigadiers – found themselves called to sit in judgment on their General's fitness for office. Probably not what William Booth had had in mind.

Lieut-Colonel Marpurg's position as 'Chief Secretary in-charge' of Denmark had proved to be the most borderline, but as he was officially 'in command' of the territory on the qualifying date he was summoned. So here he was, the only chief secretary in a meeting of commissioners and territorial commanders.

He had found it distinctly embarrassing that when he left for London some days previously it was he who got on the train at Copenhagen Central Station while his territorial commander, Colonel David Wickberg – who by then had been territorial commander for more than a month – stood on the platform and waved him off.

There was not an inch of space to spare in the wood-panelled conference room. It had obviously proved a work of art to fit into the room tables and chairs for 63 members plus two recorders plus the legal adviser. 'As far as Sunbury Court is concerned,' the Chief of the Staff had written to the members some days earlier, 'we are doing the very best we possibly can with the accommodation at our disposal. This is the only place around London where we can meet with any hope of quietness and comfort.'[1]

When Lieut-Colonel Marpurg had been shown round after his arrival, it had been explained to him that Sunbury Court – a Georgian mansion in the village of Sunbury-on-Thames, 16 miles from the heart of London – had belonged to a noble Irish family until it was converted into a riverside club. The club had failed and the house with its extensive grounds had been bought by the Army in 1921. The derelict property had since been restored and redeveloped for use as a residential centre. It was now the Officers' Training Institute. The residential facilities, however, were more spartan than comfortable, with members having to share rooms – some of them three or four to a room.

Most of the members were resident at Sunbury Court, but some travelled in each day. Commander Evangeline Booth commuted from her London hotel and the Chief of the Staff from his home. The other four members of the Booth family present – Mrs Booth and her two daughters, Commissioner Catherine Booth and Colonel Mary Booth (Territorial Commander, Germany), and her sister-in-law Commissioner Mrs Lucy Booth-Hellberg (International Travelling Commissioner) – had rented a small house, 'The Cottage', in Sunbury village and stayed there. The house was within walking distance but for convenience and to avoid journalists they usually travelled by car between the cottage and Sunbury Court.

Because of the intense public interest in the High Council, Salvation Army officers were posted as guards at all entrances to the grounds. Police officers were on duty at the main gate throughout. They had a cold time for the weather was frosty and foggy with occasional spells of snow for the duration of the Council. Special passes were issued to members and supporting staff. All the leading national dailies had sent journalists to cover the event, and they commandeered a tea-shop near the main entrance as their headquarters. Members of the High Council had been requested not to communicate individually with the press. From time to time the press were fed official information through news bulletins, but for the most they were reduced to watching the comings and goings – and to speculation on their meaning.

Seating in the conference chamber was in order of seniority with the most senior leaders near the small platform. As befitted the only chief secretary in the room, Lieut-Colonel Marpurg was in the outer semicircle of seats near the back – but this allowed him to survey the scene as a whole. It was an impressive sight: 63 leaders, every one of whom had served under William Booth himself, some from the Army's earliest days. He noted how the Commander – by far the most senior commissioner present – dominated the room, and how when Mrs Booth entered all eyes turned towards her and how for a moment even the murmur of conversation ceased. Both of them had taken the trouble to speak at some length with him. They – and he – knew that his vote was as valuable as that of the most senior leader present.

Lieut-Colonel Marpurg had done his homework and knew that if 16 of the 63 persons present were to vote in support of the General the task of the High Council would quickly be over – possibly in a couple of days. As he looked round the room he could identify the seven requisitioning commissioners. How much or how little support did they have, he wondered? All the others in the room were asking themselves the same question.

He tried to spot the known supporters of the General. There were of course the four members of his family. Then there were the four International Headquarters commissioners who had openly declared that they would stand with the General: Commissioner John Cunningham, Commissioner Theodore Kitching, Commissioner John Laurie and Commissioner Allister Smith. That made it eight.

There were also others whom it was assumed would support the General. There was Commissioner Samuel Brengle of the USA, who had so vigorously defended his General when he was attacked by William Atwood. There was Lieut-Commissioner Gunpei Yamamuro, the first Japanese Salvation Army officer, who was an ardent admirer of Bramwell Booth and the author of the only biography of him that had so far been written. There was Commissioner Albin Peyron from France, related by marriage to General and Mrs Booth and known to be sympathetic to the General's position. That made it 11.

As Lieut-Colonel Marpurg looked round the room and thought of the long-standing personal links of respect, admiration and affection that every one of these members had with Bramwell Booth, he was convinced that out of the remaining 52 it would not be hard to find a further five who would support the General – bringing the total to the needed 16.

A message to the High Council signed by 183 staff officers in Britain had been handed to him as he entered the room. As he read it, it seemed to him to sum up with sensitive eloquence the feelings and hopes of numberless Salvationists around the world – but he wondered how Mrs Booth would react to it:

We share with you and the whole Salvation Army an undiminished admiration and affection for our General, who has so splendidly led us

173

through long years, and deeply regret that the crushing burdens of office, combined with the weight of years, have resulted in such a serious breakdown in health as to leave the Army without responsible leadership. We are glad, therefore, that in harmony with our constitution, means are to be explored and plans devised whereby the Army may immediately enjoy that personal and vigorous leadership so necessary to its maintenance and progress through the world.

Tuesday 8 January 1929

Precisely at 10.30am the Chief of the Staff as the convenor of the Council opened proceedings. He welcomed the members and led them in a time of prayer and worship. A roll call was then taken. All members who had been summoned were present and correct, with the one exception of Commissioner Elwin Oliphant. There were no challenges about the membership of the Council. The Chief of the Staff announced that the first business of the Council in accordance with the Supplementary Deed of 1904 was for it to elect a President and Vice-President.

His own name was immediately proposed for the presidency, but Commissioner Higgins declined and instead proposed Commissioner James Hay, the territorial commander for New Zealand. This suggestion met with the immediate approbation of the Council, and Commissioner James Hay was elected President, with Lieut-Commissioner William Haines, Managing Director of the Salvation Army Assurance Society, being elected as Vice-President.

The President at once took charge of proceedings and the members of the Council soon felt reassured in their choice. Commissioner Hay was strong and decisive and quickly revealed a mastery of all the issues. He was also sensitive, and above all, he proved to be absolutely impartial.

The Chief of the Staff had forewarned Commissioner Hay that he would be nominating him.[2] The 'storm pilot' had thought long and hard about whom he would like to take charge of the ship. Commissioner James Hay was recognised by all as one of the

Army's most dynamic leaders. The Chief of the Staff also knew that in his relationship with Bramwell Booth, James Hay had moved from being a trusted colleague to being on the periphery. He would therefore bring sensitive understanding born out of personal experience to his leadership of the Council – but could be trusted to be scrupulously fair.

James Hay, a Scot, had risen like a meteor through the ranks of the Army in Britain and by the age of 29 was already the field secretary responsible for 3,000 officers. Following appointments as chief secretary in Britain and Principal of the International Training Garrison he was appointed territorial commander of the vast Australasian Territory at the age of 44. Commissioner and Mrs Hay arrived in Melbourne in 1909 and were to be there for the next 12 years. His command comprised not only the whole of Australia but also New Zealand.

Under his energetic leadership the work grew to such an extent that in 1912 he proposed to International Headquarters that New Zealand should become a separate territory of its own. This was done, but the work in Australia continued to expand to such a degree that in 1920 he was asked to draw up plans for the work in that country to be divided into two separate territories when he farewelled.

A sign of the regard and admiration that General Bramwell Booth had for James Hay is that when the General conducted the congress in Australia in 1920 he confided to him that his next appointment would be National Commander of the United States of America as Commander Evangeline Booth would shortly be taking up a new appointment. 'I was to say nothing for the time being until all had been completed,' he records in his autobiography.[3] Then 'what was regarded as a settled matter' changed. The Commander did not farewell, and in 1921 Commissioner James Hay was instead appointed British Commissioner in succession to Mrs Booth, with the General suggesting that he 'should aim at doubling Salvationism in Britain'.

From the beginning Commissioner James Hay felt shackled in his new appointment. This was partly due to the administrative structure in Britain whereby in reality it was the General who was the 'territorial commander' – an arrangement that was to last right up to 1990. As British Commissioner, James Hay was not responsible for the Army's social work, training, editorial, trade, finance and property in Britain. His only domain was corps work. That he did not control property was especially galling for him. During his 12 years in Australia he had opened on average a new hall or building every 10 days.

The feeling of being shackled also related to General Bramwell Booth's insistence that his children be 'consulted' on territorial policy. The fact that James Hay had spoken to the General about the need for constitutional reform added to the tension.

After six months Commissioner James Hay asked the General to be relieved of his task and said that he was prepared to take 'the least of the territories'. This brought a rift in their relationship. Three months later he was appointed as territorial commander to South Africa, and Mrs Booth resumed command of the British Territory. After some years in South Africa Commissioner Hay was appointed territorial commander for New Zealand, the country that once had been but a part of his large Australasian command. However, he went with good grace and with his trademark drive soon injected new dynamism into the territory. 'Hay halls' sprang up everywhere. It was from this appointment – and with this background – that he came to the High Council.

Getting started

While the world waited impatiently for the outcome of the High Council, the whole of the first day was devoted to procedural matters. Retired Commissioner John Carleton – by now aged 80 – was called upon to be the recorder, and Colonel Gerald Freeman, Secretary to the Chief of the Staff, was appointed as assistant recorder. It was carried unanimously that Mr William Frost should be present throughout as the legal adviser to the High Council. These three were not members of the High Council. The minutes record that it was also 'unanimously carried' that 'a message of love and sincere sympathy with the General in his illness be despatched to him'.[4] Before the morning had ended, the greeting from the Council was on its way.

A resolution moved by Commissioner Catherine Booth, that 'shorthand notes be taken of the proceedings and these be submitted to the General's counsel only', was lost by 'a large majority'.

A resolution proposed by Commissioner John Laurie, that Mr Frederick Sneath, the long-standing personal legal adviser to General Bramwell Booth, be permitted to be present to advise Mrs Booth on behalf of the General, was similarly lost by 'a large majority'.

The High Council felt that the taking of shorthand notes and the presence of Mr Sneath would change the nature of the event. Instead of being an internal and private gathering of Army leaders that was seeking through prayer and discussion to discern the right way ahead, it would take on the nature of an impeachment trial.

Commissioner John Laurie then proposed, 'that the General be represented by Mr William Jowitt, King's Counsel, as per Deed Poll 1904 which provides for such a possibility', but 'as a result of subsequent discussion Commissioner Laurie withdrew the resolution'.

The mention of Mr William Jowitt KC on the very first day of the High Council sent tremors of apprehension down the spines of all who were aware of the significance of this announcement. William Jowitt was one of the most brilliant figures in the legal world. Now aged 44, he had been the youngest King's Counsel when he 'took silk' at the age of 36 and had also been a Member of Parliament. There had already been rumours that he had been retained by the Booth family – and this was now being confirmed – but nobody knew for what purpose his services had been secured. The fear that the General might seek to circumvent the calling of the High Council by appealing to the court for relief as sole trustee and persuading it to appoint his nominee in his place still lurked in the shadows. Was it for this purpose that Mr Jowitt had been retained?

Mr William Jowitt KC was in fact to play a decisive role not only at the High Council but also in the events that followed, when, as Sir William Jowitt, he became Attorney General in the government. Some years later, as Earl Jowitt, he rose to be Lord Chancellor in the reforming government that took office following the Second World War. The Booths were living up to their dictum: when it came to legal advice only the best was good enough.

Though the first day of the High Council was fully taken up with settling these and other procedural matters, the agenda paper provided for members left no one in doubt as to the main purpose of the Council. Before them lay the text of the Resolution of Adjudication to be proposed by Commissioner David Lamb and seconded by Commissioner Wilfred Simpson. It was couched in legal terms, but there was no escaping the sheer awfulness of what the words conveyed, nor the heavy and inescapable responsibility that rested on each member in having to decide whether to vote for or against the resolution:

> That this meeting of the High Council of The Salvation Army, deeply regretting the necessity, doth hereby in exercise and furtherance of the powers and duties conferred on the Council by the provisions of the supplemental deed poll of July 26, 1904, adjudicate William Bramwell Booth unfit for office as General of The Salvation Army and remove him therefrom.

Tomorrow would surely be the fateful day.

Wednesday 9 January 1929

All the sessions at the High Council commenced with a devotional period during which fervent prayer was offered to God for guidance. On the Wednesday morning Commissioner Samuel Brengle was asked to take part. He writes: 'It was the 44th anniversary of the day God had sanctified me and my soul was mellow, full of peace and love. The President asked me to read the Bible and that also gave me an opportunity to give my testimony and tell how sacred the day was.'[5]

Following devotions, 'Commissioner Catherine Booth directed attention to the resolution respecting the appointment of Mr William Jowitt KC to speak on behalf of the General, and an arrangement was arrived at that the time for moving the resolution would be immediately preceding the adjudicatory resolution'. In other words, the resolution had not been withdrawn, it had only been deferred.

The President then asked the Chief of the Staff to read the letter that General Bramwell Booth had written to the members of the High Council on Sunday 6 January.

That the General had written immediately stirred expectations. The General had not addressed his leaders since the previous May when he had penned the letter that he hoped would once and for all close down the debate about constitutional reform. He had then said: 'I have neither the power nor the desire to make any such change. I received our "system" from the Founder's hand as a sacred trust, and I cannot abandon that trust. I do not believe that you would ask me to do so.' Now seven months had passed. The General had had time for reflection, events had moved on, and the High Council had been called. What line would he now take? Members leant forward in their seats, anxious not to miss a word, as the Chief of the Staff read:

My dear Comrades,

The calling of the High Council to remove me from office is a great shock.

I could have understood the commissioners might have been asked to consider whether I should continue in office, but the fact that the Council has been called leaves no room for doubt that the commissioners who requisitioned the Council were influenced by a desire to deprive me of the power which belongs to every General of The Salvation Army, under our Foundation Deed, of appointing or naming the manner of appointing their successor.

Whether their action is right, may God guide you to judge.

Had I been asked to resign, it would have been a very different matter, and I should not, on my own account, have much regretted the request. The doctors say that I shall get well, but in any case it will take a few months. I cannot tell – at times I feel very low. If it be God's will, how gladly I shall return to my post.

Will you give me time?

I made arrangements, when I went on rest, that the Chief of the Staff and Mrs Booth should act on my behalf as far as possible. I did not then anticipate so long an absence. As it is likely to be still further prolonged, it seems to me it would be a strength to the Army at a time which must now be regarded as critical, that I should place the administration in the hands of a Council. This I propose to do, appointing

The Chief of Staff as President.

Commander Eva Booth.

Commissioner Catherine Booth and probably two commissioners of International Headquarters as members.

Mrs Booth will wish to remain with me.

Further, as all commissioners and territorial commanders are assembled, I take the opportunity of saying that ever since I received the Memorandum from the Commander in October 1927, asking me to make certain changes in our constitution, I have been anxiously and carefully considering the whole position, and was still at work on the matter when I was ordered away and told it was imperative to rest as completely as possible.

It was in my mind to appoint a Commission to receive the various opinions, and to co-ordinate and examine their value and practicability and to discover:

1. What changes are desired.

2. Whether they could be brought about without endangering the stability of the Army or our method of work.

If the responsibility be mine when the Council has adjudicated I shall, after conference with the Chief and before the members of the Council have left, appoint such a Commission.

I love the Army. I love its teaching. I love more than ever its unity. Do not let us do anything to endanger either. I would have come to meet you, but I am not equal to the effort. God bless you all. Your affectionate General,

Bramwell Booth

The letter was received in silence, but every member was quickly trying to assess the implications of what the General had written. It was a call for middle ground to be found. The General was in effect saying: 'Do not adjudicate me unfit now, give me more time to recover my health, and in the meantime I will delegate the running of the Army to a council and immediately set up a commission to consider constitutional reform.'

The tone was very different from last May. In many ways it seemed a reasonable proposition, but there were some disconcerting features. For the Army to be led by an administrative council, even temporarily, seemed a significant departure from the historic policy that the Army should always be under the oversight, direction and control of one person, and for the High Council to be regarded as an authoritative body that could decide such major change of policy seemed in conflict with the High Council's narrow remit. Members had frequently been reminded that the one and only function of the Council was to adjudicate on the General's unfitness for office – and if found to be unfit, to elect a successor.

Was it not anyway too little too late? Bramwell Booth would remain the sole trustee. The Army had been leaderless for seven months and the doctors had just said that they 'believed' the General would need a further six months before he could return to work, but he might never return. The calling of the High Council had been traumatic for the Army. That it might have to be recalled within a few months was an unwelcome prospect.

Commissioner Albin Peyron suggested that the meeting be adjourned so that members could consider the General's letter. This received little support. Members seemed anxious to move on.

The President was also acutely aware of the danger of the High Council being blown off course by the General's intervention, finding itself working to an agenda set by him, and getting itself

181

bogged down on the details of the compromise proposal. With the Council being empowered to deal only with the one issue of whether the General was fit or unfit to be General, this had at all times to remain in view. He therefore announced that any member wishing to speak to the General's letter could do so during the discussion on the General's fitness or unfitness for office.

The Resolution of Adjudication was the next item on the agenda. It seemed that crunch point had already been reached. 'This meeting of the High Council ... doth hereby ... adjudicate William Bramwell Booth unfit for office as General of The Salvation Army and remove him therefrom.' Commissioner David Lamb was due to present it to the Council. Consideration of this agenda item would trigger the matter that had been left pending – whether Mr William Jowitt should be permitted to address the Council on behalf of the General.

At this point Commissioner Lamb brought yet another surprise to that morning's meeting. He asked the President's permission to give way for the time being in order that Commissioner Henry Mapp might present an alternative resolution, which would be seconded by Commissioner George Sowton (Territorial Commander, Australia Eastern Territory). The President agreed and Commissioner Henry Mapp moved his proposed resolution:

That this High Council of The Salvation Army, having received the letter signed by the General under date 6th January 1929, desires to place on record its high appreciation of the life and labours of the General and joins with him in gratitude to God for his partial restoration to health, and expresses the hope that his improvement may be maintained.

The Council being however unable to see the practicability of the suggestions made by the General, and realising that it is most unlikely that at the General's advanced age he can ever recover sufficiently to again take up the burdens under which he collapsed, takes the opportunity of requesting him to cooperate with the Council in securing the future welfare of the Army. To that end – with the General being, as his doctors assure us, capable of considering important questions and giving decisions thereon – the Council resolves that the President, Vice President and five members of the High Council be deputed to see the General and suggest that he should now retire from office retaining his title of General and continuing to enjoy the honours and dignities attaching thereto.

In proposing the resolution, Commissioner Henry Mapp quoted the General's words to the Council: 'Had I been asked to resign, it would have been a very different matter, and I should not, on my own account, have much regretted the request.' He then argued that if leaders such as Commissioners T. Henry Howard, John Carleton, Frederick Booth-Tucker and others had been asked to retire when they were still healthy and strong, how much more should the principle of retirement also apply to the General now that he was no longer able to bear the burden of office.

After Commissioner George Sowton had seconded the motion, member after member rose to speak in support of the resolution. In writing to British staff officers some days later, Commissioner Samuel Hurren described what happened:

The scene last Wednesday morning when it was decided to ask our beloved General to retire from office was one which none present will ever forget. The whole assembly was moved to tears as one after another pleaded with Mrs Booth and the General's family to persuade our Leader to relieve himself of the heavy burdens under which he collapsed.[6]

One speaker began with the words: 'This is the saddest day of my life.' And Lieut-Commissioner William McIntyre spoke for virtually everyone present when he tearfully pleaded with Mrs Booth 'not to drive the dear old General up hills he cannot travel'.

'Never shall I forget the emotion of speakers,' recalls Colonel Charles Baugh (Territorial Commander, India North Territory), 'nor the wave of tenderness as officers pleaded that the General and the Council be spared the agony of an adjudication "unfit". This was the highest note of the Council – the spontaneous heart tribute of affection to a lifelong warrior and leader.'[7]

Commissioner Mapp's proposal that the General should be asked to retire was another search for the middle ground, but this time it was much more in accord with the feelings and wishes of the Council. Commissioner Samuel Hurren voiced those feelings and wishes when he said that 'the resolution which has been submitted for our consideration has given gratification and ease to all of us'.[8]

'Everyone wanted to find a way to avoid adjudicating him unfit,' recalls Commissioner Samuel Brengle. 'All wanted to avoid the pain of such a vote and earnestly desired to shield him from any hasty, harsh, or false judgment from the world which might follow such a vote.' The proposal that he be asked to retire was therefore welcomed 'with eager hope and a great sigh of relief'.[9]

As the morning meeting came to an end, that relief was sensed in the buzz of animated conversation as members moved towards the lunch room.

The turn of events had come as a surprise to the Booth family. What was to be their strategy now? The press representatives at the main entrance to Sunbury Court were bereft of hard news and had therefore to make the most of what they could observe from their vantage point. Their description of the comings and goings during that Wednesday lunch hour tells its own story about the reaction of the Booth family to the unexpected development:

Commissioner Catherine Booth, daughter of the General, made repeated journeys in a closed motor-car during the day between Sunbury Court, where the Council was sitting, and a little villa close by, which is rented by the Booth family. She dashed to and from seven times in less than an hour, accompanied by a uniformed secretary. They had with them piles of documents.

The General's supporters were constantly in telephonic communication with him from the villa. Commissioner Catherine Booth and Colonel Mary Booth, another daughter, hurried there after the Council had adjourned for luncheon.

The two women were joined by Commissioners Kitching, Laurie, and Cunningham, also among the chief supporters of the General. They remained in close consultation for nearly an hour with their legal representatives. Mrs Booth stayed during this time at Sunbury Court. Colonel Bernard Booth, a son, arrived during the afternoon.[10]

A factor the Booth family had to handle was that Doctors Weir and Milne opposed the idea of a deputation being allowed to visit their patient. However, in deference to an appeal by the family, who feared that a refusal to receive the deputation would be misinterpreted, they withdrew their objection, stipulating only that the General 'should not be agitated by a discussion'.

Wednesday afternoon

The afternoon session did not commence until 3pm and discussion on the retirement resolution continued. The High Council was galvanised when the three women who dominated the scene spoke in succession – the General's sister, the General's daughter and the General's wife – each of whom was a possible successor to the General.

The Commander, in this her first intervention, said that in their deliberations they must 'seek first the interests of the Army' and hold to this. Then, secondly, they must 'seek what is best for our beloved General. He has stood the impact of the rigours of war for half a century. It is right that he should now retire. Why not? What raises the conflict? Is it not unkind and cruel for anyone to try to stop it happening? To retire is honourable.'

Commissioner Catherine Booth spoke briefly, reminding the Council of the General's request to be given time to recover – her main speaking was to come later in the Council.

Then Mrs Booth rose to the defence of her husband in a forceful speech tinged with tenderness. As she poured out her heart and recounted the events of the preceding year, she could hardly conceal her emotion. There was the dismay at the unjust accusations of nepotism, the pain at the animosity from Commissioner Booth-Tucker, the grief at the Commander's agitation and circulation of private correspondence to leaders, and the hurt

185

of the General at finding on his desk the previous March the letter from the nine commissioners – 'a hurt from which he did not recover'. There was the continuing breakdown of the General's health and how impossible it had proved to shield him from worry and anxiety about the Army's future. Then had come the shame of the calling of the High Council. 'He knew when the Founder prepared the 1904 Deed he meant the High Council to be empowered to deal only with *an unworthy General*. It seemed almost as though we who loved him most should hope for his death in order that he might never know.' Now the General was simply asking for more time to recover. Was that not a reasonable request?

Such was the cost to her of her words that she left the council chamber when she had finished speaking. After a moment of silence the President asked if others wished to address the Council. No hands were raised. It would have seemed out of place for anyone to follow such a plea from the heart.

The President therefore put to the vote the retirement resolution proposed by Commissioner Henry Mapp. It was carried without any dissenting votes. Mrs Booth did not return for the vote, and the General's supporters did not vote in favour of the motion – but neither did they vote against it.

Drama

Darkness was falling as the afternoon session continued with the reading of the full medical certificates issued by the doctors. Commissioner Hugh Whatmore then proposed that the delegation that would visit the General should carry a letter from the High Council signed by every member. There was discussion about the composition of the group. It was felt that the group should consist of members who were personally close to the General. It was agreed that, in addition to Commissioner James Hay as President, and Lieut-Commissioner William Haines as Vice-President, the members would be Commissioner Samuel Brengle, Commissioner George Mitchell (Territorial Commander, Sweden), Commissioner John Cunningham, Lieut-Commissioner Gunpei Yamamuro, and

186

Colonel Mrs Annie Trounce (Territorial Commander, Southern India).

Then the lights went out.

Sunbury Court had been hit by a power cut. 'Almost simultaneously a door was flung open,' the singularly well-informed press was later to report, 'and a breathless junior officer hurried into the room and groped his way through the darkness to the presidential dais. He handed Commissioner James Hay a note and made a hasty retreat. By the aid of a flash lamp the President read out the note, and then ensued a scene which will be long remembered by every delegate present.'

'That note', continued the news item, 'contained the information that an officer of the Army had been to Campfield Press, the Salvation Army Printing Works at St Albans, stopped the edition of *The War Cry* then on the presses, and ordered the insertion of General Bramwell Booth's letter of 6 January.'[11] This was the letter in which the General asked to be given time.

When the President announced this to the Council and informed members that the presses were now rolling again, pandemonium ensued. Who was responsible for this breach of High Council confidentiality? Anger increased as it was realised that the letter must have been delivered to Campfield Press even before it had been read out to the Council. In the shimmering light of the candles that had quickly been secured, everyone turned towards the Editor-in-Chief, Commissioner Theodore Kitching. He admitted that he was the one who had given the order, and there was an immediate rush of speakers who one after the other condemned this action.

What was to be done? With the presses rolling the Council felt it had to act quickly. It immediately ordered the removal of the General's letter from *The War Cry* and the destruction of every copy containing it. The instruction was phoned through to Campfield Press and resulted in 20,000 copies being destroyed. The Council also set up a committee of members to investigate the matter.

In the cold light of the next day the facts turned out to be not quite what they had seemed in the candlelit confusion of the previous evening. It was discovered that legally it was the General, not the High Council, who controlled *The War Cry*, and the High Council had not had the right to remove the letter or destroy the printed copies. Neither had Commissioner Kitching acted on his own initiative. The General himself had instructed him to insert the letter – and the Chief of the Staff had been aware of that fact. However, none of this was known that Wednesday evening.

Because of the dramatic developments that had taken place the session did not end until 6.50pm, and the President announced that there would be no further sessions that day.

Later that evening Mrs Booth left for Southwold. The members of the press missed nothing, and by keeping in touch with their colleagues camped outside the General's home were able to inform the world that in 'Mrs Booth's Dash to Southwold' she had 'travelled the distance of more than 120 miles in little over three hours, arriving in a mud-bespattered motor-car', and that she had then 'gone direct to the General's bedroom on the first floor and had talked to him for a considerable time'.[12]

Back at Sunbury Court, as the members felt their way in candlelight to the dining room for their evening meal, they remained deeply disturbed by the fact that the General's letter had been passed to *The Way Cry*.

There was to be worse news the next day.

Chapter Twelve

A Deputation of Seven

Thursday 10 January 1929

THE Chief of the Staff had asked for copies of all the main national newspapers to be delivered early to his home so that he could read them in the car on his way to Sunbury Court. On that Thursday morning, 10 January, he froze when he saw the headlines in the *Daily Mail*. 'Dramatic Salvation Army Surprise – New Council to Act for Him – Daughter, Sister and Three Commissioners – Deputation to the General.'

The press had obviously learnt of the decisions taken the previous day at the High Council, and it was clear that the *Daily Mail* had in its possession a copy of the General's 'Will you give me time?' letter of 6 January. When the Chief arrived at Sunbury Court it was to find the Council in an uproar. Not only had an attempt been made to get the General's letter inserted into *The War Cry*, it had also been passed to the press.

When the Council met for the morning session it was decided that in the light of this leak to the press from supporters of the Booth family, the response to the General's letter from the High Council would also have to be released. The text of the resolution about a deputation visiting the General to suggest he retire from office was therefore issued to the press that morning accompanied by the following statement:

It had been intended to make no communication to the press concerning this resolution until the General had had time to receive and consider it, but in view of the fact that the terms of the General's letter had been communicated without the knowledge of the Council to one of the London journals, the Council decided to release for publication the terms of the resolution.

It was an important turn of events, for from that moment documents and information were openly released to the press by both the Booth family and the High Council. The public in general and Salvationists in particular therefore had a daily grandstand view of what was taking place. The regular bulletins issued by the High Council also became more informative in their content.

Commissioner David Lamb submitted to the Council a draft of the letter which the deputation of seven was to present to the General. 'This was approved subject to minor alterations,' read the minutes. 'The Council then adjourned till 2 o'clock in order that the letter from the High Council to the General might be typed ready for the signatures of the members of the Council.' When the Council met again that Thursday afternoon, not only Mrs Booth but also Commissioner Mrs Lucy Booth-Hellberg were absent.

The members of the Council found at their places a copy of the letter. The original, awaiting their signatures, lay on a table just in front of the platform. The members read the text in deep silence:

Dear General,

The commissioners and territorial commanders assembled at the High Council send to their General renewed assurance of their love, specially in this hour when illness prevents him from conferring with them.

For this reason it has been thought advisable by the High Council to send to you a deputation of officers to express verbally the love and esteem in which we hold you and to hand to you this letter with a proposal, which we trust you will accept as coming from loving hearts whose sole desire is the glory of God, the salvation of the world, the continued success of our Army, and your own personal welfare.

We are here to consider the difficulties which have arisen owing to your very prolonged and unfortunate illness, which we all deeply deplore, and which nevertheless has placed the Army in a most unhappy position.

We need scarcely assure you that we have all been praying about exercising our minds ever since the High Council was convened with a hope of finding some happier solution to the problems that confront us than an adjudication as to your fitness would afford.

Until last Wednesday week you were so ill that you were not even allowed to be told that the High Council was about to meet, although it had been summoned in November last after your prolonged absence from your place at the head of the Army.

We are glad to know you are somewhat better and able to give a little consideration to the present situation, and we are praying that your health may be sufficiently strong to enable you to cooperate with us in arriving at a solution which will secure to you the fullest recognition of your great services and your unfailing devotion, and obtain also from the Army the leadership that the circumstances now demand.

At today's meeting of the Council a resolution was passed that a deputation should wait upon you to suggest that you should retire from office, retaining your title of General and continuing to enjoy the honours and dignities of the same. We are encouraged in submitting this resolution to you by the remarks made by yourself on the question of your retirement and contained in your letter to us. We therefore beg of you to embrace the opportunity of relieving yourself of a burden which at your time of life has proved to be far too great, and to retire from your responsibilities with full honours and dignities, and so emphasise once again the high ideal which you have so eloquently preached to us by word and example.

The cold phraseology of a formal resolution will certainly fail to convey to your mind the love and kindly feelings which were repeatedly manifested during our discussion and which accompany this proposal.

We assure you again that we are and always shall be mindful of this valiant fight you have waged for so many years, of the manner in which you supported and strengthened the hands of your father and our Founder, and in the years of your own Generalship have led the Army forward to victory. But we know you so well that we are certain you will put the interests of the Army first by accepting the proposal which is now before you, and which has been made necessary by the failure of your health after more than half a century of unceasing labours.

The history of our Army is a long record of acts of self-denial, and its pages are bright with the stories of individual self-sacrifice.

Your name has stood high upon these records. We want it always to remain there as an inspiration to others of an absolute devotion of every power to the great purpose of the salvation of men, and of an equal readiness to sacrifice every personal consideration that might hinder the achievement of that glorious end.

Now, in your closing years, tired, frail and unable longer to lead us forward, we would tenderly urge you to relieve yourself of your impossible task, and assure you that your place in our highest respect and our hearts' warmest affections is for ever unalterably fixed.

May God evermore grant you the guidance and consolation of his grace.

As members finished reading they bowed their heads in silent prayer – but it was now time to sign. The President invited those members wishing to sign to come forward one by one in order of seniority to write their names on the document. There would be no rush. Everyone present understood the immensity of what they were about to do. As delegates saw first of all the Chief of the Staff – he who had stood with his General through thick and thin – move to the table followed by the Commander – the General's own flesh and blood – the delegates could no longer contain their pent-up feelings. Wednesday had been just a foretaste of the emotion that Thursday would bring.

'The scene was indescribable,' wrote F. A. Mackenzie, the religious correspondent of the *Daily News,* a friend and admirer of the Army and a keen observer of the religious scene. Based on accounts from those present, he penned: 'Women and men alike wept; some were almost in a state of collapse; some felt that their hands could not move to trace their names. "Forty years ago, he encouraged me when I was a boy; now I ask for his retirement," said one. "It is the signing of the Covenant over again," said another.'[1]

'As the members of the Council walked solemnly up to sign their names, all felt it to be a sacramental act,' wrote Commissioner Charles Jeffries.[2] 'I shall never forget the agony of signing my name,' recalled Commissioner George Jolliffe, who at that time was Governor of the Men's Social Work in Britain. 'I saw more strong men in tears then than I shall ever see again, I hope.'[3]

Some members had remained seated when it was their turn to sign. All eyes were therefore on Commissioner Catherine Booth when she was due to sign. Looking directly at the President she exclaimed in a clear voice: 'Never!' – and remained seated.

When the last signature had been appended the President called on the members to sing the song 'O God, our help in ages past'. There was not a dry eye in the room.

With Mrs Booth and Commissioner Mrs Lucy Booth-Hellberg being absent there were 61 members in the room. Fifty-six of them signed. The remaining five who had not signed were Commissioner Catherine Booth, Colonel Mary Booth, Commissioner John Laurie, Commissioner Theodore Kitching and Commissioner Allister Smith. Commissioner John Cunningham – a committed supporter of the General – had signed whilst later making it known to his colleagues that signing the letter was as far as he was prepared to go. The 56 signatures at the foot of the letter made it clear that, with the sole exception of Colonel Mary Booth, every territorial commander in the world wished the General to retire.

That evening the delegation of seven headed by the President set out on their journey to call on the General at his home in Southwold. They carried the precious letter from the Council with them together with a copy of the resolution. The President also went armed with a formal retirement letter, drafted by Mr William Frost, for the General to sign should occasion arise.

The ever-alert press at the main gate watched them leave in 'two powerful saloon cars' and also reported that Commissioner Catherine Booth had departed separately. The deputation had decided to stop for the night in Ipswich so that they could arrive in good time on the Friday morning, hoping also that this would enable them to throw the press off their scent. Journalists, though, soon located them at the White Horse Hotel in Ipswich and kept the nation informed of their progress.

Friday 11 January 1929

When the seven set off the next morning for the 25-mile drive to Southwold they were followed by 14 press cars filled with journalists and photographers.[4] The deputation arrived at 10.05am. The official report of the visit, signed by the seven, which was not only communicated to the High Council but also made available to the press and published in full in *The War Cry*[5], gives us a minute-by-minute account of what happened:

'Mrs Booth and Major Olive Booth received us. Mrs Booth expressed regret that she did not have earlier intimation as to our arrival. She said she had one telegram rather late, about 6 o'clock Wednesday evening, but we pointed out that we had sent two telegrams, one being despatched about 12.30pm on Thursday. We had confirmation of this from Major Olive, who was reproved by her mother for not intimating the receipt of that telegram.

'Brigadier Bertha Smith [the General's nurse] came to us with great emotion, expressing her entire confidence that the General was going to get better – that he was better – much better than he had been, but that the cruel things likely to be said would hurt him. Perhaps, as a nurse, she wanted to warn us not to say certain things, but she was obviously much agitated.

'Mrs Booth said she could not arrange for us to see the General until a later hour, and had wired us to that effect. We, however, had left prior to its delivery. It was pointed out that our telegram indicated that we were quite prepared to wait until any hour that might be convenient.

'Mrs Booth was courteous and kind and pressed us to have some tea, which we were glad to have, as the morning drive was cold. It was finally arranged that we should come back after the General had had food, say about 12.30pm.'

The delegation drove to Lowestoft – followed by some of the press cars – to have lunch. Meanwhile the press remaining outside the General's house watched a drama unfold. At noon Commander Evangeline Booth arrived, 'having come at top speed from London', accompanied by her secretary, Colonel Richard Griffiths. The Commander asked to see the General and was admitted to the house. When the seven returned at 12.50pm they found the Commander awaiting them.

'I may never see him again, Hay, I must see him,' she said to the President. Recalls Commissioner Hay: 'I had to persuade her not to force anything, that Mrs Booth had placed a guard on the stair and she would only cause a scene. She was dissuaded and ultimately left with her secretary by road.'[6]

The official report continues: 'Commissioner Catherine, who quite understood the object of our visit, asked that she might take the letter to the General. We handed this to her, together with the copy of the resolution in respect to the retirement of the General, and these were taken to his room by the commissioner.

'We pointed out that we were quite in their hands in respect to the number that should go in the General's room, but the commissioner said the General would wish to see all members of the deputation.

'Brigadier Bertha Smith came for us about 15 minutes later and then we had our interview with the General. Mrs Booth and Commissioner Catherine were present in the bedroom all the time.

'The General seemed to remember us all, and spoke a word to each quite tenderly, asking about wives and casually referring to our work. The documents referred to were lying on the bed before him. He spoke of having read them. He said he had a great trust passed to him by the Founder, but that the proposal we had made required time – "I must have a little time". Turning to the President he said, "The old General had a great fight for one-man control. You believe in that."

'As it was evident the General could only keep his thoughts connected by our not interrupting him, we withheld any remarks at this point. He referred to his health and again to having received his trust from the Founder and from God. He said he realised what we were asking, and added, "But I must have light to see what I must do, and how I must do it. I have had some trouble in my soul. God has given me very gracious feelings in the years gone by. Perhaps he wants me to do without them now."

'We endeavoured to speak to him through his acousticon, but he did not seem to catch our expressions, and Commissioner Catherine suggested that she should repeat our words. She did so, but we think the deputation was impressed that he was not quite following or was not quite able to follow our statement that the Council felt tenderly toward him and that they wished him to consider the document before him, and after taking a little time for consideration, give us his answer.

'The General went away from his subject, one would say as if he had certain intentions in his mind to speak on other questions, and he followed, so it appeared, the preparation of his mind. For example, he spoke of the new Denmark Hill building, asking us in general if we had been there. We intimated we had not. He made some almost jocular remarks that Brengle would perhaps say that it was too ecclesiastical, and Mitchell might say: "What about Hoxton?" and Hay and Whatmore would say: "I got the idea in Melbourne." All this, however, was said very slowly.

'The General still fingered the document, revealing his feeble nerve-distressed hand, and added: "I must have a day or two to think". After making a further remark or two to the members of the deputation, it was apparent he had said as much as he was able to say.

'Mrs Booth suggested to the General that he should pray with us, and we were about to suggest the same. This seemed to give him a little freshening of thought and grip of his memory, and he prayed slowly but tenderly for "these men and their families". He prayed that "these men might act aright". He spoke to God of his health, mentioning his hope that God would come to him and help him quickly. He prayed for God's guidance in this matter, and referred to his extremity and that God might make an opportunity out of that. He thanked God for the help we had given him, and used the expression: "Help them to help me now, and help me to do the right thing in the right way." He also prayed for India.

'The prayer – as were his other words – was slow and one would say an effort. The President started to pray for the General, and, possibly not hearing him, the General started off again in prayer. Then he stopped, and the President completed the prayer, after which several of us shook hands gently with him, kissing his hand, and wishing him all blessing.

'It was quite evident the deputation could not wisely stay longer, and any personal pressure that he might go through the document and give us an indication that he accepted our representation was quite beyond him at the moment. As both Mrs Booth and Brigadier Smith, together with Commissioner Catherine, felt that this was just about as much as the General could then stand, we left quietly. He made no special remark as we left the room – indeed we rather felt that he was not noticing that we were leaving.

'While the President was in the house, it was made very clear to Commissioner Catherine that the Council does not want to go on with the adjudication as unfit. We want the General, as she well knew, to grasp the serious significance of 56 members, including every territorial commander in the world except Colonel Mary Booth, requesting him to retire from his position – a position which he was now quite unable to fill.

'We showed the commissioner that time to consider should not be calculated as from this moment – that is to say, as from between one and two o'clock today – but rather from the time that the General became aware of the point the Council had come to, and that we would return, or two of us would return, say tomorrow or Sunday. The commissioner, however, felt that either of these days was hardly giving the General the time that was needed.

197

'We had to point out that in the ordinary procedure of business we should reach the important question – the adjudication vote – by Monday, and we must beg that she should get the General's signed answer in our hands by Monday morning. We pressed on her that she could not expect, and must not expect, the Council to wait. They are assembled – we pointed out – to do what is now perfectly understood. Thus, and in similar terms we pressed the matter. The commissioner said: "Yes, but *I* must get it to you. Can't we send it to you?" To which our final words with her on this point was: "Yes, by Monday morning at the latest."'

The report ended with an assessment of the General's appearance: 'We think that the General looked frail, and extremely weak, pale and declined in general condition. His eyes have little animation, his hands are feeble, and it is quite evident that he has not much ability to turn or move in his bed. His speech is with difficulty, but it is coherent, and remarks previously thought out can be given expression to without confusion, though it is quite clear that in 15 minutes his power to do this has gone, and he probably does not recover until he has had a little rest. Indeed he took nourishment twice while we were in the room.'

At about 2pm the members of the deputation left the house, got into their cars and sped back to Sunbury Court.

Saturday 12 January 1929

The High Council had not met that Friday, though many members had gathered in small groups to pray for the General and the deputation. When the High Council re-assembled on Saturday morning the members were anxious to know the outcome of the deputation's visit. Every member was present except for Mrs Booth, who had stayed in Southwold.

The President read the deputation's report. It was fully understood that the General needed time to consider the decision, and members noted that they would have his reply by Monday morning. After the reading of the report the President gave his personal impression of the General's condition and called on each member of the deputation to do likewise.

The members of the delegation had in fact been even more shaken by the sight of the stricken, shrunken and aged figure they saw lying in bed than their carefully measured written words indicated. This became clear in their verbal comments. Even those considered closest to the General were now openly expressing their hope that he would retire. Lieut-Commissioner Gunpei Yamamuro exclaimed: 'It would be cruel, cruel to ask him to go on.' Commissioner John Cunningham admitted: 'If he were my father I would have fought as strongly as any of the family – but as I saw him yesterday I would advise my father to accept retirement.' Commissioner Samuel Brengle said: 'He is a broken man. A bent stick comes back but a broken one never comes back.'

'The unanimous opinion amongst them was that the General's work as we have known it is at an end,' is how Commissioner Samuel Hurren summarised their comments.[7]

Members of the family again asked that the General be given time. 'Do we not believe in a God who performs miracles?' pleaded Commissioner Mrs Lucy Booth-Hellberg. However, a sea-change in the attitude of Council members took place that morning. Whatever the ins and outs and rights and wrongs of the long-standing debate about constitutional reform, the simple fact the High Council now faced was that their General had come to the end of his time. If he did not choose to retire there could be no escape from the next step – he would have to be removed from office on the ground of broken health.

Whilst members considered what they had heard, the atmosphere was suddenly jarred. As the minutes record it: 'Commissioner Catherine Booth informed the Council that Ensign Jane Lambert was present at the interview of the deputation with the General and took shorthand notes.' The commissioner had the transcript with her and wished it to be entered into the record of the High Council.

In the discussion that ensued it emerged that Ensign Lambert had been seated behind a screen, that the delegation had not known she was there, and that she must have been too far from the bed to hear all of the often subdued conversation. Council members were irritated at what seemed an underhand approach. Commissioner Catherine Booth said she was surprised by this reaction as the ensign had followed the delegation into the room, and she had assumed everyone saw the ensign enter. In the end it was resolved that the President would receive the transcript as an unofficial record and compare it with the official report, but the incident made an unfavourable impression on the Council.

The rest of Saturday was spent discussing procedural points and how best to communicate with the public and with the Army family. Yet in reality the Council was in limbo until the reply from the General arrived.

Sunday and Monday 13/14 January 1929

On Sunday 13 January members of the High Council attended worship meetings at London corps. During the day a message was received from Southwold: the General's reply would not reach the High Council until Tuesday morning.

Monday 14 January was therefore another day of waiting. Commissioner Brengle used part of it to record his impressions for the benefit of a colleague back home: 'The High Council is impressive. There are some bright people here. Catherine is putting up a stiff fight, but the High Council is almost of one mind that a change must come.' He tells of the visit to see the General in Southwold and how they had found him 'feeble, pale, thin, tremulous and much wasted in flesh'. He continues:

> My emotions were mixed, a mingling of pain and chastened joy. Pained seeing him who I have loved, lying helpless and pressed by such duties and demands and faced with such momentous decisions. And joy at

once more looking into his face and seeing with my own eyes whether or not he is fit for his great office with its daily grind of work on worldwide problems which involve both the spiritual and physical welfare of millions in more than 80 countries.

He is certainly unfit at his age, and in his helpless condition for his job, if he does not retire and we have to adjudicate, I shall have to vote against him. There is no alternative. He is wholly incapacitated, and I do not believe he can ever sufficiently recover to do his work.

As we started to go he said: 'Brengle, I am sorry you have to share in this pain.' I kissed his poor, wasted hand and, I suspect, looked upon him for the last time.[8]

Chapter Thirteen

The Council Acts

Tuesday 15 January 1929

AFTER the long wait the members of the High Council approached the council chamber on Tuesday morning 15 January anxious to hear the General's reply to their request that he retire. The press had kept them in touch with developments over the weekend and on Monday. Many of the articles were mere speculation, but members had become increasingly concerned at what appeared to be stories based on leaks and briefings from supporters of the Booth family.

There had been press speculation on whether the Army's constitution permitted the General to retire from office. 'An official of The Salvation Army said to our reporter yesterday,' reported the *Daily Mail*, 'that the General has no power to retire. If he does so, and I think that is highly improbable, he will be acting illegally.'[1]

Other sections of the press had speculated along different lines. Given the negative connotations in Army circles of the word 'resignation', would the General be legally required to *resign* his office or could he just *retire* from it? On this point *The Times* correctly commented: 'Legal opinion has been taken on this matter, and the advice has been given that the expression of a desire to retire would be sufficient for all legal purposes.'[2]

There had also been continual press speculation about whether the General would appeal to the courts. That Mr William Jowitt had been retained had been widely reported. On Monday the *Daily Mail* had headlined 'Talk of Going to the Courts' and the *Daily Chronicle* had announced 'Legal Fight Likely' and had asked 'Will an Injunction be Sought?'[3] Views diverged as to the basis on which an application to the court might be made.

There had also been intense press speculation about what the General's reply would contain. The Southwold correspondent of the *Evening News* had reported that 'great secrecy is being preserved here regarding General Booth's reply to the High Council so that no discourtesy shall be shown to the Council'.[4] The *Daily Mail* had announced on Monday morning that it would be: 'No from the General – Flat Refusal to Retire.'[5]

Now on Tuesday morning the Southwold correspondent of the *Daily Mail* was informing readers that following 'receipt of a communication from Miss Catherine Booth who is at Sunbury and who is in close touch with members of the High Council, there has been a dramatic last-minute change in the situation'. The reporter continued: 'The General has strengthened his reply and I gather that there is now little doubt that the differences between the High Council and the General will be finally settled only in the courts.'

The members of the Council were getting weary of having to rely on the press for their information and looked forward to receiving direct word from the General. However, the press reports had prepared them for what that word might be.

On that Tuesday morning Mrs Booth's seat in the council chamber remained empty.

While the Council awaited her arrival it occupied itself with discussion on procedural points. When after an hour she still had not arrived, and no word had been received, the Council adjourned and preparations for the taking of the official photograph of the Council began. By this time members were concerned for her safety.

Mrs Booth eventually arrived at 11.30am and delegates learned that due to the treacherous ice and snow conditions her car had skidded and been involved in an accident. Fortunately, though Mrs Booth was shaken, she was unhurt.

When the members assembled in their overcoats outside Sunbury Court for the photograph they learnt that Mrs Booth,

Commissioner Catherine Booth, Commissioner Mrs Lucy Booth-Hellberg and Colonel Mary Booth had declined to participate. So the official photograph of the 1929 High Council – famous in Salvation Army history – was taken without four of its key members. Three non-members were in the photograph – retired Commissioner John Carleton, the recorder, Colonel Gerald Freeman, the assistant recorder, and Mr William Frost, the legal adviser. That Commissioner Carleton was seated prominently in the front row next to the Chief of the Staff was an unspoken but eloquent tribute to his influence at the High Council.

Tuesday afternoon

By 3pm the winter day had begun to darken, a chilling wind was blowing and thin snowflakes were beating against the window panes. The weather outside reflected the bleakness within felt by the delegates as they assembled to hear the General's response. They feared the worst. The President read the letter from the General:

My dear Comrades,

On 11th January 1929, I received the deputation from the High Council and carefully read the letter and copy of the resolution they brought me. I do not doubt that both the letter and deputation originated in the highest motive, nor do I doubt that you hold me in love and esteem.

We have worked together for many years. The chief object of my life has, as you all know, been the well-being of The Salvation Army, because I believe that the well-being of the Army is wrapped up with the well-being of the world at large. This work is far bigger than any individual or group of individuals.

The wisdom of our Founder decided that The Salvation Army should always be under the oversight, direction and control of some one person. It has pleased God to call me to that position.

Now I am asked to relinquish a sacred Trust, which in the sight of God, I solemnly accepted. I should not be justified in laying down that Trust unless I believed I were no longer able to carry out its responsibilities.

I have therefore thought it my duty to turn to those medical advisers who have attended me through my illness, to ascertain from them whether, in their opinion, I am likely to regain my health and strength. I am advised that, in all human probability, and subject to God's Providence, I shall, in a few months, be fully recovered.

Having this medical report, and bearing in mind my deep obligations to the Founder and to the Army, I am bound to ask myself whether I should be justified in laying down the Trust committed to me.

Such a question answers itself. I cannot do so. I have sworn to preserve the Trust committed to me. I should fail in my duty to the Founder and to the Army if I did not, so long as there is reasonable prospect that health and strength be given me, cherish and fulfil that Trust. This reason alone is sufficient to determine my decision.

But when I am advised that, were I to take any other course, serious internal controversy would almost inevitably arise, and further that the work of the Army might be interfered with by a lawsuit of the utmost magnitude, I am confirmed in the rightness of the decision which I have already made.

Nevertheless, it is not without regret that I have to announce to you that I could not, in any case, assent to your request, for while coming as it does after the summoning of the High Council, and in reply to my request for time, it amounts to little less than a threat of expulsion should I fail to comply with it.

Further, it comes after certain alterations in our Foundation Deed have, so I am informed, been publicly suggested.

Were I to yield to a request for retirement presented under these conditions, I should not be acting in the strong and consistent manner which the Founder would have desired.

I cannot but be disturbed to read in your letter that you are here to consider difficulties which have arisen owing to my illness. I have not been informed what these difficulties are, but I cannot understand how they can concern the High Council.

It does not appear to me that anything has arisen with which the Chief of the Staff is not fully competent to deal, particularly with the Special Council which I wish to appoint.

I now learn from Mrs Booth that since I went away on rest, letters have been received showing that a number of you feel some method should be adopted to appoint succeeding Generals other than the mere naming of his successor by the General for the time being.

I am strong in the opinion that this is a question of grave import to the Army and you know from what I have already written my view of it.

But I am deeply concerned for the unity of the Army, and to help me preserve this, as well as to secure consideration of this question apart from pressure of time and personality, I will avail myself of the alternative provided for in our Foundation Deed of 1878.

Should I die or otherwise vacate office before such time as the Commission appointed to consider this question has arrived at a conclusion acceptable to me and to the necessary number of commissioners, I will leave the final choice of my immediate successor to the commissioners of The Salvation Army.

I do not want to judge you, but it seems to be a strange thing that I cannot be given time to recover.

This is the time of the Army's greatest need and I pray that God may direct and rule your hearts ... Yours affectionately,

Bramwell Booth

The councillors were stunned. The General's rejection of retirement was unequivocal – on principle and because now it would be under duress. True, the General offered a major concession. If he were allowed to continue as General he would not nominate his successor but would instead allow the commissioners to choose the next General, but even that offer was hedged with qualifications. Was it not yet again too little too late? What struck members of the Council was the air of unreality that pervaded the letter. The General was writing as if the pleas for constitutional reform had only arisen in recent months while he had been away. Also, though his confidence that his health and natural powers would be restored had to be admired, did it have any basis in reality?

What most alarmed many of the councillors was the General's cryptic reference to the possibility of 'a lawsuit of the utmost magnitude' if he acceded to their request to retire. Members were not quite sure what the General meant. They wondered who exactly would bring such a lawsuit if he retired. Or was this a veiled reference to the possibility that he himself might appeal to the courts? The fear that he might do so still lurked.

The councillors were not only stunned, they were perplexed and dejected. Why, they wondered, was he not willing to lay down the burden, especially now that he was even prepared to give up the power to nominate his successor?

The President sensed the mood of the meeting and, as the minutes record, 'moved the following resolution which was seconded by Commissioner Brengle: "That the High Council, having read the General's reply, sincerely regrets that he does not see his way to adopt the suggestion of the High Council and retire from office." Upon being put to the Council the resolution was carried with six members dissenting.'

The reply from the General had not changed the thinking of the members of the Council. There was to be no more time. To the great disappointment of Mrs Booth and the other members of the family, the Council then moved on to the next item on the agenda.

The next item was whether the vote on the Resolution of Adjudication should be by secret ballot or by signed ballot with the voting list being made public. After debate it was decided 'that immediately after the voting papers have been counted, the President shall make an announcement to the Council of the result of the voting with the names of those voting for and against the resolution respectively'. On a matter as grave as deposing a General no one was to be permitted the luxury of anonymity. Each member had to stand up and be counted.

The Resolution of Adjudication is moved

One week after the Resolution of Adjudication had first appeared on the agenda paper, Commissioner David Lamb now moved 'that this meeting of the High Council, whilst regretting the necessity, does hereby ... adjudicate William Bramwell Booth unfit for office as General of The Salvation Army and remove him therefrom'.

Commissioner David Lamb covered the historical and legal background in detail. He dealt with Clause 2 of the Supplementary Deed 1904 and explained why it had been right to proceed under Subclause 3 of that clause rather than Subclause 1. He then paid tribute to the service of Bramwell Booth, but lamented the decline of his natural powers and the manner in which his devotion to his father had gradually become devotion to his family circle. He ended: 'I submit to you, then, with great conviction but great regret, that General Bramwell Booth is unequal to the task, and I beg you accordingly to support the resolution which I have moved and which is now before you.'

Commissioner Wilfred Simpson seconded the motion. He spoke of the influence that Bramwell Booth had been on his own life, but also drew attention to the 'signs that the vigour of the General's powers, both physical and nervous, have deteriorated'. It was for the sake of the Army's future and unity that he had signed the requisition. 'But I cannot see', he ended, 'how anyone in this room can with an approving conscience say other than that the General is at this moment unfit; or question whether, in view of the serious condition in which he has been for the past eight months or more, and in view also of his very advanced years, he will again be fit to adequately discharge the duties of his high office.'

When Commissioners Lamb and Simpson had finished speaking, Commissioner Catherine Booth immediately asked permission to move the following resolution: 'That the General be heard by Counsel [Mr William Jowitt] at this meeting of the High Council – day to be fixed.' The resolution was seconded by Commissioner Allister Smith. An intense debate ensued. What could Mr Jowitt possibly add to what is being said, some asked. Are *we* not the General's advisers? Are we not seeking to leave no stone unturned in our efforts to help him? When the resolution about inviting Mr Jowitt was put to the vote only eight members voted in favour. However, the refusal to allow the General to be represented by Counsel was in fact a misstep by the High Council.

The Council then adjourned until Wednesday morning at 10 o'clock. The scene was set for the decisive debate of the Council the next day.

That Tuesday evening the General issued a statement to the press gathered outside his home in Southwold that was published in all the major newspapers the next day. In that press statement one can see right into Bramwell Booth's heart and mind. He began it by rehearsing his 54 years of incessant toil for the Army without a break, and how as a result of 'bulletins indicating that my recovery was doubtful' issued in November, the High Council was called:

> But it should be clearly understood that the Founder instituted the powers under which the High Council could be called for the sole purpose of turning out of office a General who was spiritually unfit, and of electing a successor if that were done ... An important point of the deed is that, in declaring the General unfit, the High Council has power to set aside his nomination of a successor.
>
> The High Council has met to adjudicate upon my fitness for my position, and with a desire to discuss proposals for radical changes in the constitution of The Salvation Army. Legally the High Council has absolutely no power even to propose, let alone make, any changes in the constitution.

The General in his statement then summarised his 'Will you give me time?' letter of 6 January to the High Council and commented: 'I am informed that my letter to the Council was scarcely considered, and I was asked in reply to retire from office under what amounts to nothing less than a threat of expulsion. The only ground for this request, as far as I can ascertain, is that I am ill.' He continued:

> Why should I retire? My leadership at the moment may not be what it was; but what guarantee or assurance have I that I should be replaced by one who would seek first and foremost to maintain the principles of The Salvation Army?

I have carefully and prayerfully considered the entire question in all its bearings, and much as, in some respects, I should welcome complete rest and relief from responsibility, I feel I should be less than a man, let alone the leader of a great religious organisation, if I agree to the request at a time when, as I understand, there is agitation to change the foundation upon which it rests. Therefore I am compelled to refuse to do so.[6]

Wednesday 16 January 1929

On Wednesday 16 January, for the second morning running, the Council got off to a bad start. The minutes tell the story. 'The President informed the Council that an anonymous letter and telegram of a misleading character had been sent to many parts of Great Britain and overseas – the following was the text:

Do you realise that the doctors say the General will recover within six months, the General has asked the High Council to give him time, and the reply to this is a demand for his retirement? Is this fair after the General's lifelong work? The Chief of the Staff is well able to carry on during the General's continued absence. There is a growing indignation amongst the British public at the Council's action. Do you desire the General to be given time? If so telegraph immediately the Chief of the Staff, Sunbury-on-Thames.

'The President said that the telegram was evidently sent out with the intent of misleading the recipient to suppose that the communication had been sent by the Chief of the Staff. The Chief of the Staff knew nothing of the matter and entirely repudiated the action.'

In fact, the first the Chief of the Staff knew about these messages was when the local postmaster sent a messenger-boy round to Sunbury Court to ask the Chief to pay the surcharge for outgoing letters that had been insufficiently franked! Then had come the telegrams in response – addressed to him! Reported the *Daily*

Chronicle: 'By this evening more than 300 telegrams of reply had been received and answers were still pouring in. The local post office had had difficulty in coping with the rush, and messengers on foot have been delivering messages all day.' The reporter had got it right when he concluded his piece with: 'The episode is bitterly resented by the majority of the delegates as a piece of subtle and underhand propaganda.'[7]

Commissioner Theodore Kitching then moved a resolution, seconded by Commissioner John Cunningham, which was supportive of the General's case: 'That the Council be asked to formulate and hand to the General or his legal advisers a statement in writing specifying in detail all the grounds on which it is alleged he is unfit for office.' However, members were reminded that no such requirement was specified in the 1904 Supplementary Deed, and this resolution was lost – only eight members supporting it.

At this point the Chief of the Staff made a personal statement. The minutes read: 'Commissioner Catherine Booth had requested him in his official capacity as Chief of the Staff to hold a Salvation Army Court of Enquiry as to the allegations against the General's children, and that he was giving favourable consideration to the suggestion, which would therefore be dealt with after the termination of the present High Council.'

The Resolution of Adjudication is discussed

Having disposed of all other business, the President of the High Council then turned again to the Resolution of Adjudication and called on Commissioner David Lamb to read the resolution once more. When this had been done the President invited members of the Council to speak in favour of or against the motion that the General should be adjudicated unfit for office and be removed therefrom. The President decreed that nothing in the nature of charges against the General would be permitted, only the sharing of personal experiences and impressions. The Council was not a court trying the General, but a council seeking to adjudicate on his fitness or unfitness to be General.

Those supporting the motion found themselves in a predicament. They had been given to understand that from a legal point of view 'unfitness' had to be more than physical unfitness. It weighed heavily on them that if it was a matter of the General being 'permanently incapacitated by physical infirmity' only, then on the basis of Subclause 1 of the second clause of the Supplementary Deed 1904, he could have been removed from office by four out of five commissioners engaging in a 'write-in' without the High Council needing to have been summoned.

They were now proceeding on the basis of Subclause 3 that spoke of the High Council adjudicating whether the General was 'unfit' – a word the clause did not define. Yet at the same time, especially following the report of the deputation, the General's *physical* unfitness had become the one and only and seemingly all-sufficient issue on which to base any adjudication. Most speakers navigated carefully between these constraints by making the General's declining powers the key issue and ascribing to his health-breakdown any perceived deficiencies in his leadership style.

'It was not a question of one section of the Council attacking the General's honour and others defending it,' explained one of the requisitioning commissioners later to F. A. Mackenzie. 'We all regarded ourselves and the Council as a whole as guardians of the General's honour.'[8]

For the next 12 hours, with only brief interruptions for meals, one after the other, the members of the High Council shared their experiences, speaking in support of the motion that the General was unfit or against it. Those speaking in support of the motion spoke with great sorrow, but their cumulative experiences clearly conveyed the picture of someone who, because of the impairment of his natural powers, had developed an unacceptable style of leadership. Those speaking against the motion that the General was unfit highlighted his achievements, the way he was recovering his health, and pleaded for him to be given more time.

Commissioner Samuel Hurren emphasised that the General's nervous problems had been of long standing: 'I hope it will not be considered to be too far a call backward, but I would observe that even in the years 1913/14, when I was in almost hourly touch with the General as secretary to the Chief of the Staff, I saw something of the shadow of the approach of this meeting. My diary for the years mentioned contains more or less frequent references to the General's increasingly nervous state, or his being gravely burdened with details, of his drifting into a state of arrogance, a condition in which often everyone and everything was out of order, until the General, I know from what he said to me, himself feared a collapse even at that time.' Commissioner Hurren said he had noticed 'a gradual deterioration in what might be called acuteness of comprehension of what has been suitable to the moment'.[9]

Lieut-Commissioner Gunpei Yamamuro said: 'We will never forget the General, but he is now worn out, no longer able to carry the burden, and we cannot expect him to return.'

Commander Evangeline Booth intervened twice. She too spoke of her brother's gradual decline, but did not evade the issue of reform. 'The General appeals for more time to enable him to look at the constitution,' she said. 'But we have been appealing for reform for years and he has done nothing!'

The Commander referred to her letter of 9 April 1928 – copies of which she had had printed 'for the convenience of members of the High Council' – and reminded the members of the time when travelling with the General between San Francisco and Seattle she had knelt by his side in the train and had 'with all sisterly affection' implored him to bring about reform. He had then replied, 'Well, Eva, perhaps the time is soon at hand.' Yet when she had presented him with her Fifteen Points he had responded that he had neither the power nor the desire to alter the constitution.

'Five years ago I wrote to him that I thought the General's burdens were too much,' she said. 'There is not one thing I have not told him. If he would not, and if Mrs Booth would not, listen to *me*, then what chance stood others?' She ended on a dramatic note: 'I did my best and I have failed.'

Lieut-Commissioner Isaac Unsworth told of his interview with the General during which, in response to the suggestion that there be consultation about reform, the General had accused him of 'joining the enemy'.

Commissioner Hugh Whatmore defended the requisitioning commissioners, saying that they could have been impeached if they had not acted. He told how even 14 years earlier he had wondered whether the General was really coping, and spoke of the shock of seeing the decayed state of the General when he visited him in Southwold the previous September. Referring to the retirement request he concluded sadly: 'The attitude of the General is as I can't understand.'

When Commissioner Samuel Brengle stood to speak, many expected him to address the Council in support of the General. However, what he understood as an implied threat of legal action by the General in his letter had been the final breaking point for him. He spoke of his intense affection for the General and of the shock he had received when he heard the General's reply, and then with a masterful and memorable word-picture described his inner reaction: 'When I was once in Italy I visited a picture gallery, with a room dark, save for an illuminated painting of the head of Christ. I treasured memories of that picture and sorrowed when later I heard that a vandal had slashed his knife across it. In my heart I long carried a darkened room, and in it an illuminated portrait of the face of our General. But when I read the General's letter, this portrait was slashed.'[10]

Speaking against the motion that the General was unfit, Commissioner Theodore Kitching reminded the Council of the magnitude of the General's achievements and described how he had seen his health improving in recent weeks when visiting him. 'When we welcome him once again, let us do so as our Leader, as our General.' Commissioner John Laurie also spoke of the remarkable improvement in the General's health that he had seen when he recently called on the General with a notary. 'He is thinking of us. There is no bitterness on his part. I cannot vote but according to my convictions.'

Commissioner Allister Smith called on Council members to ask themselves: 'What would Jesus do?' Commissioner Mrs Lucy Booth-Hellberg in an emotional address gave a warning to members: 'How great and terrible must be the consequence of interfering with God's anointed.' In a brief intervention Mrs Booth declared: 'There is no man here to take this saintly man's place.'

Commissioner Catherine Booth speaks

The family had designated Commissioner Catherine Booth to be their main spokesperson. It was not until 9.30pm that she rose to speak. She had a difficult task. She knew that 56 of her 62 hearers had wanted her father to retire – and had been disappointed by his refusal. It was late in the day. Her audience was tired. She furthermore had the double handicap of being not only the daughter of the General but also of being thought to be his nominated successor. Would some think she was pleading not only for her father but also for herself? She spoke for one hour and 37 minutes.[11]

Catherine Booth began by referring to what some other speakers had said, and mentioned that Commissioner Samuel Brengle 'misunderstood the reference to law in the General's letter'. She pointed out that the General had said in his letter that 'he had been advised that to *comply* with the High Council's demand to retire would lay the Army open to a lawsuit, and that this was an additional reason for *not* complying. A very different thing from a threat to go to law!'

With great forensic skill Catherine Booth then criticised the evidence that had been presented about her father's state of health. The report of the deputation that visited him to ask him to retire was misleading in that it did not allow for the strain that the General was under. The earlier statements by the requisitioning commissioners about the General being unable 'to attend to the most vital or, indeed, the most trivial duties of office' were not only wrong but at variance with what the Chief of the Staff had said about the General's ability 'to discuss and decide important business matters'.

216

'The commissioners have printed several versions of the statement that *The Salvation Army is without a Head*,' she continued. 'The Salvation Army is not without a Head. It has, on more than one occasion, had a *sick* Head. Once it had a *blind* Head. Once it had a *dying* Head. But, thank God, since its birth on Mile End Waste, The Salvation Army *has not yet been "without a Head!"*'

She took the requisitioning commissioners to task for saying that 'many of the vital interests of our vast organisation are seriously affected'. Had not the General made appropriate arrangements? Had the Chief of the Staff not given vigorous leadership to the Army? 'If this Council had met to appoint a new General,' she added in a comment that no one failed to notice, 'would not Commissioner Higgins be the man of its choice?'

Commissioner Catherine Booth then summarised her father's incessant programme of activities before he was taken ill, and how the doctors had declared that the illness had followed an expected course and that complete recovery was hoped for. Members of the High Council had themselves been ill from time to time, she said. 'Is the General the only one of its leaders who may not be given time to be ill, and time to recover from illness?'

She moved on to sensitive ground. 'I want to ask the requisitioning commissioners another question: "Why did they call the High Council directly they knew that the General's life was in immediate danger?" What could be the point of calling us from the ends of the earth to adjudicate as to the fitness of a dead man? Had Bramwell Booth died before the seven commissioners had laid their requisition on the Chief's table, would they have been sorry? *Yes*, but not because the armies of Christ had lost a valiant Captain, *but because they would have been too late to requisition the High Council.*

'I learn from the newspapers and elsewhere that there is a desire on the part of some to change the Army's form of government ... The General was in the midst of investigating the position when he was taken ill ... He was not only preparing for the gathering of actual opinions as to changes desired, but obtaining all kinds of data relative to the deeds themselves … Now that he is getting better, should we not all rejoice that it would appear to be God's will to spare him to help the Army at this time of special need?

'His letters to the Council. Would you *read* them? How I wish we had had time to consider them … I plead with you, give the General a chance, give the General's plan a chance. Then *you* leave him free to retire. You know him. Is he the man to hang on to what he cannot perform?'

Commissioner Catherine Booth moved to her peroration. 'God has brought the General back from the grave, back to life, back to the Army! Why? That the High Council of The Salvation Army may declare him unfit for office? If you cast out Bramwell Booth in his sickness you will affront the memory of his father and rob the Army of an integral part of its being. I appeal to you – do not rob the Army of the General! Do not rob the General of the Army! Chief of the Staff, commissioners, territorial commanders who constitute the first High Council of The Salvation Army, I appeal to you in the name of God to declare Bramwell Booth fit to continue General of The Salvation Army!'

There was a hush as Catherine Booth resumed her seat. It had been powerful – but had it been powerful enough?

'It was something to see her standing against all the others,' wrote Lieut-Commissioner Gunpei Yamamuro in his diary that evening, 'but the tide was already set and no one could change it.'

The Chief of the Staff speaks
The President allowed time for everyone to reflect on what they had heard. Then at 10.40pm he called on the Chief of the Staff to speak.

The Chief of the Staff began by reading the letter from Mr William Frost in which the lawyer recounted for the information of the High Council the legal advice that he and Mr Stamp would have offered to the General the previous October had they had opportunity to do so – namely that 'the General's highest duty to his Trust' was to vacate office and instruct the Chief of the Staff to convene the High Council 'for the purpose of receiving his resignation and electing his successor'. The Chief of the Staff told the Council that he had shared this advice privately with Mrs Booth at the time.

The Chief of the Staff then spoke of how throughout his life he had been filled with affection for the General. He had never anticipated that he should work so closely with him. It had been a privilege beyond words to be called to serve a leader of such ability and integrity. Whether they would next meet face to face in Heaven or on earth he would be able to say to him that he had served him 'with my best ability'. He had watched the decline of his powers with great sorrow. The General's task was not that of a figurehead. It was quite wrong to suggest that the Army had not suffered during these nine months of his absence.

'Are we to allow the Army to suffer longer? I want no other General. Honoured he has been and honoured he will be while life lasts. My heart would refrain from judgment, but reason must come to the throne. I shall have to vote in that way which my conviction calls or leave – history will do the rest.'

The Resolution of Adjudication is put to the vote
The Chief of the Staff had spoken for half an hour and the time was now 11.10pm. 'The President informed the Council', record the minutes, 'that although he had intended to speak to the adjudicating resolution, in view of the lateness of the hour he would refrain from doing so, and the voting would be proceeded with.' Commissioner Hay then called on everyone present to lay aside personal feelings in their voting and to put the interests of the Army above everything else. He then read out once more the words of the Resolution of Adjudication.

After a time of silent prayer, the names were called one by one. As the most senior member present, the Chief of the Staff was the first to break the silence with his footfall as he went up to the President's dais, received his voting paper and entered the small voting room adjoining the platform.[12] He emerged a few moments later, placed his completed and signed ballot in the urn in front of the dais and returned to his seat. The Commander was the next to move forward. One by one the members rose to their feet to vote. The stillness was absolute. Despite the lateness of the hour there was no sense of rush. That master of words, Commissioner Samuel Brengle, was later to describe the scene:

> The night was a night long remembered. The last vote was not cast till after midnight. The silence of a death chamber was there. You could hear men breathing labouredly. Hearts were well nigh breaking. It was much like the night my darling lay dead. The old order was passing, breaking away for the new. A long life, with a glorious record into which honour and love and sincerest praise had poured, was passing behind dark and threatening clouds. He came to his high place on the high, calm seas of worldwide acclaim and popularity and esteem won by his father, but now he was passing beyond the horizon on a dark and stormed-tossed sea.[13]

After Brigadier William Ebbs (Officer Commanding, Italy) had cast the last vote, the tellers – Commissioner Henry Mapp and Commissioner John Cunningham – counted the votes in the presence of the Council. The tension was almost unbearable as after opening each ballot paper they intoned whether it was 'for' or 'against'. Fifty-six of the members had signed the letter asking the General to retire. How many of them would be prepared to take the next step of voting for his deposition? After unfolding the last ballot and adding up the figures they handed the final result to the President.

At 15 minutes past midnight on the Thursday morning, the President announced that the 'resolution relating to the adjudication and removal of General William Bramwell Booth has been duly passed by a majority of not less than three in four'. Of the 63 members, 55 had voted for the resolution and eight had voted against.

The eight members who had voted against the resolution were the three members of the Bramwell Booth family together with Commissioner Mrs Lucy Booth-Hellberg, plus Commissioner John

Cunningham, Commissioner Theodore Kitching, Commissioner John Laurie and Commissioner Allister Smith.

Bramwell Booth had been deposed. The Salvation Army was without a Head.

A wave of emotion swept through the room as the full realisation of what they had just done hit members. It was with choked voices that they sang in closing:

> *When we cannot see our way,*
> *Let us trust and still obey;*
> *He who bids us forward go*
> *Cannot fail the way to show.*

By this time it was 12.30am on the Thursday. Knowing that members needed time to rest and to prepare for the next stage of the High Council, the President announced that there would be no meeting of the Council on the Thursday. The High Council would meet again on Friday 18 January at 10.30am to elect the new General.

Had the High Council elected the next General on that Thursday, history might well have taken a different course.

When everything had ended in the early morning hours of that day, the four women of the Booth family who had supported the General walked in single file out of the conference room. They had done all they could to stop him from being humiliated, but it had not been enough. Mrs Booth and Commissioner Mrs Lucy Booth-Hellberg were able to contain their grief but Commissioner Catherine Booth and her sister Colonel Mary wept openly. Some members of the Council tried to comfort them, while others broke down in tears and prayed aloud. Because the hour was so advanced, arrangements had been made for the four women to stay in the main conference house for the night.

At 2am Mrs Booth asked Catherine to phone her brother, Staff-Captain Wycliffe Booth, in Southwold so that he could share the outcome of the vote with his father in the morning.

221

'It was not until breakfast time that the news was gently broken to the aged General by the captain,' reported the Southwold correspondent of the *Daily Chronicle*. 'For fear that the High Council's decision, which had been reached some days earlier than the General had anticipated, might cause him a shock, Captain Booth only hinted indirectly at its nature. The General, however, seemed to understand the full import of his son's remarks, and, after bowing his head and praying for a few moments, he said, in a calm voice, "Very well."'[14]

Chapter Fourteen

Black Friday

AFTER the rest day on Thursday, members of the High Council reassembled on Friday 18 January at 10.30 in the morning. They were refreshed, but it was going to be a difficult day.

Not everyone had rested on the previous day. The President of the High Council had written a formal letter to Bramwell Booth enclosing a copy of the resolution by which he had been removed from office. The requisitioning commissioners had issued a press statement that began: 'The result of the vote is a complete vindication of the seven commissioners who requested the calling of the Council.' Many members had spent time in informal conversations about the future of the Army under the new order that was about to be ushered in.

The press speculated about what Bramwell Booth would do next. 'Decision to be Fought in the Courts' proclaimed the *Daily Express*. 'No Appeal to the Courts' answered the *Daily News*, whose usually well-versed writer, F. A. Mackenzie, informed readers that 'this assurance has been given me by one of the General's closest adherents in the High Council'. *The Star* meanwhile quoted a 'semi-official source' to the effect that 'Bramwell Booth was likely to leave it to the Army to take legal action against him to divest him of the trust which he holds'.

Mrs Booth had stayed in London for meetings with advisers on the Thursday, and had then journeyed to Southwold in the evening. In the wintry conditions her car had been involved in yet another accident, spinning around twice on the icy road before coming to a halt, with only the skill of the driver preventing a serious crash. She did not arrive home until after midnight. Mrs Booth did not return for Friday's meeting, and Commissioner Mrs Lucy Booth-Hellberg was also absent.

On that Friday morning it was the turn of the Chief of the Staff to be affected by the wintry conditions. As he was being driven to Sunbury Court on the North Circular Road a lorry coming from a side road was unable to stop and the two vehicles collided. 'I thought that he must be killed for the back of the lorry was lifted up and fell on the bonnet of the car,' reported Mr Colin Williams later to the journalists outside Sunbury Court. 'I saw the accident in my rear mirror. I did not know that he was Commissioner Higgins. I asked him where he wanted to go, and offered to drive him to Sunbury Court. We chatted all the way here, but he did not disclose his identity at all, and made no reference to the accident. I have never seen a man so cool after such a narrow escape.'[1]

The meeting of the High Council commenced as always with a devotional period. Following the time of prayer, Commissioner David Lamb moved that the High Council be formally adjourned until Saturday morning 'in order that the members might have time to consider the various aspects of the appointment of the new General'. What Commissioner Lamb was proposing was that the Council should meet as a 'committee of the whole' or as a 'conference of leaders' in which there could be informal discussion about the future leadership of the Army without the formality of an actual meeting of the High Council.

The minutes continue: 'After some discussion by several members of the Council, the Chief of the Staff suggested that the Council, as such, be adjourned only until 2.30 that afternoon in order to give members an opportunity of expressing their views. This was agreed.' To emphasise the informality of the occasion, the President and Vice-President stepped down from their chairs.

Constitutional reform is discussed
The meeting that followed was historic. For the first time ever the Army's commissioners and territorial commanders were gathered

together and could speak openly and freely about constitutional reform, but they were gathered without the one person who could take action – the General. Many of the leaders spoke, among them a number who had not previously participated. The discussion revealed a wide span of thinking on the subject.

Lieut-Commissioner William McIntyre pleaded for the impossible burden on the General to be lifted through the appointment of trustees to handle the business side. Commissioner Karl Larsson (Territorial Commander, Norway) counselled caution about going too far. 'I believe in one-man government as per our deed poll,' he said. 'Every man wants the man above him to be controlled, but if we make too many adjustments we might have a giant tied down by a committee.' However, arrangements for finance and property needed to be worked out, he said, and the General should serve for a set term or a fixed retirement age should be established.

Commander Evangeline Booth began by speaking of the frustration suffered by territorial commanders because of the limitations placed on their authority. 'One-man government stops at the General's door,' she said. She then moved on to the need for reform. 'According to the newspapers I am a possible nominee, but how can I possibly accept unless it is understood that there will be changes. We cannot go back to our commands without a settlement.'

'Whoever is the General,' she continued, 'should agree in principle to changes to the constitution being made with the support of two thirds of the commissioners *with* the General, or by three fourths of the commissioners *without* the General.' There must have been a collective drawing in of breath at these final words. The Commander was proposing that the commissioners should be able to outvote the General – as the Annual Conference had been able to do under the 1875 constitution.

The Commander summarised her proposals: 1. The General's sole right to make an appointment should be abrogated. 2. The General's own appointment should be for a set term of years, but with the possibility of re-election. 3. The General's retirement age should be fixed. 4. Territorial commanders should be granted greater powers commensurate with the size of their commands.

Commissioner Albin Peyron said that it 'would be wrong to go against the nomination of the General – but the General should submit the name of the future General to the commissioners'.

When retired Commissioner Carleton intervened everyone leaned forward so as not to miss a word. 'We must not tie ourselves down,' warned the aged statesman, 'but orders and regulations should not be compiled by one person, and promotion should not be in the hands of any one individual.' He was strongly in favour of an Advisory Council to the General, and said that this had been in the mind of William Booth who had stated to him: 'I am all for an Advisory Council and I will have one.' Commissioner Carleton hoped that the next General would appoint a number of commissioners 'to go into the matter of reform exhaustively' and that any changes might be given legal standing by a Royal Charter.

Commissioner Samuel Hurren commented that 'the fewer alterations legally the better', but that these should include that the General be elected for a set term of years, that there be an Advisory Council to the General, that the General be subject to his own orders and regulations, that officers be protected by being able to appeal to a panel, that promotions be on the advice of a 'small and efficient council', and that property holdings be on the basis of 'a perpetual succession' to avoid a great upheaval every time there was a new General.

When lunch time approached not everyone who wished to speak had yet been heard, but it was decided to stay with the programme for the day that had been agreed.

Nominations

When the leaders gathered again at 2.30pm, it therefore was for a formal session of the High Council. Commissioner Henry Mapp proposed and Lieut-Commissioner William Haines seconded 'that this Council shall proceed with the election of the General by having nominations by ballot'. This was unanimously carried.

Nomination papers were then distributed and members were invited to nominate the person they felt should be the next General. The nomination papers were not to be signed. Through this process five members of the High Council were nominated: Commissioner Catherine Booth, Commander Evangeline Booth, Commissioner James Hay, Commissioner Edward Higgins and Lieut-Commissioner Charles Rich (Territorial Commander, Canada West). Of these, Commissioners Catherine Booth, James Hay and Charles Rich immediately declined. The Chief of the Staff and the Commander accepted nomination and became candidates for the office of General of The Salvation Army.

Informal discussions on reform continue

After a brief refreshment break, it was decided in a change of plans to continue the informal discussions of the morning. A number of councillors contributed. Colonel Narayana Muthiah (Territorial Commander, Madras and Telegu, India) endorsed the concept of an elected General but wondered whether future elections should be held by letter or cable to avoid expense. Lieut-Commissioner Richard Holz called for the General to be elected for a fixed term of between five and 10 years, and to work with an 'executive' council rather than an 'advisory' council. What needed to be resolved was whether the General should be under the council, or the council under the General.

Commissioner Henry Mapp then spoke: 'I want The Salvation Army to be an army. The Salvation Army should be under the control of one person and that person should be the General. But there must be limitations to the General's authority.' He addressed some of the ways in which this might be achieved. In this connection he recognised the limitation of authority that the High Council itself had. He said that the legal advice received was that the High Council could not impose any conditions on the person it elected.

Late in the afternoon, when darkness had already fallen outside, Lieut-Commissioner William Haines, the Vice-President, indicated that he wanted to speak. The 56-year-old Vice-President was best known for the work he had done with the Army in France and Belgium during the First World War. His health had suffered as a result but he was still spoken of as a veritable human dynamo. He had not said much during the Council, but whenever he had intervened it was with a natural authority that made everyone listen.

That afternoon, recalls the Commander in a letter to her chief secretary, 'Haines made a never-to-be-forgotten effort to inspire the Army to free itself from the bondage in which we find ourselves, of forbidden speech, forbidden thought, forbidden conscience, and forbidden action'.[2] By way of illustration he related how General Bramwell Booth had said at a meeting of the Salvation Army Assurance Society board that 'it was not what *they* thought, but what *he* thought' that mattered. At this, Commissioner Catherine Booth rose and challenged him – and did so for a second time before he had finished.

Tragedy

'Haines practically dropped dead after his address,' continues the Commander in her account: 'It was too much for him – his face grew whiter and whiter as he talked. The High Council adjourned briefly upon the conclusion of his speech. Naturally everybody went out of the room. As I was going, I looked back, and saw him standing, his tall figure erect, under the blaze of an arc light. I told him his words would be of service to the Army as long as the flag waved, and congratulated him on his courage and the heroic stand he had taken.

'I went upstairs heart-sick – worn out – hungry and cold – hungry because I cannot eat, and cold because we are always cold over here. Brengle went up with me. Haines had left the council chamber, and he almost immediately collapsed. They laid him on a sofa. He had a cup of tea and seemed better.'[3]

When the members of the High Council had partaken of refreshments, they returned to the council chamber where the President declared that Mr Frost had an important announcement to make.

'Mr Frost informed the Council', record the minutes, 'that he had just received notification from his city office that General Bramwell Booth had obtained an injunction from the High Court to prevent the Council from proceeding with the election of a new General and that the hearing would probably be taken on Monday 21st January.' This was immediately after the weekend. The President announced that the High Council would therefore adjourn until the day after the court hearing, and would meet again on Tuesday 22 January, at 10.30am.

The announcement was matter-of-fact but it was as if a bomb had been tossed into the council chamber. The members of the High Council were devastated by the turn of events and grimly shook their heads as they looked round at each other. 'The shepherd has turned against the sheep,' said one. Wrote the Commander: 'I shall never forget the faces of the men.' The feared prospect that had lurked in the shadows had suddenly become a reality.

The members began to leave the council room. 'Haines, lying on the sofa outside, noticed the people coming out again and asked why we had adjourned,' recalls the Commander. 'Somebody said to him, "The General has taken out an injunction." Carleton was beside him and Mapp. His secretary, who happened to be there, held his head with his hands. Haines just gasped and said, "Oh, how did they find out?" – and died. His face turned almost black. The doctor later said it was the shock in his poor state of health – his muscles tightened so around the heart that it strangled him.

'You can never imagine the scene,' continues the Commander. 'Hurren rushed up to me, his own face as white as death. He said, "Haines has gone!" and burst into tears. Haines's own Colonel, who is a saint, wept like a child. In fact nearly everybody was in tears. Think of it, within the hour in which the injunction was taken out, Haines was dead! I ran downstairs and said aloud: "A martyr to the cause!" The whole Council took it up.'[4]

The press at the gates recorded a dramatic episode: 'One little soul who would have saved the commissioner's life if he could was a boy in the uniform of The Salvation Army, who was ordered hastily to fetch spirits. He ran half a mile to the nearest hotel, arrived breathlessly, cried, "Give me a bottle of brandy! It doesn't matter what it costs!", and slapped a pound note on the counter. "Take the cork out," he cried. He took the bottle, put his thumb on its mouth, and was out of sight in a moment, dashing along the dark road to Sunbury Court. He rushed through a group of photographers, almost upsetting one tripod, and beat on the closed gates for admission. All the efforts were unavailing. The Vice-President did not rally and died almost immediately.'[5]

The injunction

Shaken by the death of their Vice-President, the councillors could be seen conversing in small groups as they awaited further details about the injunction that Bramwell Booth had secured.

The injunction that Mr Justice Eve, sitting in the Chancery Division of the High Court of Justice, had granted that morning was a temporary injunction. It stopped the Council from acting on its decision to depose the General and elect a successor until the matter could be considered at an injunction hearing. At Monday's hearing Mr Justice Eve would decide whether or not to lift the injunction. If he lifted the injunction the High Council would be able to proceed with its business. If he did not, it was likely that the Council would have to await the outcome of a full lawsuit. It was a grim prospect.

The key issue therefore was the grounds on which the temporary injunction had been obtained. When the members were informed of the grounds they were shocked.

The application for an injunction had been made on behalf of General Bramwell Booth by Mr Wilfred Greene KC, and was based on two points:

1. That the Deed Poll of 1904 was not legally valid because a Trustee of a charitable Trust cannot alter the Trust at will, and
2. That the High Council's procedure was a violation of the Deed Poll and contrary to the principles of natural justice. The General had been deprived of the ordinary right of being allowed to put his case before the Council, and no medical evidence as to his fitness had been considered.

It was the first point that was devastating. Based on the fact 'that the [1878] Deed of Constitution did not contain any power to revoke or vary the provisions thereof', Mr Wilfred Greene was contending that:

a) Neither the Founder nor anyone else had the power to alter or add to the provisions of the 1878 Deed of Constitution,
b) The provisions of the 1904 Deed were and are inconsistent with the Deed of Constitution, and if valid would deprive the General for the time being of his rights and powers under the Deed of Constitution,
c) The 1904 Deed was and is therefore wholly void as to the provisions conferring power to remove a General and appoint a successor.[6]

The injunction also expressly prohibited the High Council or the Chief of the Staff 'from destroying, interfering with, or permitting the destruction of, or interference with, the "sealed envelope" containing the statement of the General as to his successor or the means to be taken for the appointment of a successor, or the said statement itself'.

This was not the feared appeal to the court by the General for the court to appoint his nominated successor as the sole trustee. Neither was it an appeal to the court on some technicality in the interpretation of the 1904 Deed. It was worse. Bramwell Booth's lawyers were contending nothing less than that the Deed of 1904 was legally invalid – that in legal terms it did not exist and had never existed. Therefore there was no such thing as a High Council, and therefore the General had not been removed from office.

The terms of the injunction in effect undermined the legal foundation on which the Army had stood for a quarter of a century – and which Bramwell Booth had helped lay. It is little wonder that the councillors were perplexed – and dismayed.

The reaction of the councillors

None of the High Council members had been present when on a wintry day in 1878 Mr Cozens-Hardy pleaded with William Booth to include a clause in the Foundation Deed that would give him and his

231

successors power to vary the deed. Only Bramwell Booth had heard Mr Cozens-Hardy warn that unless there was such a clause in the trust document, the trustee of a charitable trust could not alter the trust at will – the very words that were now being used in the injunction.

Many members of the High Council, however, remembered that it was Bramwell Booth himself who had masterminded the 1904 Supplementary Deed on behalf of his father, and how those great constitutional lawyers, Asquith, Haldane and Sargant, had endorsed the deed as legally valid.

Several High Council members had also been present at the International Staff Council in 1904 when William Booth, after carrying the draft document with him for seven years, had executed the Supplementary Deed in the presence of the Army's leaders.

Moreover, some of the High Council members had been in attendance in 1912 when Bramwell Booth on becoming General had signed a deed confirming that he accepted office not only on the terms of the 1878 Deed but also on the terms of the Supplementary Deed of 1904.

Was it really possible that he was now contending that the Supplementary Deed had been legally invalid all along and was therefore worthless?

The dismay of the councillors turned to apprehension. What if Mr Justice Eve upheld the injunction? The prospect was too awful to contemplate. The High Council would have no alternative but to challenge Bramwell Booth in court, but preparations for such a case might take many months and the trial was likely to be long and difficult. It was obviously essential to get the injunction lifted at Monday's hearing.

The dismay felt by the councillors at the General's action had not only to do with the grounds on which the injunction had been sought. A principle was at stake. For the General to take the Army to a secular court to resolve an internal issue was against the Army's orders and regulations, and these were based on biblical teaching. The press was not slow in quoting the actual regulation for the information of its

232

readers: 'In no case may Salvation soldiers go to law in the ordinary way with respect to differences which may exist between them. This is positively prohibited by the Holy Spirit and must never be practised – 1 Corinthians, Chapter 6, Verse 1.'[7] The regulation had been reissued in Bramwell Booth's name as recently as 1927.

The four International Headquarters commissioners who had stood by the General's side in the adjudication vote were more than dismayed. They felt badly let down. They had understood from comments made by Commissioner Catherine Booth at the High Council that the General would not take the matter to court. They remembered especially her response to Commissioner Samuel Brengle in which she dismissed as completely unfounded his fears that the General would take legal action. Whatever the rights and wrongs of that issue – and perhaps the General only took his final decision at the very last moment, at a time when Commissioner Catherine Booth had already given her assurances to the Council – the four commissioners felt that they had been misled.

They therefore decided to withdraw their support and informed Commissioner Catherine Booth and the Council accordingly. So strong were their feelings that the next day they asked the press office at International Headquarters to tell the media that:

> Commissioners Laurie, Cunningham, Smith and Kitching were four of the eight members of the High Council who supported the Booth family and refused to assent to the adjudication of the General as unfit. They have now dissociated themselves from such action, and have refused the family further support. This action was taken on the ground that Commissioner Catherine Booth, speaking for the family, had several times given the High Council the assurance that no legal action was contemplated.

The High Council as a whole felt let down in another sense as well. When the Council had deposed Bramwell Booth in the early hours of Thursday morning, it had not rushed to elect his successor. There was no need to hurry. No court action threatened. The Council 'had been positively and frequently assured by the family that no such step would be taken,' records the Commander.[8] Had the new General been elected later that same day, Bramwell Booth would have been faced with a different situation, for the 1904 Deed clearly laid down that:

> After any person has been elected General of The Salvation Army and accepted office, his election shall not be invalidated by any flaw in the summoning, constitution or proceedings of the High Council, or by any error in any matter or thing in anywise relating to such election or to any removal or vacation of office by any prior General.

Whether Bramwell Booth in such circumstances would have held back from challenging his elected successor in court we shall never know. Sections of the press, however, gently mocked the Council for its failure to act swiftly. 'The reformers were caught talking,' said one.[9]

On Saturday 19 January the members of the High Council received an acknowledgement from the General in response to the letter the President had written him to notify him of his deposition. 'My first responsibility', replied Bramwell Booth, 'is to ascertain whether under the circumstances which have now arisen, it entitles me to relinquish my Trust as you desire. I am advised that in the interests of the Army, I am not at liberty to do this until the legality of the position has been tested.'[10] The response did not calm the apprehensions of the councillors.

The reaction of the Chief of the Staff

No one had been more thunderstruck than the Chief of the Staff when he heard about the step the General had taken. Something snapped within him that day. On the Saturday he penned in sorrow a bitter note to his leader. This letter was meant to be private, but when it was later read out in open court it became available to the press. Salvationists also read it in the Supplement to *The War Cry* that was issued following the court hearing:

> I am afraid that what I am going to say will very much grieve you, but the position now is one in which I could not conscientiously hold my peace. I have all through these unhappy proceedings done my utmost

to do nothing which could in the least be interpreted as being antagonistic to you, and I think that Mrs Booth will agree that my address to the High Council was one in which I spoke in the highest terms of your integrity, your ability and your leadership.

I regret, however, that your action in securing an injunction has entirely changed my view upon one of the main grounds of my confidence. I held on, in spite of many things which I have been bewildered about, to the belief that you had no selfish interests in endeavouring to continue in office in spite of your enfeebled condition of health. That is shattered, and I can only see in your attitude a determination to try to keep the power and position which has been yours in The Salvation Army, even if in trying to do so you bring ruin to The Salvation Army.

That you could be guilty of going to the courts and securing an injunction upon the plea the 1904 Deed is *ultra vires* [beyond a person's legal power] has so stirred me and produced such indignation that in the interests of the Army, which to my surprise you say in your letter *you are seeking to secure,* I have consecrated myself to resist to the last drop of blood I have, this attack upon a Trust which you received from the Founder, and to which his name was attached, and which he and you have said over and over again, was made in the highest interest of The Salvation Army.

General, you have alienated the sympathy which was felt for you. You have isolated yourself from the comrades who have served you all these years. Even the men who have stood by your cause in this difficulty have had now to step aside, so that the plea you are making is a purely family one, and, in the light of all that will be revealed, that will be apparent to the world.

I am grieved beyond words. My heart is stricken, but I brace myself for whatever demands may be made on me.[11]

The same day the Chief of the Staff also wrote to all staff officers:

I could never have believed that General Booth could have dealt such a ghastly blow at the Trust passed on to him by his predecessor. The 1904 Deed was the work of our Founder, assisted by his son Bramwell, heralded by both as an additional safeguard for the Army's protection. General Bramwell Booth accepted office 'upon and subject to the terms not only of the said deed poll of the 7 August 1878, but also of the said deed poll of the 27 July 1904'. (I quote from his acceptance of office document.)

Now he has appealed to the court to declare this deed *ultra vires*, and should he be successful – which I do not think he will – the Army will be left without this part of our foundation, upon which we have built for nearly twenty-five years, and God alone knows what legal complications may ensue.

It seems unthinkable that General Booth could have adopted this course of action, and the only charitable construction I can place upon it is that he is in too enfeebled condition to fully appreciate the seriousness of his action.[12]

By taking the matter to court, Bramwell Booth forfeited most of the remaining goodwill towards him and his family. Letters of protest poured into International Headquarters from all over the world. No one could miss the groundswell of condemnation that flowed from press, public, officers and soldiers. Taking the dispute to the courts, it was felt, had been a tragic mistake.

Nevertheless, perhaps even this dark cloud was not without its silver lining, reflected Commander Evangeline Booth. 'What they thought to be evil against us has turned out for our good. The family now stands absolutely alone. Not a single supporter.'[13]

For the Commander herself, though, such was the personal agony of that black Friday, 18 January, that when she returned to her hotel room that evening she sat down and penned a personal letter to Commissioner James Hay, President of the High Council, in which she withdrew her candidature for the Generalship. 'I will be more useful if I stay as the Commander than as the General,' she wrote.

When the High Council adjourned at the end of that Friday, the members hoped that the injunction would be lifted at the Monday hearing and that they would meet together again as a Council on the Tuesday.

However, they were about to become nomads. It would be nearly four weeks before they assembled anew at Sunbury Court.

Chapter Fifteen
Booth versus Hurren and Others

MR JUSTICE EVE had never known space in his court in the High Court of Justice to be in such great demand. Long before the doors opened, the street milled with journalists and Salvationists. With just a few exceptions, all members of the High Council were there. As soon as the doors opened there was a rush for seats, but many were unsuccessful. When Mr Justice Eve noticed that some members of the High Council had not been able to get a seat, he invited them, in the highest Army tradition, to join him on the platform! 'It was a unique sight', reported the *Daily Express,* 'to see the High Court judge embedded in a setting of Salvation Army uniforms.'[1]

Mr Justice Eve looked down on a glittering array of legal talent. Counting King's Counsel alone, on one side appearing for General Bramwell Booth were Mr Wilfred Greene KC, Mr William Jowitt KC and Mr H. B. Vaisey KC. On the opposite side appearing for Commissioner Samuel Hurren and the other requisitioning commissioners were Mr Gavin Simonds KC and Mr Gilbert H. Hurst KC, and appearing for the Chief of the Staff, Mr Stuart Bevan KC. Given the close relationship there had been between Bramwell Booth and Samuel Hurren, there was a sad irony in that the legal action was known as 'Booth v. Hurren and Others', but this was simply due to the fact that Commissioner Hurren had been the first to sign the letter of requisition.

The date was Tuesday 29 January 1929 – 12 days after the injunction had been served. It was later than anyone had wanted. The hearing had been postponed and then postponed again. In the intervening time Mr Justice Eve had worked hard to persuade the

237

contending sides to settle their difference without pursuing litigation, saying that 'the continuance of the proceedings will prejudicially affect a great and beneficent institution'. Yet despite every attempt it had not proved possible for the parties to come to a meeting of minds.

For the members of the High Council it had been an unwelcome delay. On the previous Tuesday – 22 January – they had all travelled to the International Training Garrison at Clapton, East London. In the morning they had met there for an informal meeting of High Council members at which they had signed statements in preparation for the injunction hearing. In the afternoon they had all attended the funeral of Lieut-Commissioner William Haines. The Chief of the Staff conducted the funeral and the event drew a vast attendance of officers and soldiers, some saying that nothing like it had been seen since the funeral of the Founder. With the court hearing in central London being the next event on the horizon, the London-based commissioners had moved from Sunbury Court to their homes, and many overseas members had found alternative accommodation in the capital. Sunbury Court was therefore no longer the place where the action was and the press had moved away.

The press, however, had not been idle during the 12-day interval and had speculated freely on how the dispute might be settled. A shortage of hard facts was no deterrent. The *Daily Herald* had even announced that 'a ballot of all enrolled Salvationists, including the rank-and-file members, will be taken to decide the issue between General Bramwell Booth and the High Council!'[2] Though the story had no factual basis the paper followed it up some days later with a report that balloting had been heavy, especially in the north of England!

The hearing opens
The action brought on behalf of General Bramwell Booth before Mr Justice Eve, recorded the court reporter of *The Times*, was 'to restrain the members of the High Council from acting on the resolution passed early on Thursday morning, January 17th, which, after

declaring that General Booth was unfit to remain in office, purported to remove him therefrom'. The action was against the High Council as a body, and Commissioner Edward Higgins separately as Chief of the Staff. General Bramwell Booth was applying for the injunction to be made permanent. The High Council wished it lifted so that it could proceed with the election of a new General.

In the injunction hearing a series of affidavits – sworn written statements – prepared by the parties to the action would be presented as evidence and argued by counsel for the respective sides, after which Mr Justice Eve would give judgment.

For General Booth

As *The Times* reported,[3] Mr Greene (for the General) opened provocatively. For some time, he said, there had apparently been a desire among certain members of The Salvation Army to bring about radical change in its constitution. The present situation was the culmination of that effort. Without any self-seeking motive or any regard to his own personal position, the General was opposing what he conceived to be an attack on what was laid down by the Founder and on the trusts which he had carried on.

Mr Simonds (for the requisitioning commissioners) interposed at this point and said that this was a most extraordinary opening! There was not a word in the written statements to support such a suggestion. The action of the High Council had not been influenced by any such consideration, and he strongly protested against the insinuation.

Mr Greene responded by saying that his opening was based on a paragraph in the statements submitted. He then went on to say that there were two grounds on which he sought to test the legality of what had been done at the High Council. The first raised a question which sooner or later would have to be decided – namely the legal validity of the 1904 Deed, which laid down certain rules by which the General might be deprived of office. The second point was as to the procedure under that deed – whether, if the deed were valid, the procedure laid down under it had been adhered to.

On this second point, Mr Greene argued that it raised the broad principle whether or not, under the terms of that deed, the High Council, adjudicating on the question of the unfitness of the General, were bound to formulate the charges and were bound to give him an opportunity of being heard. The General wished to know what charges had been formulated against him and wished to have the opportunity of meeting them. At the meeting of the High Council called to consider his removal, charges were made and speeches delivered containing suggestions against the General's conduct which must have influenced those that heard them.

The General held the view, continued Mr Greene, that had he the opportunity of meeting those who were making charges he would be able to persuade the High Council that there was no real ground for his removal. The General, he contended, must be given fair opportunity of meeting the charges against him, and if the result were to confirm the resolution which had been passed he must and would accept it. His Lordship had been asked to preserve the *status quo* until the matter could be finally determined because if the High Council, having deposed the General, were to proceed to elect another, the defects in their procedures were automatically cured.

Mr Vaisey (also for the General) then outlined the history of the 1878 and 1904 Deeds, and described the build-up to the present crisis as seen from the perspective of the General. He read a sworn statement by Mr Frederick Sneath, the General's personal lawyer, giving further details about these deeds. Mr Vaisey also referred to the medical certificates that had been issued, and read out and commented on the General's letters to the High Council. He further read out the bitter letter that the Chief of the Staff had written when he heard that the General was taking the matter to court.[4] The reading of a short corroborative statement by Commissioner Catherine Booth concluded this part of the presentation.

For the High Council
Mr Gavin Simonds (for the requisitioning commissioners) said that the first statement which he had to read was sworn by 53 persons,

all members of the High Council who voted for the resolution passed on 17 January 1929 – other than William Haines who had died and the defendant Edward Higgins, Chief of the Staff, who was separately represented.

Mr Simonds affirmed that the General had been very ably represented at the High Council by those who had argued against the resolution, and that it was quite untrue to suggest that the High Council refused to hear anyone on behalf of the General. The Council only refused to hear legal advocates, but they allowed the General's wife and children and his supporters on the Council the utmost freedom of speech. Moreover, the letters which the General sent to the Council were read and considered. It was also untrue to suggest that there had not been a fair and proper adjudication.

They did not agree to the presence of legal advocates, continued Mr Simonds, because they regarded the affair as a domestic matter and felt that in the interests of The Salvation Army and of the General the proceedings of the High Council ought to be kept strictly private. The General's daughter, Commissioner Catherine Booth, made the last speech on behalf of the General, and she gave the Council to understand that the General had no intention of going to law.

Mr Simonds next read a lengthy affirmation by Commissioner Hurren and six other commissioners that presented their views on the history of the deeds and background to the present crisis.

Following this, Mr Stuart Bevan (for the Chief of the Staff) read a statement on behalf of Commissioner Higgins, which among other things said that the General's last attendance at headquarters was on 12 April 1928, and that since then in no sense whatever had the operations of the organisation been under the oversight, direction or control of the General in his own proper person. In his statement the Chief of the Staff also declared that, speaking for himself and for all members of the High Council who had voted with him, they were above all things anxious not to take any course that was in any way unfair to the General or an infringement of his rights. They had acted with a single eye to the welfare of The Salvation Army, which was the life-work of them all.

For General Booth

In a further submission read by counsel for the General, Commissioner Catherine Booth contested the statement in the evidence presented on behalf of the High Council that before the submission and discussion of the actual resolution of adjudication nothing was said or done that could possibly be construed as any sort of reflection on the General. She asserted that the mover of the resolution [Commissioner David Lamb] had alleged that a change had come over the General, and that he had withdrawn his counsel from the most trusted officers and given it to his family. Further, that a speaker in support of the resolution had stated that during the summer it had freely been said that the General's mind was affected.

In her statement, Commissioner Catherine Booth also alleged that before the formal meetings of the Council a number of informal meetings were held, to which she was not summoned, at which the position of the General had been discussed. By means of those informal meetings, and otherwise, an enormous amount of propaganda had been carried out in favour of removing the General and so preparing the position for appointing his successor. Resulting from agitation originating in America, a group among leading officers of the Army had for some months expressed a desire to change the constitution of the Army, and there was no doubt that the requisitioning commissioners and those in favour of the changes had taken advantage of the General's illness to endeavour to remove him and nullify his appointment of a successor.

With this the court broke for lunch.

A crucial statement

Following the lunch interval Mr Greene (on behalf of the General) made a crucial statement, which in the few seconds it took for it to be made totally transformed the nature of the hearing.

Mr Greene said that the action being brought was based on two grounds – the legal validity of the 1904 Deed and whether correct procedures had been observed – but that in view of the evidence filed he was not justified in asking for a temporary injunction on

242

the ground of any suggested invalidity in the Deed Poll of 1904. The present application must be based on the *procedure* of the High Council on the assumption that the 1904 was a valid document.

It is clear that the members of the General's legal team had decided already in their preparation for the injunction hearing not to pursue the first point, for at no time did they argue the issue. They must have concluded that to seek to prove in court that the 1904 Deed was legally invalid was too complex and too vital a matter for an injunction hearing.

The issue hinged on the finest of legal points. Did or did not the 1904 Deed 'vary' the 1878 Deed? If it did it was legally invalid. Enormous consequences therefore rested on the answer given to that question. The members of the General's team also knew that the legal validity of the 1904 Deed would be defended by the Army with all the force it could muster, and that the Chief of the Staff had spoken for virtually the whole of the Army's leadership when he had declared that he would resist the attack on the deed 'to the last drop of blood that I have'.

The General's legal team must also have realised that to prove the 1904 Deed to be legally invalid would be a monumental challenge for them. Much more by way of evidence would be needed than the sworn statements they had thus far received. The legal team would have to show that the three most eminent constitutional lawyers at the turn of the century had been mistaken in their advice – and one of them, the highly respected Lord Justice Sargant, was still alive and might be persuaded to speak in defence of his creation. The team would also have to get round the fact that when Bramwell Booth became General in 1912 he at that point accepted the legality of the 1904 Deed when he executed a deed stating that he accepted office not only on the basis of the 1878 Foundation Deed but also of the 1904 Supplementary Deed.

The right setting for such a legal battle was not an injunction hearing. It would require a full trial.

A huge collective sigh of relief must have gone up from the members of the High Council when they heard Mr Greene's statement. The 1904 Deed was to be assumed to be legally valid for the purposes of the hearing. The legal existence of the High Council was therefore not under threat. All they now had to deal with was whether they as a Council had observed correct procedures. If errors had been made, these could surely be put right.

The hearing continues

After dropping his bombshell, Mr Greene continued his presentation on behalf of the General – dealing only with the matter of procedures.

The High Council was convened for the purpose of declaring the General unfit, he said, but it was a question of unfitness without specifying any ground for such incapacity.

At the meeting on January 15th, he averred, various charges were made by speakers against the General which were totally unconnected with the question of his physical unfitness, and they might have influenced the majority to declare him unfit. It was said that he was guilty of favouritism, and penalised officers who differed from him on policy, and those statements were made by one or more of the judges [members of the High Council] without any evidence to support them. It was a charge of general unfitness which might involve both his physical and mental capacity. The resolution proposed left it open to any members of the Council to bring forward any grounds of unfitness he pleased.

On this note the court adjourned for the day.

When the court assembled the next day, Mr Greene, concluding his speech on behalf of General Booth, contended that the resolution of the High Council was void and useless because the Council had not heard General Booth.

Mr Jowitt, speaking also for the General, said that there was very little he wanted to add. He gathered that the members of the High Council were rather suspicious of lawyers. At this Mr Justice Eve commented that he hoped that they would go away from there without that suspicion.

Continuing, Mr Jowitt said that he was not impeaching the good faith of the members of the High Council in the slightest degree, but it was a fundamental principle of justice that no man should be condemned for anything behind his back. There was no difference between physical, mental or moral unfitness. All the authorities supported that principle.

For the High Council

Mr Gavin Simonds (for the requisitioning commissioners) took the opportunity to plead with the General and his legal team not to challenge the validity of the 1904 Deed through further legal action. The Deed of 1904, he said, provided in the establishment of the High Council the single safeguard against the evils of autocracy which might become despotism, which in turn might become tyranny. The deed was the only safeguard against a man clinging to office in such circumstances.

'I beg General Booth to think twice and thrice again,' he continued, 'before he challenges this deed, which in honour and loyalty to the trust which his father reposed in him, and in duty to the Army, he is bound to maintain in its unchallengeable integrity.'

The single question in this case, he added, was whether the General was fit or unfit to carry on, and unfit for physical reasons only ... The General was saying to the High Council: 'The time is a critical one for the Army, I am unable to direct its affairs, and I will place the administration in the hands of a council.' What more could anyone say in the General's defence after such a declaration? It was as clear a statement by him as any statement could be that he could not exercise the directional power which he ought to as General. The High Council accepted that statement, and asked him to retire. The conclusion at which they arrived was the only conclusion to which reasonable men could come on the facts presented to them by the General himself. To say in those circumstances that the General was condemned unheard was preposterous.

Mr Simonds further contended that the fact that some member of the High Council might have said that quite apart from physical incapacity he did not think General Booth ought to retain his office ought not to vitiate the decision to which the High Council came. In a meeting of 63 people one could not prevent some people making observations which had better not have been made.

If General Booth was unfit it was the duty of the Council to remove him, he concluded. 'Nothing else has guided or influenced, or will guide or influence, their deliberations than the fact that in his old age he is unfit to sustain the burdens of his office.'

For General Booth

Mr Jowitt (on behalf of the General) then returned to the point that the General had not been properly heard by the High Council. It had been suggested by some that even if the injunction was granted and the General was represented by legal counsel, the High Council would come to the same conclusion. He hoped, however, that each member of the High Council would disregard what had been done before and would, after hearing the General, come to a right conclusion whether it was impossible or improbable for him to resume office.

The judgment

In giving judgment, Mr Justice Eve noted that though relief in the action was claimed on two grounds, the motion had been argued on the second ground only – namely that the High Council had failed to observe the elemental principle that no judgment should be pronounced against a party who had not had the opportunity of appearing and being heard.

He also noted – significantly – that the motion had been argued on the second of those grounds only, because the evidence dealing with the first disclosed a state of things which could only be solved at the trial of the action.

In summing up the provisions of the 1904 Deed for removing a General from office, Mr Justice Eve said that he would accept the view, for the purposes of his judgment, that the situation could have been dealt with, had the commissioners been so minded, under Subclause 1, but the matter was dealt with under Subclause 3.

In other words, Mr Justice Eve accepted that the matter could have been handled by a 'write-in' of the commissioners. If four in five commissioners were satisfied that the General was 'permanently incapacitated by physical infirmity' he could have been removed from office without the High Council being called, but he noted that the matter had been dealt with under Subclause 3, by which the High Council had been summoned to adjudicate on the fitness or otherwise of the General.

His Lordship then reviewed events since the calling of the High Council, remarking that it was quite impossible to read the affidavit of the Chief of Staff, Commissioner Higgins, without appreciating that the absence from the control of the General had brought about serious results to the organisation of The Salvation Army.

Regarding the letter sent to the General proposing that he should retire, Mr Justice Eve commented that this must have brought home to the General's mind the fact that there was no suggestion of any ground other than that of physical weakness having been put forward as a reason for holding the meeting of the Council and of suggesting his retirement.

His Lordship observed that when the General replied to the effect that he could not relinquish his position and that he could not desert his Trust, there was a clear issue between the adjudicating body and the General. On the one hand, the attitude of the High Council was that the General had been ill for a long time, that his condition was unpromising so far as his early recovery, and that having regard to his age and the length of his illness he would not be able within a reasonable time to sustain the burdens of his office. On the other hand, the General was not prepared to acknowledge that the hopes of his recovery were likely to be falsified.

The Council met, continued Mr Justice Eve, and, not unnaturally, after a lengthy deliberation they came to the conclusion expressed in the resolution which they passed. Into the merits of that conclusion it was not the province of the court to enter. That was a matter for the High Council alone, and he had no power to review it or any right to express any opinion as to its correctness or not.

He thought, however, that it was legitimate to observe on the evidence before the court that the conclusion would appear to be based solely on the question of the General's health and on no other ground. He had from counsel (Mr Simonds) representing the majority of the High Council the statement made in court that it was on that ground alone that the decision was arrived at.

On the matter of whether the Council ought to have come to any conclusion without giving the General an opportunity of being present in person or by duly authorised agents, he could not help thinking that a mistake was made – a perfectly innocent mistake he doubted not – that they did not give General Booth an opportunity of stating the grounds on which he was seeking to continue in office for the present.

The conclusion he arrived at on the whole matter, continued Mr Justice Eve, was that there should have been that opportunity. The High Council had not yet broken up, and it was not a matter that called for any long delay. In those circumstances any injunction made must be limited in terms so as not to prevent the Council from at once rectifying the mistake. He must therefore grant an injunction to restrain the defendants from acting on the resolution passed on January 17th until after holding a meeting of the Council and until after the General had been given an opportunity of urging, either by himself or by others, why the resolution declaring him unfit should not be enforced.

Mr Greene (for the General) said that the resolution was either good or bad.

His Lordship replied: 'It was bad. The injunction will be to restrain the High Council from acting on that or any resolution declaring the General unfit until after the holding of the meeting. The meeting ought to be held soon.'

Mr Greene said that he could not mention a date, as the General had to be consulted and his instructions taken.

The hearing was at an end.

Mr Justice Eve had expressed the hope that the matter might be resolved without any long delay. That hope was not to be fulfilled.

The members of the High Council gathered in the council chamber at Sunbury Court. The photo is taken from the back of the hall. Commissioner James Hay (President) stands on the platform. Seated, right, on the platform is Lieut-Commissioner William Haines (Vice-President) and, left, Mr William Frost

Above: The deputation of seven that visited General Bramwell Booth in Southwold.
Left to right: Commissioners John Cunningham and Samuel Brengle. Lieut-
Commissioner Gunpei Yamamuro. Commissioner James Hay. Colonel Mrs Annie
Trounce. Commissioner George Mitchell and Lieut-Commissioner William Haines.

Left: The Chief of
the Staff,
Commissioner
Edward Higgins,
heads the processio
at the funeral of
Lieut-Commission
William Haines,
which was held in
Clapton Congress
Hall. In the second
row Commander
Evangeline Booth i
flanked by
Commissioner Her
Mapp on the left an
Commissioner
George Mitchell on
the right.

above: Outside the High Court – left to right: Lieut-Commissioner William McIntyre, Commissioner Johannes de Groot, Lieut-Commissioner Richard Holz, Lieut-Commissioner John McMillan and the Chief of the Staff, Commissioner Edward Higgins.

right: Mr William Jowitt arrives at Sunbury Court accompanied by an officer 'armour-bearer'.

below: The City of London pays its last respects to General Bramwell Booth as his funeral cortege wends its way from International Headquarters to Abney Park Cemetery. Three and a half thousand uniformed Salvationists marched in the procession.

Left: General Evangeline Booth and Commissioner Catherine Bramwell-Booth in conversation before the opening of the 1939 High Council.

Below: Commissioner Catherine Bramwell-Booth, aged 94, speak at the 1978 International Congres in Wembley.

Chapter Sixteen

The Council Waits

AFTER a break of only a day following the court hearing, the members of the High Council met on Friday 1 February 1929 to consider the judgment that had been given. They did not return to Sunbury Court, but instead met at the Auction Mart, 155 Queen Victoria Street, near to International Headquarters. Mrs Booth did not attend.

Mr William Frost read the verbatim report of the judgment given by Mr Justice Eve, and then gave his views on the outcome and answered questions from the members.

Mr Frost emphasised the relief it had been to discover that the General and his legal team were not going to press the question of the legal validity of the 1904 Deed at the injunction hearing. The matter of procedural errors made by the Council could be corrected, and by correcting them the injunction would automatically be lifted. This would enable the High Council to proceed with the election of a new General.

Regarding the procedural errors, Mr Frost explained that Mr Justice Eve had ruled that it had not been sufficient for members of the High Council to speak in defence of the General because as members of an adjudicatory body they were all cast in the role of 'judges'. The General had to be represented by someone quite independent of the Council, someone without a vote.

The worrying aspect, continued Mr Frost, was that the General and his team had not abandoned the challenge to the legal validity of the 1904 Deed. They had only postponed it until they had gathered all the evidence they needed for a full trial.

This was bad news. The earlier threat of the General possibly appealing to the courts had been like a vague fearsome prospect lurking in the background. It was being replaced with something far more threatening. A very specific sword of Damocles now hung by one slender hair over the collective head of the Army's leadership, a sword that could at any time come plunging down.

If at a trial the 1904 Deed was declared legally invalid, Bramwell Booth would be restored as General, and any successor elected by the High Council would have to stand down. In such a scenario, Bramwell Booth's eventual successor would be the person whose name was in the 'sealed envelope'. Until the matter was finally resolved in a court of law, the 'sealed envelope' had to be preserved intact and unopened. No one could therefore relax until the matter was settled.

Mr William Frost also drew the attention of the High Council to two further positive outcomes in the judgment given at the hearing. Firstly, Mr Justice Eve had accepted that it was in order for the issue to be dealt with under Clause 2, *Subclause 3* of the 1904 Deed. In so doing he had endorsed the legitimacy of the High Council being called to adjudicate on the General's fitness or unfitness for office.

Secondly, the injunction hearing had clarified that the 'unfitness' referred to in Subclause 3 could include *physical* unfitness. Mr William Jowitt had helpfully declared that 'there was no difference between physical, mental, or moral unfitness'. The General's breakdown in health and continued physical incapacity was therefore an all-sufficient reason under Subclause 3 for removing the General from office. The High Council need not have considered any other aspects of unfitness but could have rested its case on the one issue of health. However, it took the injunction hearing to clarify the point.

Had this point been clear from the outset, some things better left unsaid would not have been said at the High Council.

Following the briefing by Mr Frost, Commissioner David Lamb submitted the following notice: 'That on one day next week convenient to the General or his representative I propose to move a resolution asking the High Council to adjudicate General Bramwell Booth unfit for office *on the ground of ill-health* and to remove him from office accordingly.'

The High Council then resolved to issue an invitation to the General 'to attend the High Council one day next week, either in person or by a representative,' asking him to indicate 'whether he will attend personally or by whom, and that the General be informed that the High Council will be pleased to hear any evidence he may desire to submit either orally or by statutory declaration'.

The General's health

The invitation extended to the General to attend the High Council in person was not just a matter of courtesy. The family kept saying that he had made a remarkable recovery, but no one knew for sure. Some members of the Council thought that he might make a supreme effort and come himself to address the Council – and knew the decisive impact that might have. Others read the situation differently. To them the 'fight' was not coming from Bramwell Booth but from his family and their advisers. The Commander verbalised this sentiment when writing a personal note to her chief secretary during the weekend following the court judgment:

> Just how far the General is back of it there is no telling. The family try to make out that he is improving, but there is absolutely nothing but their own word to back this up. They do not let people see him, and such statements as purport to come directly from him are so clearly not his that one cannot but believe that he is rather the tool in the hands of his family than the chief actor.
>
> Take, for instance, his letter to the High Council of January 14th [in which he turned down the invitation to retire]. Did that man, so sick and feeble that he could only with difficulty follow the letter brought to him by a deputation from the High Council on January 11th, dictate or even formulate in principle the text of his reply? He never did! Not only is the wording not his, but very few of the sentiments show the special and peculiar colouring of his mind. Someone else is not only writing for him but thinking for him.

I do not say that he does not assent to what is done. He no doubt does, but he would just as quickly assent to some other course if that course were presented to him and backed up by the same people.[1]

Events flow

While the High Council awaited the General's reply, events did not cease – nor did the battle for hearts and minds. The family sought by every means possible to present the General's case in the most favourable light and to emphasise that he was recovering rapidly and was in full control. A series of initiatives on their part increased the tension.

On 31 January – even before the High Council gathered in the Auction Mart to review the judgment – Commissioner Catherine Booth met openly with the press for the first time, and in her statement said that 'General Booth is getting up daily for an hour or two and is progressing well'. She continued:

It is very unfortunate that the delegation that visited him got a wrong impression. They were greatly taken aback by the difference in his appearance. Probably none of them had seen him since his illness, and the fact that he looked very much thinner gave them the impression that he was much more ill than was really the case.

I think the High Council very much misunderstood the reason for his going to the courts. Some are trying to rake up the idea that it is against Army principles. It is if you have a personal quarrel with anyone. But this is not a personal quarrel, and as far as going to law to seek guidance on legal points is concerned, well, we are constantly doing it.

It is an appalling thought to me that the High Council cannot think out a better plan than to meet again, simply to make a good resolution instead of a bad one. I wish with all my heart that we could reach an agreement which would meet what the Council wants – which is really the power to elect the General's successor. They are more anxious about that than about turning out the General.

One of the strongest reasons why the General does not wish to retire at this juncture is that he knows quite well that there is this agitation afoot, which began in America, to get certain changes made in the Army's constitution. But if you are going to change the Army's

252

constitution, should not the thousands and thousands of other officers, local officers and soldiers also have a voice?

I feel that the High Council might yet realise that they have made a mistake.[2]

On Saturday 2 February *The War Cry* included a four-page supplement 'issued by instruction of the General'. General Bramwell Booth still had control of *The War Cry* and copies of correspondence between the General and the High Council had already appeared, as had the full report by the deputation that visited him in Southwold. The supplement contained the General's letter to the High Council of 14 January, in which he declined to retire, and also the full report of the proceedings before Mr Justice Eve as reprinted from *The Times* – an item that covered nearly three pages in small type.

On Sunday 3 February – the next day – General Bramwell Booth returned unexpectedly to his London home in Hadley Wood, near Barnet. Everyone wondered whether this meant that the General was preparing to address the High Council personally. The press made the most of the development: 'Secret Dash from Southwold' headlined the *Daily Mail* the next day with equally dramatic sub-headings: 'Bed-chair in a Motorcar – First Time Out in Three Months – Will he face High Council?' The *Daily Herald* considered it a 'Bombshell for the Council!' The family said that he was unlikely to address the High Council personally, and explained that the General had returned to London because his health had improved so much that he could now undergo a course of specialised medicine he needed for his complete recovery. Yet the question hung in the air – would the General after all come to Sunbury?

On Monday 4 February the General's legal team took out a 'summons for direction' in a legal action to have the 1904 Deed declared invalid. It was only a small step, a necessary step to initiate what would be a long legal process, but it was hugely significant. For by it General Bramwell Booth was letting it be known that he intended to pursue the matter of the legal validity of the 1904 Deed to a full trial. The sword of Damocles still threatened.

When the members of the High Council met informally that same day at the Auction Mart to review progress they had the distinct feeling that the battle for hearts and minds was not going their way. This was reinforced when they learnt that the General was planning to use that week's issue of *The War Cry* – dated Saturday 9 February – to state his case even more fully. The members of the High Council decided that they would have to issue a statement of their own in which they could present their own side of the story. This would be in the form of a four-page supplement to go out with that edition of *The War Cry*. However, while the supplement was being prepared, news favourable to the General's position continued to flow.

On Tuesday 5 February the *Daily Chronicle* announced that 'General Booth Blames "Man from Texas"'. The cause of the General's ill-health, the paper informed its readers, was 'the campaign which, since late in 1926, has been carried on over the signature of "The Man from Texas" among staff officers, undermining the General's authority and asking for the complete abrogation of the 1878 Deed Poll'.

Mr George Pollard intervenes

On Wednesday 6 February wide publicity was given to a letter written by a Mr George Pollard to the High Council in support of the General. 'When I learned a few weeks ago', he began, 'that the General was lying ill at Southwold with no one at hand to help or advise him at the most critical period of his wonderful life, I got in touch with him. I went to see him and found him anything but helpless as far as his mental powers are concerned. I was with him for the greater part of an hour and found his mind and memory as clear as I have ever known it. I set to work to help and advise him by every means in my power and I intend to continue to do so.' The letter went on to criticise the Council. 'I regard the whole action and attitude of the High Council towards the General as ungrateful, harsh, unchristianlike, and unjust.'

What gave the intervention by Mr George Pollard special significance was that he was a former commissioner of The

Salvation Army and was personally known to many members of the Council. He had had a remarkable career as an officer. In 1883, when he was a young captain aged 20, William Booth had sent him, together with 19-year-old Lieutenant Edward Wright, to pioneer the Army in New Zealand. His success there had been so extraordinary that when after just nine months he called his newly formed Army together for a congress in Dunedin, it already consisted of 30 officers, 600 uniformed soldiers, five brass bands, and 5,000 converts! No hall in the city was large enough to contain them all.[3]

On his return to England, George Pollard had risen rapidly through the ranks, being promoted to commissioner at the age of 31, 'becoming the first Chancellor of the Exchequer in 1896, and becoming, perhaps, the closest confidant of William and Bramwell Booth in the decade 1894 to 1904'.[4] He resigned his officership at that point on the grounds of ill-health, but soon recovered to become a leading figure in J. Lyon and Co, a company which with their tea shops and corner houses was the equivalent of the coffee bars of today. Now aged 66 he was prominent in the business world but a controversial figure within Army circles.

Mr George Pollard proposed that a small group of commissioners should form a commission to work with the General on the constitutional question – and offered his services to the commission. However, the members of the High Council were not disposed to accept advice from one who had left them for the world of business. Besides, he had not endeared himself to them by writing that their refusal to grant the General time to recover was 'repulsive' and that 'such a request in similar circumstances would be readily granted by any third-class business house'.

Mr Maurice Whitlow writes

The very next day, Thursday 7 February, Mr Maurice Whitlow, another former Salvation Army officer and now a special correspondent for the *Daily Express,* allied himself with the General's cause. He had served on International Headquarters as an adjutant, was currently a local officer at a London corps, and was personally known to the General. Mr Whitlow gave an account of an interview he had had with the General at his Hadley Wood home – 'the only interview the Head of The Salvation Army has granted since the beginning of his illness in May last year,' stated the paper.

I found General Booth reclining in his bed, supported by pillows, but astonishingly alert and active. His keen brown eyes twinkled with recognition as I entered the room. In regard to the present controversy he spoke with vigour, clarity and sustained argument.

'Tell the Salvationists', he said, 'to keep on with their work whatever happens. They must tell the story at the corner of the street just as though there was nothing the matter.

'Tell the public that Bramwell Booth is not going to fail in the trust committed to him by his father. For 54 years that trust has been my first consideration.'

I put the leading question: 'Tell me, Sir, what was the real reason for your appeal to the courts?' He turned to me in reply with another of his keenly appraising glances. 'In my position as a trustee,' he commented,' I am bound in honour to do all that I can to protect The Salvation Army Trust. I have never had the dread of the law that some of our officers have.'

Then with a smile he said to me: 'You know, members of the High Council have themselves often advised me in the interests of the Army to take legal action, and have sometimes been eager to do so, even when I did not myself think it necessary. Perhaps in a little while these same men will see that I did for the Army the only thing an honourable man could do.

'What would you have done?' he asked after a pause. 'The men who are appointed to act as my legal advisers tell me that a certain action is necessary. I cannot reasonably say, "You be hanged".' He suggested hastily that perhaps it would scarcely be appropriate that he should be quoted in these exact words, but that I would doubtless be able to substitute something that would 'look more respectable'.

'I am rejoiced to see you so much better than I had hoped,' I said. 'If the High Council give you time to recover, will the work of the Army have been crippled by your prolonged absence?'

'I am much better than I was,' he replied. 'Indeed we were only saying this morning that I was a different being. While I have been away the Chief of the Staff has had power to carry on. No one has proved that the work has been hindered.

'While I have been ill I have been thinking about the future. I want to help widows with families more than we have ever done. I want to send more boys across to Australia and Canada, and I want to reinforce our missionary fields with better men and women than ever.'

It was indicated to me that my time was at an end, and the General, following his usual practice, prayed for me before I left. In the course of his prayer he referred to events of which we both had knowledge that happened more than 20 years ago.

In the course of conversation with Mrs Booth I learned that the doctors declare that within six weeks the General will have recovered as much weight as will restore him to his normal physique.

The General responds to the High Council

On Friday 8 February – nine days after Mr Justice Eve had given judgment – the members of the High Council met once more in the Auction Mart to hear the General's response to their invitation that he or a representative attend the Council.

Mr William Frost informed the Council that Mr William Jowitt KC, with Mr Frederick Sneath as his instructing solicitor, would attend the High Council in order to address it on behalf of the General. In the light of this information, the Council decided that the two King's Counsel who had represented the Chief of the Staff and the requisitioning commissioners at the injunction hearing should also be invited to be in attendance, together with their respective solicitors.

The venue for the meeting would be Sunbury Court and the date of the meeting would be Wednesday 13 February 1929 – a full 14 days after the court judgment. The Council took the opportunity of settling a number of procedures for that meeting.

Advance copies of *The War Cry* dated 9 February 1929 and the High Council's supplement were distributed to members and were carefully studied.

The General puts his case in *The War Cry*

The War Cry included a number of items in defence of the General's decision to resort to the courts. One of them was a message from the General himself:

> Many of you are no doubt asking yourself, 'Where does the General stand?' Well, the General stands where the General has *always* stood. I stand for the constitution of The Salvation Army as interpreted by the [1878] Foundation Deed.
>
> It is the greatest grief of my life so far, that doubts and fears as to the rightness of the Founder's plan should have arisen in the minds of capable and thoughtful men who have done splendid work for the Army. But I see no middle course. I must follow the Army flag and adhere to the Foundation principles, that splendid heritage that the Founder bequeathed to us.

Another article dealt with the legal position. It reiterated the point that 'the trustee of a Trust once created, even though that trustee be its "creator", has no more right to endanger its existence or to encroach on its rights than a parent has the right to kill or mutilate his own child'. The Salvation Army is a Trust, said the article, created by William Booth by the 1878 Deed Poll, 'and no one, not even the Founder, had or has the right of encroaching upon the stipulations of the original Deed Poll except as officially authorised by law'.

> It was never intended that the 1904 Supplementary Deed should contain anything which might endanger the principles or even the very existence of the Trust originally created … The High Council was not created to function as an executive or legislative body, but purely and solely for the purpose of safeguarding the Trust and to maintain it permanently and inviolate … Neither the High Council nor the Trustee himself has any authority to introduce principles which are foreign to the original Trust Deed of The Salvation Army. The General would be unfaithful to The Salvation Army, and to the Trust itself, if he did not put forth every effort to prevent a possible interference with the original purposes and principles of the Foundation Deed Poll of August 7, 1878.

A further article stressed that going to court in this instance was not in defiance of orders and regulations. The Army had frequently resorted to the law to defend its interests when these were threatened from outside. Even internally, orders and regulations made clear that a bandsman who refused to deliver up his instrument rendered himself liable to legal proceedings. This was not a personal quarrel between soldiers but an action undertaken in defence of a sacred Trust.

The High Council responds in a Supplement to *The War Cry*

Three hundred thousand copies of the four-page supplement prepared by the High Council were printed and distributed with *The War Cry* dated 9 February.[5] The supplement, in addition to providing news items and quoting favourable press comments, put the High Council's position in forthright terms:

The statements made by, or on behalf of, the General in the current *War Cry* consist partly of appeals to sentiment, partly of special pleadings and also, to a certain extent, of misrepresentations. In our opinion, based upon legal advice we have received, there was, and is, no legal necessity for the General to go to law, and least of all to ask, as he has done, that the courts should declare the Deed of 1904 to be null and void.

The statement made by the General in his message that 'doubts and fears as to the rightness of the Founder's plan' have arisen in the minds of the members of the High Council, is entirely misleading. 'The Founder's Plan' for the Army included the Supplementary Deed Poll of 1904; both that Deed and the High Council which it brought into being were planned by him. Doubt concerning it, and fear of the consequences of its operation against themselves can exist only in the mind of the General and his family – certainly not in the minds of the members of the High Council.

It is common knowledge that the General assisted in the framing of the Deed which he now attacks ... The General, moreover, by Deed signed by him holds his office as General subject to the Deed Poll of 1904.

It cannot be too clearly understood that the General is not proceeding at law in defence of The Salvation Army but in defence of his own personal position as Trustee and General, and that his action is not taken against outsiders but against The Salvation Army as represented by the Army's principal leaders throughout the world, now constitutionally assembled as the High Council.

It is of interest to note that the President of the High Council, Commissioner James Hay, received from the General's solicitors, under date 5th February, a letter in which it is stated that if the proposal to adjudicate the General unfit is not carried when the High Council next meets, this would result in the discontinuance of the legal proceedings and that this would leave both the General and the commissioners unfettered to consider any constitutional questions. This confirms the fact that the General's legal action rests on personal grounds and that 'the attack' on the 1904 Deed is unnecessary for the purpose of defending the Trust.

In writing to staff officers on 7 February, the Chief of the Staff had been even more pungent. Yes, William Booth did go to law, 'but the Founder never went to Law against his own people, nor did he resort to Law to nullify his own Deeds!' Perhaps 'it may have been necessary that the courts should be called upon to say whether the transfer of the Trust, from one General to another was in order – seeing that the General was unwilling to part with it – but that could have been done, as the General and his advisers must know, in a simple, non-contentious manner, in which both sides could have taken part without feelings of resentment'. He continued:

If the General's attack upon the 1904 Deed succeeds, then, at a stroke, we are back to the 1878 Deed, under which neither the present General nor any nominee of his could be removed from office for any cause whatever.

This leads us to the true explanation of the General's action. It is really taken in the hope that the High Council will be declared illegal, and that he, in spite of his continued inability to act because of physical weakness, shall be reinstated without there being any power to remove him or any successor whom he might choose to appoint. What a catastrophe all this is!

Commander Evangeline Booth had written to the Salvationists in the USA – a letter that was widely reported in the press: 'How heartbreaking to every true Salvationist is the spectacle presented by the unworthy actions of our General at the end of his long, and hitherto honoured, career. He has violated both the letter and the teaching of the New Testament by haling his brethren into the secular law courts. This he has done despite the entreaties – literally with tears – the pleadings, the prayers, of his wisest and ablest and most responsible officers from all over the world. By his attack upon the Supplementary Deed Poll of 1904, the General has aimed a cruel and heartless blow at the very foundations of the Army's constitution – a foundation laid under divine guidance by our beloved Founder himself.'

Also, in a personal note to Bramwell, signing herself 'your sister wounded and grieved', the Commander had written: 'Dear Bramwell, let me once again say to you that I do not think there is anyone who can protect you from the storm of obloquy which in my opinion is certain to overwhelm you and your family if you persist in your present course.'[6]

Mr Frank Smith joins the fray

No sooner had Salvationists absorbed the contents of the *The War Cry* of 9 February and its supplement before another bombshell exploded. In the *Sunday Express* of 10 February 1929 yet another former officer entered the fray. It was none other than ex-commissioner Frank Smith rising to the defence of his chief of old.

In his early years as an officer Frank Smith had lit up the Army sky. In 1884 William Booth had sent him to take command of the Army in the USA when Thomas Moore defected, and after three and a half years as William Booth's 'commissioner' there he had returned to London to work closely with the Founder on social projects, becoming in time the Army's first social commissioner.

Feeling that he could ameliorate social evil more effectively as a politician, Commissioner Frank Smith resigned as an officer in December 1890 and took up work with the Labour movement. In

1901 he returned to officership – as the divisional commander in Bolton holding the rank of brigadier – but three years later he reverted to the political field. He stood unsuccessfully for Parliament 12 times before finally being elected a member in the autumn of 1929 at the age of 76.

Under the banner head of 'The Plot to Oust General Booth' the lead in the *Sunday Express* began: 'In this the first "inside" story of the battle for the control of The Salvation Army, ex-Commissioner Frank Smith, formerly Commander in Chief in America, "spills the beans", as he vividly expresses it, in a series of sensational disclosures. He tears aside the veil that has hidden the High Council's conclaves and shows how "American aspirations, American envyings, and American intolerance of anything which has British control" is the real motive power behind all the plotting.'

'I say that the General's troubles began in America,' wrote Frank Smith. To him the root of the problem was 'this popular American sentiment allied with the personal ambitions of Commander Eva'.

The Commander, who herself had taken American citizenship, was sensitive to the undercurrent flowing whereby the reform movement was labelled as an American take-over. It had even been whispered that if she became General, International Headquarters would move to New York. However, the overt attack by Frank Smith on her and her American colleagues so incensed the Commander that it was only with great difficulty that she was restrained from taking out a writ against the paper.

The General releases a press statement

On Tuesday 12 February, the day before the High Council was to reassemble at Sunbury Court, wide publicity was given to a statement that the General issued through the Press Association to defend his recourse to the law. With the legal advice he had received, he wrote, he had virtually had no alternative, but he also made a new claim: he had gone to law not to attack the 1904 Deed but to defend it:

To infer that my action implies a desire on my part to destroy the 1904 Deed is entirely without foundation. In fact whether action under the Deed, now contemplated for the first time, compels an immediate decision by the courts as to its validity or not, it will and must be my first duty to enlist the best possible advice with a view to enquiring into its alleged faults and ambiguities, that the Deed may be altered and strengthened as found necessary. I consider it of vital importance to The Salvation Army that the essential features of the 1904 Deed remain a part of our constitution.

Not all the press accounts were favourable to the General and his family. On the same day, Tuesday 12 February, the *Daily Chronicle* reported that Commissioner Catherine Booth had written to the staff of the Women's Social Work – of which she was the leader – regretting that she could not be with them as much as usual because of the High Council. She had received in reply a letter signed by 152 members of the London staff saying: 'We think you ought to know that we are definitely and entirely with the Chief of the Staff and the High Council in these circumstances.'

Search for a compromise

While outwardly the battle for hearts and minds was proceeding, behind the scenes both sides had explored the possibility of reaching some form of accommodation. The family sought a compromise along the lines already outlined by the General. Bramwell Booth would remain in office, the stigma of him being declared 'unfit' would be erased from the record, a commission on constitutional reform would be appointed, and he would waive the power to appoint his own successor.

On its part, the High Council prepared draft papers by which the adjudication resolution would be rescinded if the General, after all, retired voluntarily and gave an undertaking that he would 'carry out and facilitate with the least possible delay or expense the transfer to any new General to be elected by the High Council of all property and rights vested in him in the capacity of General of The Salvation Army'.[7]

The gulf between the two sides was wide. As early as the weekend immediately following the court hearing, the Commander had written to Colonel W. F. Jenkins about the efforts being made by the family: 'Now that everything is against them, they no doubt see the wisdom of compromise. Catherine this weekend is trying to see as many of the High Council as she can – evidently preparing them for something. Or trying to. But the High Council are absolutely set in their views that no compromise can even be considered that means the loss of one step of the ground we have gained at such a tremendous cost.'[8]

Mrs Booth asked the recently retired Archbishop of Canterbury, Lord Randall Davidson, to arbitrate between the General and the Council, but Lord Davidson turned down the request on the grounds that he was disappointed that the General had gone to a secular court instead of composing his differences in the privacy of the council chamber. He believed that it would have been better for the General to retire as he himself had done. He also said that he had contended for some time past that the constitution of the Army needed remodelling.[9]

Twenty-four hours before the Council was due to re-assemble at Sunbury Court, the press reported that two former prime ministers of Britain had been invited by 'a representative, acting on behalf of the General' to mediate. Mr David Lloyd George had intimated that 'he did not think the moment an opportune one for his intervention'. Mr Ramsay MacDonald had 'expressed his willingness to put his best services at the disposal of both parties if they mutually agreed to approach him'.[10]

The chance of that happening was nil.

The stage was therefore set for the final showdown at Sunbury Court the next day.

To the eleventh hour Bramwell Booth hoped that a way might be found to avert the impending tragedy, and on the eve of the High Council coming together again he wrote yet a further appeal to his colleagues.

Chapter Seventeen

Day of Decision

FOR the members of the High Council it felt strange to be back at Sunbury Court again. Twenty-six days had passed since they last met there. When the President called the meeting to order at 10.30am on Wednesday 13 February 1929, all members were in their places except for Commissioner Wilfred Simpson who was ill. Mr William Jowitt KC with Mr Frederick Sneath as his attending solicitor were also present. So also were Mr Gavin Simonds KC and his solicitor Mr Percival Wright, who had represented the requisitioning commissioners at the court hearing. After devotions the President opened with the following statement:

> The only business on the agenda today is what is called the Adjudicating Resolution. We are dealing with this again today because, as you all know, Mr Justice Eve held that our former resolution was bad because the General's representatives were not present. They are now here, and will have the fullest opportunity of addressing you and calling any evidence they desire.
>
> 'I am sure we shall all give the fullest consideration to everything they and their witness have to say to us. And for the time being we must put out of our minds everything that has gone before and everything we have heard or read except what is now to be laid before us.

Mr Jowitt then rose and objected to the presence of Mr Gavin Simonds and Mr Percival Wright 'on the ground that they really represented defendants to High Court proceedings with which the High Council was not immediately concerned'. He argued that 'as the High Council was in the position of judges it did not require legal advice'. The minutes record that 'in order that General Bramwell Booth and his supporters might have no possible cause for complaint, Mr Gavin Simonds and Mr Percival Wright withdrew'.

When they had left, the President called on Commissioner David Lamb to move the resolution and for Commissioner Richard Wilson – in the absence of Commissioner Simpson – to second it.

Commissioner Lamb again moves the Resolution of Adjudication
'Pursuant to a notice given,' commenced Commissioner David Lamb, 'I now beg to move the resolution standing in my name and a copy of which is in your hands. It is this:

> That this meeting of the High Council of The Salvation Army doth hereby in exercise and performance of the powers and duties conferred upon the High Council by the provisions of the Supplementary Deed Poll of the 26 July 1904 under the hand and seal of William Booth, the Founder of The Salvation Army, adjudicate Bramwell Booth unfit for office as General of The Salvation Army and remove him therefrom, and doth hereby declare by way of record, that *this resolution is based upon the state of health of the said Bramwell Booth.*

'The task which falls to me at this time', continued Commissioner Lamb, 'is an easier and simpler one than that which fell to my lot on the 15th January last, when I submitted to you a resolution in terms somewhat similar to those embodied in the present resolution.

'What a trial to our patience and to our faith has this interval of waiting been – but at the same time, what an education … Since the issue now before us has been clarified to the extent that it is upon the state of the General's health we are to proceed, and that we are legally right in doing so under Subclause 3 of Clause 2 of the 1904 Deed, I can now speak with a little more definiteness and greater freedom.

'Mr Justice Eve says we have to rectify a mistake. Well, it is not difficult for us to start afresh: our whole training, our experience, our system all combine to make an entirely fresh start easy. Nor do we mind being corrected – even in public – and what would greatly distress some people, troubles us but little. If we start a song with the wrong tune, or pitch the right tune too high or too low – what do we do? We stop and start afresh! The possession of that quality is one of the reasons why we are here today as Leaders in The Salvation Army.

'Mr Justice Eve's wish that we should rectify the mistake "*at once*" has not proved to be quite so expeditious as we would have wished. Still, here we are today with Mr Jowitt representing the General. Listen carefully to what Mr Jowitt may say. He knows we did not want him, but nevertheless we are now glad to see him to represent the General, for the last thing in the world we want to do is to create the semblance of an idea that we should deny natural justice to the General.'

Commissioner Lamb then summarised the magnitude of the duties and responsibilities of the General of The Salvation Army, emphasising that only 'a strong and robust and very fit person' could discharge such a trust. 'We may be told by doctors and others that the General's health has improved: it may well be so … But my judgment tells me that the General is still a sick man – a very sick man. For that reason I ask you to accept my theory that some of the General's actions are evidence of his failing health. What then *is* the issue? It is this – is the General fit?

'He has not been at Headquarters since May of last year. You have the doctors' certificates of last month – you may have others today. You have the report of the officers of the High Council who saw the General a month ago. That concerns the past.

'But what is the position today? Instead of the General himself, we have a legal representative. If we are told that the General's health is so much improved that he is granting business interviews to certain people, and perhaps that he has even seen Mr Jowitt or Mr Sneath or both of them, we cannot ignore the fact that while he may be fit to see ex-officers he is not well enough to see his sister – the Commander – or consult with his Chief of the Staff. That is the present position.

'In the face of all this can you today have a moment's hesitation on the question? The General is unfit.

'That brings me to the question of the future ... Does anyone here honestly believe – having regard to the General's age, the state of his health last year, the state of his health this year, the state of his health today (as far as we know it) – does anyone honestly believe, I ask, that the General is now fit, or at any time in the near future is likely to be fit, to take hold of this great worldwide organisation and give it that vigorous leadership which it demands? ...

'I submit to you, then, with deep conviction but great regret, that General Bramwell Booth is unequal to the task, and I beg you accordingly to support the resolution which I have moved and which is now before you.'[1]

Commissioner Richard Wilson gave a brief seconding address after which the President asked if anyone else wished to speak. No one rose.

A further letter from the General to the High Council
Commissioner Catherine Booth was agitated by the fact that no one wished to speak and reminded the President that the General had written a further letter to the Council. The President then called on Mr William Jowitt KC to read the letter from the General dated 12 February 1929. It is a moving letter in that to the very last Bramwell Booth hoped that a settlement might be achieved:

> It cannot be denied that the Army is facing a period fraught with gravest dangers. It is borne upon me that you all and I should and must work together for the Army's sake, forgetting if need be all individual hopes and aims.
>
> Can we not find a way? I have prayed much. I have tried to meet you in the proposals I have already put before you. If you have any to make to me I will gladly give them consideration. Surely, after a lifetime of work for the same ends, we ought to find a better way than that of separation.

The doubts, newly raised, on the validity and interpretation of the Supplementary Deed fill me with anxiety. God is restoring my health, and I feel strongly I ought not to be denied the opportunity of reshaping the Deed, which it is evident will be necessary if it is to be that strength to the Army the Founder intended. I have more right than any one of you, both by experience and knowledge of the past, to act in the matter. If we work together all may yet be well, but if I am deprived of my place as your Leader the position is so complicated that loss and confusion must inevitably follow.

If the improvement in my health does not justify the doctors' expectations and meet the demands of my work I shall of course retire, but I do not think it unreasonable to expect that, when for the first time I require it, I shall have time to recover health when that recovery is confidently expected.

I have been sorely wounded, but I love you, and I think you know me well enough to know that the opinions expressed under the stress of the present circumstances will not alter my attitude towards you nor influence our future relationships.

Under God's good hand we shall yet live and work together to save the Army and to make known to the sinful and lost among the sons of men the saving grace of our Lord Jesus Christ.

I am His. You also are called in His name. Seek earnestly the guidance of the Holy Spirit, and let your decision today be according to that guidance. Yours affectionately,

Bramwell Booth

Mr Jowitt KC addresses the High Council

After reading the letter, Mr William Jowitt addressed the members of the High Council on behalf of the General in what all agreed was a brilliant and heart-moving speech.[2]

He immediately gained the attention of his hearers by assuring them that lawyers were as human and susceptible to heat and cold as everyone else, and won their sympathy by stating that 'no disaster will be greater than if a rift comes into the Army'.

He then addressed the legal position, saying that 'some feel the General has acted wrongly in challenging the 1904 Deed'. However, the General had been advised, he said, that by the law of England the 1878 Deed could not be altered, and his sole purpose in going to law was to test the legal interpretation of the constitution. It was not fair to condemn him for taking that step.

The key question was this: had the 1904 Deed *altered* the 1878 Deed? It could be argued, he said, that most important changes had in fact been made.[3]

Yet the Council today, he continued, was not concerned with the letter of the law but with its spirit. 'Your great organisation is in peril – what course is the right one to take?' He understood the reform motivation, and acknowledged that 'many believe that the time has come for a change in this democratic age'. Some might even believe the General to be a stumbling block to change.

Today, advised Mr Jowitt, members should disregard the fact that the General had gone to law – that was a point that had to be raised because of the assets involved. They should also disregard the General appointing his successor – that point had already been won. Instead they should ask on the evidence that they had: is the General fit?

Mr Jowitt appealed to the members of the Council not to dispense lightly with the great wisdom that the General could bring to the leadership of the Army at a difficult time. 'The General is progressing favourably,' he said, 'and has great recuperative powers. He may be able to take up his position again even in six months' time.'

Non-medical witnesses

Mr Jowitt then announced that he was first calling two non-medical witnesses to testify to the General's remarkable progress in health in recent weeks. With the protective shield the family had thrown up around the General the pool of potential witnesses on which he could call was small. Surprisingly, both witnesses chosen were ex-officers. Some councillors wondered whether Mr Jowitt had been adequately briefed as to the psychological disadvantage this would place them at when speaking to the Council.

The first was Mr George Pollard, the former commissioner and Chancellor of the Exchequer and now a business tycoon who had severed all connections with the Army. Because of his strictures against the Council, he was embarrassed to be there at all, and opened by saying that he had been 'pressed to come'. He spoke of his recent contact with the General and how he had found him 'anything but helpless as far as his mental powers are concerned'. He believed 'that with caution the General might before long be able to take up some of the duties of his high office'.

A number of members then addressed questions to him. Commissioner James Hay, later recalling Mr Pollard's participation, recorded that 'his testimony was weak'.[4]

The second witness was Mr Maurice Whitlow, the Salvationist journalist who had interviewed the General at his Hadley Wood home on 6 February. Describing the occasion later for the readers of the *Daily Express,* Mr Whitlow wrote: 'Mr Jowitt questioned me at once concerning the interview I had with the General, and asked me tell the High Council how I came to be the journalist who was thus privileged.'

Mr Whitlow told the Council of his past connections with the General when he served as an officer, and how he and two of his daughters were now local officers and a third was an officer who had offered for India. This information helped to break down barriers.

'I was then asked', continued Mr Whitlow in his newspaper account, 'to describe more fully what had happened at the interview.'

I told the Council that the General had referred to them collectively in terms of affection and esteem, specially mentioning Commissioner Hurren, and that I had prepared an interview of set questions but the General's alertness had rendered such preparation useless.

As soon as I had finished, Commander Evangeline Booth rose and said: 'You say the General spoke with affection of Commissioner Hurren. Did he say a word about me, his sister? Did he say anything about the times I have tried to see him, have begged with tears to be allowed to get a glimpse of him through an open door?'

'Well, Commander,' I replied, 'I was only 25 minutes with the General, and you have heard that we had a comprehensive talk. He did not mention your name.' Miss Booth murmured 'thank you' and sat down.[5]

Commissioner James Hay later recalled that the contribution by Mr Whitlow was 'of little import'.[6]

On that note the Council adjourned for lunch.

Medical witnesses

In the afternoon session Mr William Jowitt called on three doctors as witnesses. They were the General's own two physicians – Dr E. Wardlaw Milne and Dr John Weir – together with Sir Thomas (later Lord) Horder, whom the family had brought in to give an independent medical opinion. All three had examined the General two days before, and had signed a certificate dated 11 February 1929 which lay before the Council:

> We have this day examined General Booth and we are of the opinion that the General is recovering steadily from a very severe illness. We estimate the period necessary to complete recovery as already stated, that is six months from January 5th last.
>
> There is not, and never has been, any question of mental incapacity. This being so, the General is able to make decisions on matters submitted to him. He is advised medically not to engage in routine work for the period above-mentioned.

Each of the doctors spoke in turn – the testimony of Sir Thomas Horder being of especial interest. He was of the opinion that 'recovery would be a slow affair', and, recalled the President later, 'pleaded that, in having a great giant in our Founder, we may be erring to expect that every successor would be alike strenuous, long-lived and able to do all the heavy work as laid down and expected of our General'.[7] Doctors Milne and Weir remained optimistic that in time the General would regain his health.

The three doctors were subjected to intense cross-examination by the High Council. 'In answering one question,' reported a member later, 'Sir Thomas Horder answered all questions, and unmistakably confirmed the testimony of the High Council's deputation. When confronted with the duties of the General of The Salvation Army and asked if at 73 years of age and after a year's serious illness the General could return to work and meet the requirements of this task, his answer was "impossible", adding: "The General can return and do the work of a man of 73 years of age; he will be able to give decisions and counsel and advise those who must of necessity bear much of the burden."'[8]

'Several members of the High Council', remembers Commissioner James Hay, 'asked when the General might be so improved in health that he might get back to the office and so gradually get into the running? Sir Thomas Horder thought that in three months he might, and that in six months he could be doing even fuller duty. But it was quite in evidence, and even the Booths must have seen it, that even the united views of these medical gentlemen did not give any enthusiasm to the views they advocated. It was a poor case to plead at its best.'[9]

'Their testimony,' concluded Lieut-Commissioner William McIntyre, 'instead of changing the viewpoint of the High Council, confirmed them in their convictions.'[10]

As the three doctors left Sunbury Court, one was overheard exclaiming to his colleagues: 'They gave us a good peppering!'[11]

Mr William Jowitt sums up

When the doctors had left, the President invited any member who wished to speak to do so. 'Mr Jowitt', recalls Commissioner James Hay, 'had every expectation that some of our members would rise to remark on the doctors' views or the views of other witnesses, but although I asked several times anyone wishing to say anything before we heard Mr Jowitt, none got up. He remarked to me: "This is strange. They are such controlled men, so calm, so sympathetic, and yet men of evidently strong views."'[12]

Mr William Jowitt then rose and began his summing up. He reminded the members of the High Council that they were there 'on one ground and one ground only – unfitness'. It was not a matter of the General's age, but whether he was fit at 73 to undertake his responsibilities. He spoke of the tremendous contribution that Bramwell Booth had made to the creation and organisation of the Army – and said this was 'the secret of its success'. While not wanting to jeopardise the great work of the Army, he appealed to their loyalty and to their sense of fairness. He referred to the hopeful views of the doctors, especially Sir Thomas Horder's comment that the General might be able to undertake light duties within three months. He thought the General would be prepared to review the matter of retirement at that point if his health was not making satisfactory progress. The General had asked to be given more time to recover. Mr Jowitt appealed to the Council to grant their leader that request, but closed his case by strongly advocating constitutional change.

'At the close of Mr Jowitt's address,' recalls the President, 'I asked the members to stand while I thanked him and, through him, the witnesses for their evidence – all of which would be fully weighed and determined upon. I then said that when the legal gentlemen had retired we would again take our seats as the Army's High Council and would arrive at our decision. We bowed to them and they retired.'[13]

Further discussion on the Resolution of Adjudication

When the doors had closed and the High Council was on its own again, the President reminded members of the Resolution of Adjudication before them, and gave further opportunity to anyone wishing to speak for or against the motion.

Twelve members spoke – some speaking for the first time to the Council.

Commissioner Catherine Booth spoke briefly. On entering the council chamber that morning, members had found at their places a printed copy of the passionate speech she had previously made in that room together with a covering note. She read the note out aloud:

'Most of you will, I think, understand why I could not give my speech to the High Council over again. When I spoke to you my words failed to move you. I send them to you because there may be a slender hope that reflecting on them might influence you to reconsider your decision prayerfully, independently, as before the Lord.'

Commander Evangeline Booth and Commissioner Samuel Brengle spoke, but it was Commissioner Samuel Hurren who electrified the proceedings by his intervention. Perhaps overcome because of his close attachment to the General through the years, he called for a last-minute reprieve. Should not the Council, he pleaded, consider Mr Jowitt's words that the General might be prepared to review the matter of his retirement after three months, and even at this late stage seek to arrive at a definite agreement with him along those lines?[14]

It fell to another of the requisitioning commissioners, Commissioner Henry Mapp, to point out the impracticalities of the suggestion, however well meant. The High Council could hardly continue in being for three months, the cost of reassembling would be great, and any benefit gained from postponement might be small. The Army wanted and needed a decision now.

Commissioner Mapp had judged the mood of the assembly accurately, and despite a plea from Commissioner Catherine Booth for half an hour's adjournment in order that there might be an informal seeking for mutual agreement, Commissioner Hurren's proposal was not pursued.

The second vote on the Resolution of Adjudication

When the last of the speakers had concluded, the President read the Resolution of Adjudication yet again and called on the vote to be taken. 'You must as far as possible', he reiterated, 'set aside all connected with the previous adjudication and vote as your conscience directs in the light of the evidence that has just been put before you.'

Starting at 6pm the members one by one moved forward to record their votes as their names were called. With Lieut-Commissioner William Haines having been promoted to Glory and

Commissioner Wilfred Simpson being sick, there were only 61 members present at this second vote.

When the ballots had been counted, the President announced the result. Of the 61 members present, 52 had voted for General Bramwell Booth to be removed from office, five had voted against, and four had abstained.

The five voting against the resolution were the three members of the Bramwell Booth family – Mrs Booth, Commissioner Catherine Booth and Colonel Mary Booth – together with Commissioner Mrs Lucy Booth-Hellberg and Commissioner Allister Smith.

The four who abstained were Commissioner John Cunningham, Commissioner Theodore Kitching, Commissioner John Laurie, together with Commissioner Albin Peyron. The three International Headquarters commissioners had withdrawn their support for the General when he went to law, but could not bring themselves to actually vote for his deposition. Commissioner Peyron in the previous vote had voted against the General. This time he abstained.

With everyone sensing the emotion of the moment, the President made the formal announcement that General Bramwell Booth had been declared unfit for office on the ground of his health and had been removed therefrom. Once again – and this time definitely – The Salvation Army had no General.

A letter was immediately sent to Bramwell Booth by special messenger informing him of the result of the ballot. As soon as the meeting ended Mrs Booth returned to Hadley Wood to be with him, and Commissioner Mrs Lucy Booth-Hellberg also withdrew.

The time was now 7pm and the President announced that the Council stood adjourned, but would meet again at 8.15pm to elect a new General. However legally definite the adjudication this time, the Council was not going to be caught talking again.

Second nominations for General

Compared with the time it takes a modern High Council to elect a new General, the 1929 High Council moved with great despatch. When the Council met at 8.15pm nomination papers were immediately distributed. This process once again resulted in five nominations being made. Commander Evangeline Booth, Commissioner Catherine Booth and Commissioner Edward Higgins were nominated for the second time. Commissioner Samuel Hurren and Commissioner Henry Mapp were new nominees.

Those who had become aware that following the first nomination process on 'Black Friday' the Commander in a letter to the President had withdrawn her candidature for the Generalship wondered how she would respond to being nominated for a second time. In the intervening weeks a number had privately encouraged her to make herself available if nominated again. 'Amid the confusion of uncertainty,' writes her biographer, 'Evangeline Booth was assured by her friends that she could not withhold from the High Council an opportunity of having her as General if the Spirit so moved them.'[15] In this spirit she accepted nomination again, as did the Chief of the Staff. The other three nominees declined. The President then invited the two candidates to address the Council.

The Commander speaks

The Commander spoke first, and soon gripped the Council with her dramatic eloquence. She spoke of the bondage in which the Army was held and the strong yearning there was for freedom from autocracy and for the right of speech and the right of conscience. She appealed to her parents' vision for the Army and spoke of her own hopes for the future. She emphasised her international credentials and nailed the rumours about International Headquarters being moved to New York as 'folly'. 'International Headquarters', she said, 'will always be in London – where the Army began.'

On the matter of reform she said that her proposals were 'not very drastic' and that 'the details can be left to a council', but that it was vital to do *something* – and to 'do the right thing'. She continued: 'All future Generals must be elected for a set term of years, and no one 70 years old should be elected.' She reiterated that constitutional changes should be adopted with the agreement of 'two thirds of the commissioners *with* the General' or 'three fourths of the commissioners *without* the General'.

The Commander was once more indicating that on the matter of constitutional reform she would be prepared, if elected General, to be outvoted by the commissioners. She was saying in effect that the Annual Conference of the 1875 Deed would be back in the shape and form of the commissioners – at least for decisions on the constitution.

About the General's authority she said: 'The General cannot be a supreme being. All down the march of history no man has proved himself to be trusted with power without control. We must have restrictions.'

In closing she painted a powerful word-picture as she described the toil and sacrifice and even martyrdom of Salvationists as being centred on the cross. 'On the cross we hang all our hopes. This organisation is God's, and in his name we are going on and will go on to even greater things. The cross will triumph. None shall be weary. Our people shall have the victory through our Lord and Saviour Jesus Christ. The Founder when he was going to have the operation on his eyes said: "I cannot see the sun set, but I shall see it rise!" And so it will be for his Army.'

The Chief of the Staff speaks

The President then called on Commissioner Edward Higgins to speak. He began by saying: 'I think I should say to you frankly that I shall not be disappointed if I am not elected General. My plans have been made for over a year now, and were made known to the General at that time, by which I fully intended to retire from active service on the attainment of my 65th year.

'If I were left to consider my own feelings,' he continued, 'and were to follow the inclinations of my heart and mind, I should still plead that these plans be allowed to mature. But it has been expressed to me by one and another in this room that it would be hardly "playing the game" if I were to shrink from bearing some of the burdens which present conditions impose on Salvation Army leaders.

'I have therefore yielded to those views to the extent that I have not asked that my name should be removed from the list of nominees, and wish now to say that, after much prayer and the seeking of guidance, I am willing to do my best for you all and for the Army, if it is clear by the voting that will presently follow that the bulk of the Council desires me for the post.

'But I should say that whilst the Deed Poll requires a two-thirds majority to elect a General, I shall not allow my name to go to any further ballot after it has been revealed by voting that a majority, *however small,* desires someone else. I could not, of course, transfer votes to anyone, but I must then be reckoned out of the running.'[16]

The Chief of the Staff then addressed the matter of constitutional reform. He wanted the Army to remain an 'army' and hoped that wisdom would prevail so that 'we will not find democracy around our necks'. He would appoint a commission to look into the question of the successorship, term of years and age limit for the General. On the matter of the trusteeship, he felt that 'all temporalities should be held by the General', but that every possible avenue for resolving the problem of trusteeship should be explored, and that legislation might be necessary.

The Chief discussed 'one-man control'. He referred to the concept of 'the General in Council'. This was a concept that Commissioner David Lamb had been canvassing for some time whereby the General would be the 'chairman' of a small governing council. Commissioner Higgins declared plainly that he was not prepared to serve as General on those terms, but said that he had no objection to an Advisory Council to the General which would *advise* the General on top promotions and appointments together with any major changes in orders and regulations.

The vote for a new General
Commissioner Samuel Brengle felt that the speeches influenced the voting decisively. As he wrote the next day to Colonel W. F. Jenkins: 'The councillors compared the Commander's speech with the speech by Commissioner Higgins and many of them, I think, there

and then finally decided for Higgins. One most prominent commissioner told me that he was undecided until he heard the two speeches. The Commander spoke for 53 minutes, Higgins for 25. She was flowery and tried to captivate by eloquence and pathos. He was plain, specific, utterly frank and manly.'[17]

The Commander had already sensed the way the wind was blowing, and that it was not in her direction. As early as a month before the vote she had commented to her chief secretary: 'I beg of you, don't feel badly if I am not the General. You will see that Higgins will be the General, but as long as I am not too much humiliated, this is all right – the Lord will take care of me and I can come back to you all in America and we shall go ahead as never before in our lives.' She felt that the Council would choose the Chief of the Staff because his more moderate views on reform would appeal to 'both sides'.[18]

It had already been agreed that the vote to elect a new General would be in secret with ballot papers not being signed. As mentioned by the Chief of the Staff in his speech, a two-thirds majority was needed to elect a General, as contrasted with a three-fourths majority to remove a General from office.

The vote began at 11.30pm and one by one the 59 members present came forward to record their vote. The President announced the result well after midnight.

Commissioner Edward Higgins   42 votes
Commander Evangeline Booth   17 votes

That a decision had been reached in the first ballot came as a surprise to the Council. The new General was greeted with warm and yet restrained applause for members were sensitive to how the Commander might be feeling. The scene was later described to the special correspondent of the *Daily Telegraph* waiting by the gate. 'The new General, his white hair ruffled, his ruddy face flowing in the light of the electric lamps, and his blue coat undone, disclosing his red guernsey, rose to his feet and, with a tremor in his voice, humbly thanked his fellow officers for 'the position of high trust' to which they had elected him.'[19]

Commented a member of the High Council to the same reporter that evening: 'I think it will be a popular choice throughout the Army. It is a little surprising that the majority in favour of Commissioner Higgins was so large. Everyone thought that the voting would have been more even.'[20]

The Council closes

The President called on the new General to sign the Deed of Acceptance of Office. When the Deed was read, no member missed the significance of the fact that General Edward Higgins was accepting office subject to the terms of both the 1878 and the 1904 Deeds of Constitution.

After the singing of a song the President ended the High Council by praying. With the election of the new General the High Council stood *ipso facto* dissolved. It had no more purpose, power or authority. The 1929 High Council had ceased to exist.

The President announced that the General wished to meet with them all later that Thursday morning at 10.30. As the Council broke up, members moved forward to clasp the hand of their new leader and to wish him well. They then made their way out of the council chamber. By this time it was nearly 1 o'clock in the morning.

Commissioner Catherine Booth and Colonel Mary Booth left together. When asked for a comment by a press reporter at the gate, Commissioner Catherine responded with simple pathos:

'What can I say? General Booth has gone.'[21]

Chapter Eighteen

An Unexpected Sequel

'BOOTH'S Army led by a Higgins will take some getting used to,' observed the charlady to her companion when the news came over the radio early the next morning, but human nature has a way of adjusting quickly to new realities.

It began with the leaders. When they reassembled later on that Thursday morning, 14 February 1929, they met not as members of the High Council but as the Army's most senior leaders meeting with their new spiritual and executive head. As General and Mrs Higgins entered the room they were greeted with overwhelming applause.

The General took immediate charge. His inspired choice of Scripture and first words to his leaders would be long remembered. He took his text from Hebrews: 'Let us hold fast the profession of our faith without wavering; for he is faithful that promised; and let us consider one another to provoke unto love and to good works.'[1] At this time of change, he said, let us hold fast to those things that are not going to change – 'the profession of our faith'. As he urged his leaders 'to spur one another on to love and good deeds', they sensed that their relationships were already beginning to heal.

In the speeches by members which followed, Commander Evangeline Booth was particularly impressive and gracious in her words. In her speaking she read out the letter she had written to Commissioner James Hay on 18 January in which she had withdrawn her candidature for the Generalship, and revealed that among those who had sought to persuade her to change her mind was none other than Mrs Higgins. 'I therefore left the matter in the hands of God,' she said. More than one commented afterwards that, if she had given that speech the night before, the result of the election might have been different.

The press

After the meeting General Higgins met with the press. When leaving Sunbury Court in the early hours of the morning he had responded briefly to questions from journalists and had said:

> On the question of reform I can say little at the moment. We have not had time to consider that. I was elected General without any conditions except those imposed by the 1878 and 1904 Deeds.
>
> I hope there will not be any further legal difficulties. Certainly it will be my duty to protect the trust imposed upon me. If the Deed of 1904 is attacked, I must defend it. It will not be a fight between a new General and a deposed General; it would be a fight on a narrow issue.
>
> I have no idea that such a fight is coming. I do not know if General Booth will accept the decision of the Council. But if such a fight were to come, the work of the Army will go on.
>
> General Booth will retain his title, but after his name 'Retired' will be written. We do not want to take away any of the honours that belong to him. There is no ill feeling at all. Please stress that. We have nothing but love and affection for him.[2]

General Higgins was now able to expand on those remarks and to update the press on the current position:

> On the question of reform, it is my intention to appoint two commissions, one to investigate the question of future Generals, and the other to consider the all-important question of trusteeship. The first question can probably be decided without much difficulty. The second will involve many complications, including going to Parliament for an amended Deed Poll.
>
> One-man control of the Army, so far as the funds are concerned, will definitely disappear. I am in sole control of the spiritual work with many advisers around me. But it has been decided that the business side of the Army shall no longer be vested in one man.
>
> It will be necessary for me at some time to meet General Bramwell Booth for the transference of the trusteeship. There is no hurry for that

and I do not know when the meeting will be. Should General Booth be unwilling to transfer the trusteeship it will inevitably become a legal question. That is the last thing we wish, but even if that happened the work of the Army could be carried on because I, as the Chief of the Staff, hold the power of attorney – that is, banking powers which give me control of the funds.[3]

Editorial comment in the press unanimously applauded the step towards reform that had been taken. Mr Percival Wright, the tireless lawyer for the requisitioning commissioners, produced for general distribution a booklet with '101 Extracts from Newspapers'. Typical of such extracts was the comment made by Dr S. M. Berry, the Chairman of the Congregational Union of England and Wales, in the *Nottingham Journal*:

> In the early days there may have been need for the organisation to be coloured with the spirit of autocracy, but those days have long since passed. Pioneers in carrying the gospel, with all its healing influences, cannot allow their organisation to be considered as an anachronism. It would not only prove a hindrance to their work, but would also affect the confidence of the public. It is only by courage in pursuing the path of reform that they can serve the cause to which they have given their lives.

The Salvationist family

British Salvationists went out of their way to make their new General feel welcome and wanted. They had anxiously followed events in the media and in *The War Cry*. A further special Supplement to *The War Cry* for 16 February 1929 giving a full update had been prepared by the editorial staff and distribution had begun. However, when General Higgins saw a copy he felt that it would open wounds that were already beginning to heal and had the distribution stopped. Not all Salvationists therefore received the supplement and had to rely on the press for their information – but that did not hold them back.

Police were needed to deal with the crowds massed in front of International Headquarters when General and Mrs Higgins arrived there for the first time. As the General sprang out of his car he was immediately surrounded by a thousand cheering and saluting friends. 'You must all be as good as you can,' he said to them with his characteristic warm smile. 'You must all work as hard as you can. You must keep the flag flying as high as you can. Do good to all, and let mercy and justice triumph throughout the world.'[4]

These scenes were surpassed when on Monday 18 February the new General was welcomed in the Clapton Congress Hall. The occasion was also 'The Bidding of Godspeed to the High Council Delegates'. The correspondent of *The Manchester Guardian* described it as 'one of the most memorable meetings in the history of The Salvation Army'. In opening the meeting Commissioner Samuel Hurren said: 'We meet as an enfranchised Army. I see the possibility of the youngest boy or girl in this great meeting or in the village corps, however obscure in name, birth or breeding, becoming the General of The Salvation Army. We greet our new General not as a pontiff but as a big brother.'

Many commented that joy had returned to the Army – and so had largeness of heart. The correspondent, noting that members of Bramwell Booth's family were present, commented that 'they would be able to report to their father that every mention of his name was greeted with enthusiasm, and that the speakers spoke of him with great affection, admiration and tenderness'. Commander Evangeline Booth said that 'no sister ever loved a brother more than I love him'.

With sensitivity, grace and easy banter the Commander sparkled throughout the evening, and Mrs Higgins saluted her as 'the greatest woman leader the Army has ever known'.

When General Higgins rose to speak he was greeted with a thundering ovation. In describing to the congregation the events that had taken place, he returned to the nautical imagery of which he was so fond:

The changing of a Captain is a serious matter, especially when the change is made in a storm and amidst rocks and dangers which are a constant menace to the safety of the ship. In this storm it was essential to have a Captain who could be on the bridge, alert and alive to every change of current, and able to perceive the slightest indication of hidden rocks. And so, with the deepest regret and with the tenderest remembrances of the incalculable service rendered, it was decided to relieve the Captain of responsibility which health and age had made too great for him. As a result of that action I have been entrusted by my comrades with the task of leadership.[5]

In the days following the meeting in Clapton the members of the High Council began what for many were long sea-journeys back to their commands, but not without the Scottish members – all 15 of them – first being hosted for lunch at the House of Commons by their kinsman Mr Ramsay MacDonald. Some members of the High Council had been away for three months or more.

From all over the world messages of welcome and good wishes for the new General kept pouring in. Salvationists had respected and loved General Bramwell Booth, but Edward Higgins was no stranger to them and the overwhelming majority of them gladly welcomed him as their General. Though not all. Some Salvationists in Britain disagreed strongly with what had happened and wrote to General and Mrs Booth to express their sorrow and even anger. Other Salvationists found themselves torn in their thinking – but help was at hand.

On 8 March 1929, just three weeks after the close of the High Council, a book was published that more than anything else was to shape the thinking of Salvationists about the events they had watched from afar. It was *The Clash of the Cymbals* by F. A. Mackenzie. Its subtitle was 'The Secret History of the Revolt in The Salvation Army'. The book strongly supported the reformers and the calling of the High Council. With its hot topicality it became an instant bestseller among the public and Salvationists alike, with even Salvationist Publishing and Supplies Ltd promoting its sale. The book reassured the Salvationist family that what had taken place had been necessary.

The man in the street

If informed opinion was in favour of reform and accepted that what had happened was perhaps needful to achieve it, the British man in the street remained stubbornly loyal to Bramwell Booth. A monumental opinion poll on the issue was conducted within two weeks of the High Council closing when tens of thousands of Salvationists went 'door to door' to collect for the annual Self-Denial Appeal. When they did they met with a hostile reception, with refusals to give frequently being accompanied by the comment: 'Not after what you did to old General Booth.'

The financial result of the appeal was down by a third and did not fully recover until many years later. The reason for the slow return to the pre-1929 levels of support was not due to continued hostility by members of the public. Theirs had been a spontaneous gut reaction, and their traditional warmth towards the Army soon returned. It was more due to the fact that Salvationists had been put off from collecting door-to-door by the response they had encountered and the number of collectors was therefore greatly reduced. This factor coupled with the economic depression of the time 'meant almost superhuman tasks of collecting for officers,' recalled General Albert Orsborn later in his autobiography. 'Even now, nearly 30 years after our crisis, "Self-Denial" is much more an officers' battle than it should be.'[6]

Some prophets of doom predicted that the parting of the ways with the Booths would mark the beginning of the end of the Army. In this they were wrong. The Army is larger today than it has ever been. However, for whatever cause, and there are undoubtedly many, the number of Salvation Army soldiers in Britain did in fact peak in 1929.

The Commander

Before returning to the USA, the Commander made one more attempt to see her brother 'if only that we might kiss each other goodbye and pray together'. Mrs Booth, however, responded by quoting the doctors to whom she had referred the request: 'he must not be subjected to anything of an agitating nature'.[7]

288

When the Commander left from Waterloo Station on her way to the liner that would take her across the Atlantic, many hundreds of Salvationists had once more gathered to wave to her. On her arrival in New York she was greeted in the press and by Salvationists as a returning heroine.

'The Commander has been the Joan of Arc in the reform movement,' said Lieut-Commissioner Richard Holz in the 'welcome home meeting' for the American delegation, 'and the achievements and accomplishments of the High Council, that hold so much of encouragement for the present and hope for the future, are in large measure due to her untiring labours and her skilful and inspiring leadership.'[8]

However, the strain of the weeks in London had taken its toll. 'I feel like a soldier who has been in the front line of battle who has come home with many, many wounds,' she responded in the welcome meeting. 'I don't think I shall ever again be quite the same, for there are some sore places that I fear will never heal.' Evangeline was as much a highly-strung Booth as her brother, and she too, as her biographer records, 'had to face the aftermath of prolonged nervous strain'.[9] To Commissioner Henry Mapp she wrote privately: 'The nine weeks in London follow me like a black nightmare, casting a dark shadow on my path, colouring everything I have to do.'[10]

American Salvationists had taken it for granted that the Commander would return home wearing the gold braid of a General, but their disappointment was assuaged by their joy over the fact that she would remain their leader. They were also well disposed towards General Higgins. Not only was he the choice of the High Council, but most knew him from his visits to the USA as Chief of the Staff, and many could remember him from the time when for nine years he was second-in-command of the Army in America.

In recognition of her services, General Higgins promoted Evangeline Booth to Commander-in-Chief and also brought the three USA territorial commanders who were lieut-commissioners – Richard Holz, William McIntyre and John McMillan – to full rank.

The 'storm pilot' as the 'captain'

General Edward Higgins chose Commissioner Henry Mapp to be his Chief of the Staff and threw himself into the daunting task that had become his. Within weeks he and Mrs Higgins began their international campaigns. Yet if he ever needed to earn his title of 'storm pilot' it was during the next two years, for the sequel to the High Council was to prove as extraordinary as the lead-up to it had been.

General Higgins knew that those who had hoped that the High Council would usher in great constitutional reforms were saying that little if anything had been accomplished. The Deeds of 1878 and 1904 stood unchanged. One autocrat had simply been replaced by another. Some wondered out loud whether the great upheaval had been for nothing. Was there to be no gain for all the pain?

In fact the High Council had opened a door to reform that no man could now shut. The new General stood committed to the introduction of change. A symbolic sign of the new era was that General Higgins did not immediately nominate his successor by means of a 'sealed envelope', which constitutionally and according to William Booth was his 'first duty'. The precedent of Generals being *elected* had already been established, and were General Higgins to suffer an untimely death the very absence of a 'sealed envelope' would automatically trigger the calling of the High Council to elect his successor.

Another symbolic sign of change was that General Higgins forthwith discontinued the system whereby the General's allowance was paid from a private trust. Instead he received his allowance from Salvation Army funds like all other officers.

The High Council itself was not empowered to deal with constitutional change, but if General Higgins had wished to he could have immediately called a Conference of Commissioners and Territorial Commanders before the members departed for home. Mr Percival Wright had even arranged for top constitutional lawyers to stand by.

General Higgins, though, rightly judged the facts and the mood. The detailed groundwork for reform had first to be laid, and the leaders were now anxious to return home to get on with their tasks. So instead of calling a conference the General appointed the two commissions he had already announced – one to deal with the position of future Generals and the other with the matter of trusteeship – and these quickly got under way.

The sword of Damocles

The work of the two reform commissions, however, ground to a halt within a few weeks.

It became clear that General Bramwell Booth (Retired) was not prepared to accept the new reality. To what degree he was influenced by his family in this will always remain a matter of conjecture, but through his legal representatives Bramwell Booth confirmed that he intended to pursue his court action to have the 1904 Deed declared invalid. 'He cherished the hope that his right to appoint his successor would be upheld by the courts, and thus the battle for the constitution might yet be won,' records Catherine Bramwell-Booth in her biography of her father.[11] That was an understatement. If the 1904 Deed was declared invalid, Bramwell Booth would not only retain the right to appoint his successor, but would also be reinstated as General.

The Army also found itself in another extraordinary legal position. General Higgins had been elected General of The Salvation Army, but the sole trustee of its funds and properties was still Bramwell Booth. It will be recalled that when William Booth died he had in his will appointed his successor as his executor, and that 'the effect was to vest the legal title of Army property in the next General without the necessity for transfers of deeds or orders of court'.[12] The administrative control and the legal title had thus come together at the same time in the same person.

Bramwell Booth, however, was still alive, and it was therefore necessary for him personally to sign over the trusteeship to his successor. This he was unwilling to do while the trial about the legal validity of the 1904 Deed remained pending. General Higgins, as he had indicated to the press, could still operate under the power of attorney that Bramwell Booth had granted him as Chief of the Staff (and which Bramwell Booth had not cancelled). These powers, however, were limited by the provisions of the Trustee Act 1925. The system whereby Bramwell Booth signed key financial and property documents therefore had to be kept in place even after he had been removed from office.

In these circumstances General Higgins considered it of little use to continue discussions about constitutional change. 'Until the court action has been disposed of one way or the other,' reported Mr Percival Wright to Mr George W. Wickersham in the USA, 'it is very difficult to press General Higgins to go on with the reforms, as he is at present in a most awkward position, for if the 1904 Deed should be declared void, he has not been properly elected and is not General.'[13] Reform would have to wait until the sword of Damocles was removed.

In the meantime General Higgins could only press Bramwell Booth 'to bring his action on for judgment as quickly as possible'.[14]

General Bramwell Booth (Retired)

The will to fight on nourished the energies of Bramwell Booth, but the blow of being removed from office affected his health. 'After the second decision of the High Council had been made known to him, Bramwell Booth did not again speak of recovery,' wrote his daughter. 'He was touched by the tokens of love he received, such as a bowl of bulbs from The Nest – a Salvation Army home for girls. An Army captain sent him her wedding flowers, a girl from the London streets brought roses. On his 73rd birthday (9 March 1929) he was shown the piles of letters and telegrams – some he read and with a smile said: "There are some then who still love me." However, his isolation from the Army and its affairs ate into his very soul.'[15]

The Salvation Army had never had a deposed General before, and getting the protocols right did not always prove easy. As General, Bramwell Booth had received his weekly allowance from the Wisely Trust, but an unfortunate delay of several weeks ensued while the trustees of that trust sought reassurance that the provision that the trust document permitted them to make for a retired General extended to a deposed one as well.

Bramwell Booth continued to be remembered by Salvationists with the deepest affection. *The War Cry* celebrated his 73rd birthday with a major feature, proclaiming that 'the Army, and indeed the world at large, will never forget his achievements'. However, when the centenary of the birth of William Booth on 29 April 1929 approached, Bramwell Booth was disappointed that he was not asked to contribute a message to *The War Cry*. He sent his message to *The Times* instead.

It was also noticed that no member of the Booth family spoke at the great centenary celebrations in the Royal Albert Hall. General Higgins had in fact invited Commissioner Catherine Booth to speak. He had asked that there be no reference to controversial matters, but had expressed the hope that she would refer to her father. She had written back, declining the invitation, on the grounds that much that she would wish to say might be wrongly interpreted and that it was impossible for her to speak in his presence about her father. So she sat very visibly on the platform but did not speak.[16]

While the centenary celebrations took place in the Royal Albert Hall, General Bramwell Booth in his sickroom at Hadley Wood dedicated his youngest grandchild to God under the Army flag. He was the son of Staff-Captain and Mrs Wycliffe and Renée Booth and would one day become an officer whose distinguished service culminated in his appointment as territorial commander for Germany. He was named Bramwell Booth.

On the same day – 29 April 1929 – the Prime Minister, Mr Stanley Baldwin, informed General Booth that the King had appointed him a member of the Order of the Companions of Honour. Said the General: 'It is kind of the King. It will be good for the Army.'

In May 1929 Bramwell Booth's health condition again began to give cause for concern, and in June deteriorated sharply. On 16 June 1929 – four months after he had lost office – he was promoted to Glory.

Records General Frederick Coutts in the Army's official history:

Not only the Army, but the whole world, hastened to honour him in death as in life. The King and Queen sent a message of 'sincere sympathy' to Mrs Bramwell Booth. General and Mrs Higgins cancelled their congress campaigns in Scandinavia to remain in London for the last tributes to the second General.

The arrangements which General Bramwell had made for the funeral of the Founder 17 years earlier were followed almost to the letter for his own. He lay in state for two days in the Clapton Congress Hall. The Royal Albert Hall was more than filled for the funeral service on the Sunday evening [conducted by General Edward Higgins]. On the Monday the route taken for William Booth's funeral from International Headquarters to Abney Park was followed for his eldest son. Three and a half thousand uniformed Salvationists were in the procession and once again the life of the city of London was halted as the coffin passed the Mansion House along Bishopsgate.[17]

New executors

The reading of General Bramwell Booth's will caused shockwaves to reverberate. As his father had done, Bramwell Booth had in his will dated 15 August 1913 appointed his successor as his executor to ensure a smooth handover of funds and properties. However, on 28 March 1929 – three months before his death – he had added a brief codicil vesting the trust property, not in his successor, but in a body of three executors consisting of Mrs Booth, Commissioner Catherine Booth and Mr Frederick Sneath, his lawyer.

An already vexing and complicated position was thus made even more vexing and complicated. General Higgins had administrative control of the Army, but the trustee of the Army's assets was no longer Bramwell Booth but a trio of joint trustees – his widow, his daughter and his attorney.

'The effect of that substitution is clear,' declared *The War Cry*. 'It compels General Higgins to go to these three executors for the necessary legal transfer of Army property. Whether they will give the transfer without further difficulty, or whether they will insist upon the courts being referred to, is not yet clear. The executors are obtaining advice upon their position.'[18]

Until the matter could be resolved General Higgins had no option but to go to the three trustees whenever he needed authorisations regarding funds and properties for the administration of the Army. The necessary signatures were usually given without delay, but in one instance, when the General wished to initiate a particular major change of international appointments, the trustees objected on the grounds that they did not consider the changes necessary and the consequent expenditure justified. They were reminded that such judgments were the General's to make.

The sword of Damocles – the General takes action

A key issue in the new situation was whether the three trustees would continue the preparation for a trial on the legal validity of the 1904 Deed. If the court were to declare the deed legally invalid the 'sealed envelope' and its content would come back into play again.

'General Booth Case to Go On' announced the *Daily Mail* on 4 July 1929. 'General Higgins had hoped', wrote Mr William Frost to the Treasury Solicitor on 8 August 1929, 'that with the death of the late General Bramwell Booth the litigation would have died too.'[19] It had not. The three trustees were unwilling to withdraw the action. The sword still hung threateningly.

The trustees explored their options. At one point they felt that at the very least 'the person named in the envelope should have the opportunity before the funds were transferred of deciding whether to contest his or her right of succession'.[20] At another time they explored making the transfer of assets conditional on them receiving a clear commitment from the General that he would not seek to change the 1878 constitution. Summer of 1929 dragged into autumn with no movement on their part.

In the end the three trustees decided to ask for direction from the Attorney General – the chief legal adviser to the government. By this time this was none other than Sir William Jowitt himself. Because of his previous involvement in the case he asked his 'number two', the Solicitor General, Sir J. B. Melville KC, to deal with the matter on his behalf. As part of the enquiry by the government's legal team the Solicitor General met with Commissioner Catherine Booth.

The guidance the three trustees received from the Solicitor General 'was against further litigation about the validity of the 1904 Deed and in favour of a transfer of the trust property to General Higgins'.[21]

Yet the trustees were still unwilling to make the transfer, as an official statement from International Headquarters on 29 October 1929 made clear. Their ground was that the letter from the Solicitor General was only an 'opinion' and did not have the force of an order of the court, which would 'relieve them of any personal responsibility'. Continued the statement: 'This was, of course, just as well known to them when they sought the opinion as after they had obtained it, and it is difficult to see why, if they had no intention of acting upon the Solicitor General's opinion when expressed, they occasioned the expense and loss of time in obtaining it.'

The bulletin ended with an announcement:

> The opinion of counsel we have consulted says: 'It is clear that nothing but an order of the court will induce the executors to place the property and funds of The Salvation Army under the control of General Higgins, and it is imperative that such an order should now be applied for.' General Higgins, therefore, with the greatest reluctance and sorrow, has been compelled to authorise the issuing of the necessary writ.

General Higgins speaks out

Allegations that the Booth family was being victimised by the new administration had crept into the press, and General Higgins took the opportunity afforded by the announcement about the legal action to respond to them. In the *Daily News* of 30 October 1929, under the heading 'General Higgins Speaks Out At Last', he gave detailed answers to 14 specific allegations.

The words 'at last' in the newspaper heading were on target. During recent months General Higgins had been under increasing pressure from the remaining supporters of the Booth family.

In July 1929 ex-Commissioner Frank Smith had published a book in support of his former leader entitled *The Betrayal of Bramwell Booth*. Its subtitle was indicative of its contents: 'A defence of General Booth against the unwarrantable and unchristian attack made upon him by the High Council of The Salvation Army'.

In September 1929 Mrs Booth had issued a 76-page booklet – available free of charge on application – under the title *Statement by Mrs Booth*.[22] This was another spirited defence of her husband's position and included extensive extracts from her own speaking at the High Council and the full text of Commissioner Catherine Booth's speech.

Many felt that it was high time for General Higgins to speak out. Now in October 1929, his frank, forthright and persuasive replies to 14 allegations being made by supporters of the Booth family disarmed his critics and helped to diminish further the ranks of those still siding with the family. The article in the *Daily News* was subsequently reprinted as a four-page pamphlet for internal circulation.

The Attorney General intervenes

At this point Sir William Jowitt, the Attorney General, decided to intervene personally in the dispute to try to reach a settlement out of court. He asked both parties to the litigation to come separately to see him, and suggested to them that if the litigation were allowed to continue irreparable harm might be done to The Salvation Army. He asked to be allowed to suggest lines upon which the matter could be settled. He admitted that it might not be found altogether satisfactory to either side, but expressed his belief that it was in the true interests of the Army that the compromise should be accepted. The four key points in the settlement he suggested were:

1. No change to be made to the 1878 constitution during General Higgins's term of office.
2. The next General to be elected by the commissioners.
3. The 'sealed envelope' to be opened at the time of that election, not to bind the commissioners to elect the person specified but so that they might know what General Bramwell Booth's wishes had been.
4. Bramwell Booth's executors – the three trustees – to hand over the property and funds.[23]

There seemed to be grounds for compromise. General Higgins of course had no difficulty with his successor being elected, and was prepared to preserve the 'sealed envelope' until the election. He felt, though, that the electors should be free to decide whether they wished to open the 'sealed envelope' or not. However, the attempted settlement foundered on the first point – the 1878 Deed. General Higgins was not prepared to bind himself not to change the 1878 constitution during his term of office, and Commissioner Catherine Booth was not willing to concede that it might ever be changed, whether by General Higgins or by any of his successors.

The date of the court case on the transfer of assets was set for 21 January 1930. Some days before the event Commissioner Catherine Booth received an earnest plea from her aunt, the Commander: 'I appeal to you, my dearest Catherine, to render a supreme service to our beloved Salvation Army. I would beg of you to use your great influence to secure a friendly hearing of the case now pending, and acceptance of the Deed of 1904 by agreement of us all expressed in court.'[24]

Higgins versus Sneath

The action on 21 January 1930 took place in the High Court of Justice before Mr Justice Clauson. By a happy arrangement in which all involved concurred, Mr Frederick Sneath was named as the first defendant instead of Mrs Booth or Commissioner Catherine Booth. This avoided eye-catching press headlines of 'Higgins v. Booth'. Mr Gavin Simonds KC once more appeared for General Higgins, and Mr

H. B. Vaisey KC again represented the Booth family. The legal reporters from *The Times* were as always on duty.[25]

For General Higgins

Mr Gavin Simonds (for General Higgins) opened the case by recounting how General Bramwell Booth at his death had not transferred the Army's property to his successor, but instead had vested it in his three executors. They had refused to hand over the property, even in the face of the advice from the Attorney General. Mr Simonds then summarised the constitutional position and said that the three trustees did not admit the validity of the trust deed of 1904, and challenged the election of General Higgins.

Continuing, Mr Simonds said it was not for him to establish the validity of the Deed of 1904. It stood until it was upset, and it had stood for 25 years unchallenged. General Bramwell Booth, on becoming General, had executed a deed poll accepting office on and subject to the terms of the Deeds of both 1878 and 1904.

'Is that admitted?' asked his Lordship.

'Yes, it is admitted,' said Mr Simonds, and his Lordship was shown a copy of the 1904 Deed Poll signed by Bramwell Booth.

Mr Justice Clauson looked at the signature, and then ruled that for all practical purposes it placed Bramwell Booth in exactly the same position as if he himself had signed the original Deed of 1904.

'I entirely accept what your Lordship says,' responded Mr Simonds, 'but we are met with this refusal.' The three executors of the late General, he continued, said that they were in a position of difficulty because the General himself challenged the validity of the 1904 Deed. Unfortunately, that was all too true. The last public act of the man who had done such great service was to challenge the validity of the deed.

It was not known, he added, who was appointed by the testator as his successor, and if the provisions of the Deed of 1904 were invalid the appointment would be operative and the successor would be entitled to claim that any transfer by the executors to

General Higgins was wrongful. The executors therefore submitted that the envelope should be opened to ascertain who was the successor so that he might be joined as a party to the proceedings.

His Lordship: 'Assuming that there is a mistake and that the real person is one whose name we don't know, he would have no claim against the executors who acted on an order of the court.'

Mr Simonds submitted that the executors were not competent to challenge the trust that General Bramwell Booth accepted. The Attorney General assented to the view that the property should be handed over to General Higgins on the footing that the Deed of 1904 was valid, and what he (Mr Simonds) was now asking for was a declaration that General Higgins was entitled to the transfer of the property and an order for the transfer.

For the three trustees

When Mr Vaisey rose to speak for the three trustees his first words were awaited with trepidation. Would he or would he not on behalf of his clients challenge the validity of the 1904 Deed? It soon became clear what his instructions were. Perhaps the letter from the Commander had been influential.

Mr Vaisey said that he was not challenging the Deed of 1904, and that expression was a travesty of the position taken up by his clients. Neither was he opposing the claim, and he refused to have placed on his shoulders the burden of actively alleging and attempting by arguments to persuade his Lordship that the Deed of 1904 was invalid. Such an attitude would certainly be most gravely misunderstood. What they wanted was the ordinary protection which the court always afforded when persons who had come into the possession of large funds were asked to hand them over.

They were simply asking the court to authorise them to transfer the assets to General Higgins.

The judgment

In giving judgment Mr Justice Clauson said: 'The matter seems to be exceedingly simple.'

'The executors', he continued, 'have the right to say that they will not act except under order of the court, and the right course for the court to take is to order the executors to hand over the funds. I see no difficulty in making an order which, I understand, is not opposed. It seems to be all there is in the case, and if you – Mr Vaisey – are not objecting to the order in the terms I have stated there is nothing more to be said.'

Mr Vaisey: 'The executors desire to justify themselves. This is not a trumped up and imaginary question.'

His Lordship: 'I am relieving you of all difficulty. The executors are bound to act in accordance with the provisions of the Deed of 1904. I am prepared to decide accordingly. The executors have been put in a difficult position because of the view erroneously taken by their testator, General Bramwell Booth. They had no recourse but to have the matter dealt with in open court.'

Reactions

The case ended before lunch. General Higgins was greatly relieved by its outcome, which had been better than his most optimistic expectations. Mr Justice Clauson had ordered the three trustees to transfer the funds, he had given his judgment on the basis that the 1904 Deed was legally valid, and the trustees had not opposed the transfer. An excellent outcome. Yet that was not all. The three trustees had also declared in court that they would not seek to challenge the legality of the 1904 Deed.

In a subsequent press interview Commissioner Catherine Booth regretted that 'the 1904 Deed's validity was still undecided' and that the judgment had 'left them in the air' on that matter. She thought 'the Judge might have ordered the envelope containing the name of the successor to be opened so that the person named could have an opportunity of saying whether he wished to take office or not'.[26]

However, the legal status of the 1904 Supplementary Deed was never again challenged.

The 'sealed envelope'

That same afternoon an historic meeting took place in the office of General Edward Higgins. Present were the General, the Chief of the Staff (Commissioner Henry Mapp), Commissioners John Laurie, Arthur Blowers, George Sowton, Isaac Unsworth, Theodore Kitching and Mr William Frost.

From his briefcase Mr Frost brought out the 'sealed envelope' that Bramwell Booth had completed two years earlier. He read the relevant extract from the Supplementary Deed of 1904 and then ceremonially and in view of everyone placed the envelope in the open fireplace. They all watched as the flames consumed the envelope and its contents. When only ashes remained Mr Frost signed the following statement which all present countersigned:

> This is to certify that at 101, Queen Victoria Street in the City of London on Tuesday 21st day of January 1930, following upon the judgment of Mr Justice Clauson just delivered in the action 'Higgins v. Sneath', I, the undersigned William Frost, did destroy by burning unopened the envelope containing the appointment of a successor as General of The Salvation Army dated the 14th day of March 1928 and signed by the late General Bramwell Booth and delivered by him to me on that date, and that such destruction took place in the presence of the undermentioned persons, who have also signed their names hereunder.

The next day this document was enrolled in the Supreme Court of Judicature as a Memorandum of Destruction of a Document, and an official statement was made to this effect.

Within days rumours began to circulate that a duplicate of the 'sealed envelope' existed. Mr William Frost wrote to *The Times*, which published his letter on 24 January 1930, to say that the rumour was totally false. 'No duplicate of the burned document has ever existed,' he averred. He then described how he had been called to the Turkish baths on 14 March 1928 so that General Bramwell Booth could complete the document in total secrecy. Since then, he continued, the envelope containing the document 'was never for one moment out of my personal possession and control, in the vaults of a city safe deposit company (where I lodged it immediately) until I put it into the fire and watched its complete destruction on the 21st instant'.

As General Edward Higgins went home that evening after the ceremony in his office, his step was lighter. Within three weeks he would be celebrating his first anniversary as General. What a year it had been!

Now for the first time since he became General the sword of Damocles no longer hung over his head. The threat of the legality of the 1904 Deed being put to the test in a trial had gone. The legality of his election as General was sure. The envelope containing the name of the alternative General had been destroyed, and the Army's properties and funds were now to be transferred to. the rightful trustee.

At long last he would be able to turn his attention to the matter of constitutional reform.

Chapter Nineteen

Towards Reform

THE very next day General Higgins asked Commissioner David Lamb to come and see him. He explained that with the legal position now settled he wished the studies on reform to continue, but instead of having two separate commissions as previously he was going to create one new commission that would look at *all* aspects of reform. He wanted Commissioner David Lamb to become the chairman.

The task of the commission, said the General, was 'to enquire into and advise me as to any practicable improvements in the constitution of The Salvation Army, and the nature of the legal or other means necessary to carry the same into effect'.[1] The commission was to explore three reforms in particular:

1. The holding of property and funds
2. The method of appointment or election of Generals
3. The provision of a retirement age for Generals

The General and the chairman discussed possible membership. For sheer practicality the members would have to be London-based, but they wanted the group to be representative of the broad range of views that had already been expressed. The members appointed were: Commissioners David Lamb (chairman), Samuel Hurren, Charles Jeffries, Isaac Unsworth, Wilfred Simpson – all known to hold reformist views – and Commissioners Catherine Booth and John Laurie to provide the traditionalist ballast. The Advisory Commission on Constitutional Reform held its first meeting on

4 March 1930 and for the next eight months met frequently, often for day-long meetings.

On 19 April 1930 General Higgins wrote to all commissioners and territorial commanders asking them for their own views on reform. 'I gather that the commission is not finding its task an easy one,' he commented. 'That is not to be wondered at. The entire problem is difficult.'

In asking for the personal views of his leaders he shared with them something of his own attitude to reform. 'I still think,' he wrote, 'that what we have called the "three reforms" are what we should concentrate upon. They are all of far-reaching importance. Let us address ourselves principally to those points which our experience has shown to be vital. Do not let us attempt to alter anything for the mere sake of alteration, nor even because we think we could improve upon it.'

When commenting on each of the proposed reforms he skilfully showed how they were already provided for in the 1878 constitution. On the holding of assets he inclined to their being vested in a body of trustees or, preferably, a trustee company. It was 'not only improper, but almost unthinkable, that the legal title to the possessions of a great public trust should or could be left dependent upon the privately appointed executors of any man's will'. Vesting the assets in a trustee company 'would be in the spirit of one of the existing provisions of the 1878 Deed [which permitted a General to 'appoint trustees'], but would be compulsory instead of optional'.

On the selection of a new General he felt that this should be made by 'a body of leading officers'. He continued: 'This also would be in the spirit of one of the existing provisions of the 1878 Deed [the alternative method whereby a General could indicate 'the means to be taken for the appointment of a successor'], but would be compulsory instead of optional.'

On establishing an age of retirement for the General he felt that recent experience had shown the need for it. 'A General has to work and push and lead. The Army should be saved from a leaderless period occasioned by old age.' He thought 73 might be a possibility. 'Setting an age of retirement,' he wrote, 'would not be inconsistent with the spirit of the 1878 Deed, which only provided in the case of the Founder himself that the Generalship should be held for life.'

The responses began to arrive. The commission was hard at work. The matter had to be brought to decision. General Higgins therefore called all of his commissioners to meet in London at the Mildmay Centre on 11 November 1930.

The commissioners and reform

The press scented 'an atmosphere of mystery' about the conference. Perhaps the Army was facing another crisis. However, at a reception for journalists some days before the event General Higgins explained that there was 'no mystery at all about the conference'. He said: 'It is true that it is the first of its kind which the Army has ever held, but I am hoping that it will not be the last of such gatherings, and that at stated periods the leaders of the Army will meet and discuss their problems.'[2]

The Salvation Army as an 'army' had been in existence since 1878, and the fact that in those 52 years the commissioners had never before met *in conference* is a revealing commentary on the autocratic top-down style of government that had until then prevailed.

Forty-two commissioners met at Mildmay. There were six new faces. The other 36 had together lived through the trauma of the High Council. At long last, after the years of pressure on Bramwell Booth to call just such a conference, here were the commissioners of The Salvation Army met together under the presidency of the General to discuss reform. They looked forward to full and free exchanges that would guide the General in the decisions he would have to take.

General Higgins went one step further. To the surprise of all and the dismay of some he announced early in the proceedings that on matters of reform he would be governed by majority votes of the conference. The conference was not going to *advise* on reform. The conference was going to *decide* about reform.

Commander Evangeline Booth had said at the High Council that, if elected, she would abide by a three-fourths majority of the commissioners on matters of reform even if she herself disagreed. General Higgins was now going even further. He would accept the will of the conference on each resolution by a simple majority vote. This was so far from the usual Army way that Commissioner David Lamb, for one, considered that General Higgins by that announcement 'abrogated his right as General'.[3]

The three reforms

The conference had before it the Preliminary Report of the Advisory Commission on Reform. Considering that the commission had been at work for eight months, this was a surprisingly slim document of only 15 pages. Through its long discussions the commission had been able to distil each issue to its very essence and – again surprisingly – had achieved a consensus view on the reforms needed and how they might be implemented. At the conference these findings were studied, discussed and then voted on.

Regarding the holding of assets it was unanimously agreed that a 'custodian trustee company' should be formed in which the General would be the 'managing trustee' and selected commissioners the 'custodian trustees'. As the managing trustee the General would still be in day-to-day control but the custodian trustees would be appointed watchdogs who were legally responsible for ensuring that the terms of the trust were complied with. The Salvation Army would no longer be a 'one-man charity'. The vote in favour was 42 to nil.

On the matter of selecting future Generals, everyone agreed that they should be elected, but there were differences of opinion as to who the electors should be. The Advisory Commission on Reform, after considering options ranging from a small group of just the most senior 20 commissioners to a large group with national representation and many options in between, had opted for an electoral college consisting of the *full* commissioners only; that is, not including the lieut-commissioners.

There were also different opinions as to whether this electoral body should be a separate group from the High Council (with the High Council being left as the adjudicatory body to deal with emergency situations only) or whether the High Council itself would always be the electoral college. On this point the Advisory Commission had recommended that the High Council should become the electing body, but with its membership restricted to full commissioners only.

The decision of the Commissioners' Conference was that the High Council would be the electoral body, but it rejected the proposal that its membership should be limited to full commissioners only. However, in the light of the number of relatively junior officers who had been present at the 1929 High Council the conference proposed that the membership of the High Council should be restricted to commissioners (including lieut-commissioners) and territorial commanders who had held the rank of full colonel for two years before the qualifying date. This was carried unanimously – 42 to nil.

On the matter of a retirement age for the General the conference was agreed that there should be a fixed age, but should it be 73 – as the General favoured – or 70 or somewhere in between? By a majority vote it was decided that it should be 70.

Other reform proposals
In addition to these three main reforms, the conference recommended two further reforms.

It recommended that a Board of Arbitration should be established to which territorial commanders, chief secretaries and heads of department at International Headquarters who felt that they had been unfairly dealt with by the General could appeal. The board would be empowered to look into 'differences or misunderstandings or grievances of any description whatever except any such as are administrative or have direct relation to appointment or rank'. The proposal clearly reflected painful episodes of the recent past, with the experience of Colonel George Carpenter being freely quoted. The establishment of a Board of Arbitration was unanimously agreed – 42 to nil.

The conference then spent a very long time discussing whether, in addition to the reforms already agreed, the authority of the General should be further limited in some way. This was perhaps the most important debate of the conference. A foundation principle of The Salvation Army (and of the Christian Mission before it) was that the movement would always be 'under the oversight, direction and control of some *one* person'. There was no disagreement with that principle at the conference. The question was whether the General should have unfettered authority or whether that authority should be limited in some way or other, and if so how.

Should the General be required to work with a small council of senior commissioners who in certain circumstances would be empowered to overrule him? Or should the General, having listened to advice, have the power to always have the last word? In other words, was the future of the Army to lie in a return to the annulled 1875 constitution in which the Annual Conference could overrule the General Superintendent (except when named William Booth), or did the future lie with the 1878 constitution in which the General Superintendent's word was always final?

In a very carefully phrased resolution Commissioner Charles Jeffries proposed 'that it is desirable that some method should be devised by which the powers of the General should be modified'. This was put to the vote – and was lost. Nineteen voted *for* the resolution and 23 against. The majority did not wish the powers of the General to be modified. This vote was destined to become the most celebrated and oft quoted vote of the conference, for it had been breathtakingly close. Had only three more commissioners voted for the General's powers to be limited the course of Army history would have been changed – for ever.

310

Implementation

The next item on the agenda was how the agreed reforms were going to be implemented. Changing the composition of the High Council was no problem. That was covered by the 1904 Supplementary Deed which the General could vary with the consent of two-thirds of the commissioners. That consent was immediately forthcoming and, with Mr William Frost in attendance, a Deed of Variation was executed on the spot.

What about the other reforms? Would the 1878 Deed have to be amended to make them effective? If so, because of the absence of a variation clause, any changes would have to be endorsed by Parliament. Was the conference in agreement with an approach being made to Parliament?

To the great surprise of the Commissioners' Conference, the seven members of the Advisory Commission on Reform had *unanimously* recommended that the 1878 Deed should not be touched and that therefore no approach to Parliament was needed.

The opposition of Commissioner Catherine Bramwell-Booth – as she had now become – to *any* change in the 1878 constitution was well known. Hers was an opposition based on principle. Like her father she saw the 1878 Deed as a sacred trust that under no circumstances could be tampered with. She had made her position clear to the General: 'I am convinced that morally the General is not free to use his influence to change one iota of the constitution as delivered into his care by the Founder.'[4]

The opposition of the other members of the Advisory Commission to varying the 1878 Deed was based more on pragmatic grounds. If the desired reforms could be achieved *without* changing the 1878 constitution, why then change it? Even Commissioner David Lamb – the arch-reformer and chairman of the Advisory Commission on Constitutional Reform – had become so convinced that the way forward lay in working within the 1878 Deed that some accused him of having 'joined the Booths'!

Reforms within the terms of the 1878 Deed would not be legally foolproof. A trustee company would be formed – no permission from Parliament was needed for that – and future Generals would undertake not to revoke the powers of the trustees. With regard to the selection of successors, future Generals would be expected to declare openly that they would use the second provision in the Deed, with the High Council being the electoral body. The 'sealed envelope' would simply fall away as an irrelevance, as there would be no need to put such a statement in an envelope. With regard to retirement, future Generals would be expected to agree to retire at the stipulated age of 70. These, however, would be moral, not legal, commitments by the General. Legally, future Generals would still have the power to revoke the appointment of trustees, choose their own successor, and continue in office for life.

Yet, commented the Advisory Commission sagely in its report: 'The moral restraints are considerable and will be strengthened by time ... Better to take some risks and be content with something short of an ideal, rather than risk the refusal, interference, or opposition which might follow an application to Parliament to amend our constitution.'[5]

At the Commissioners' Conference, however, other voices urged strongly that having got as far as they had on the matter of reform it would be a mistake to stop short and not complete the task.

The vote on whether to take the matter to Parliament was so crucial that General Higgins announced it would be held twice. This would enable members to reflect on the outcome of the first vote before finally committing themselves on the second. The resolution read:

The General to be authorised and recommended to apply to Parliament for an Act of Parliament establishing the reforms which have been resolved upon by the conference with such modifications (if any) as Parliament may approve or require.

The outcome was decisive. In the first vote the resolution was approved 31 to 11. In the second vote it was agreed by an even bigger margin: 35 to 7. The reforms were to be cemented by an Act of Parliament. A paragraph in the official bulletin to staff officers following the conference sought to head off the anticipated criticism:

> This does not in the slightest degree mean that the Army will be founded on an Act of Parliament or that our Founder's Deed of 1878 will be supplanted by an Act of Parliament, but simply and only that Parliament will approve the one or two variations desired in the 1878 Deed and thus settle these matters once and for all.

Parliament and reform

In December 1930, a few weeks after the close of the Commissioners' Conference, General Edward Higgins submitted a Private Bill to Parliament. Its object was 'to provide for the better organisation of The Salvation Army, and for the custody of real and personal property held upon charitable trusts by, or the administration whereof devolves upon, the General of The Salvation Army'. The four key issues were:

1. A trustee company to be formed
2. Future Generals to be elected
3. The retirement age of Generals to be set at 70
4. A Board of Arbitration to be established

At the Commissioners' Conference the question had been asked whether Salvationists who were opposed to the Bill could go to Parliament to express their views. Mr William Frost had informed the conference that legally they had every right to do so and, moreover, that their views would be listened to and taken into account by Parliament. The prospect of officers and soldiers publicly opposing a Bill sponsored by their General was not welcome, but the pilot who had already steered the Army ship through a hurricane was not to be frightened by the threat of further rough seas. In yet another controversial but courageous decision, General Higgins announced publicly that he wished that 'every legitimate criticism of the proposals in the Bill coming from any section of opinion, however small, should be heard'.

The Bill was discussed in 10 sittings of the House of Commons Select Committee for dealing with Private Bills over a period lasting from 25 March to 30 April 1931. Six written petitions were presented against the Bill, each supported by counsel. Commissioner Catherine Bramwell-Booth and Commissioner David Lamb made submissions and Commissioner Allister Smith testified verbally – creating the extraordinary situation of three International Headquarters commissioners in active service opposing the General in the full public glare of Parliament. Others presenting written petitions included Mrs General Bramwell Booth (Retired) and 'Major Alexander Hogarth[6] and other officers and soldiers of The Salvation Army'. Among those giving verbal testimony against the Bill was Mr Maurice Whitlow, the Salvationist journalist who had appeared as a witness at the High Council.

The Bill was opposed on a variety of grounds, including the following: a spiritual organisation should not submit itself to the yoke of a temporal power; the reforms could be made without going to Parliament; the Army was ever evolving and the intervention of Parliament would create rigidity where now there was fluidity; the Commissioners' Conference that had taken the decisions on reform was not representative of the Army as a whole; the reforms proposed were not sufficiently comprehensive to warrant the attention of Parliament; the Bill was against the best interests of the Army.

The Honourable Mr Frank Smith, by now the Member of Parliament for Nuneaton-Warwick, produced his own printed pamphlet opposing the Bill for the information of his fellow members. Another well-argued 'opposition' pamphlet was issued from within the Army. Some extracts:

Why should Parliamentary sanction be sought for a Custodian Trustee Company, which anyway leaves the General in sole control of the disposition of the funds of The Salvation Army? ... Why should

314

Parliament decide how the General of The Salvation Army shall be chosen? ... Why should Parliament determine the age at which the General of The Salvation Army must retire? ... Why should Parliament decide how differences between the General and his principal officers should be resolved?

On the last point Commissioner Catherine Bramwell-Booth had commented caustically to Commissioner Albin Peyron, circulating the letter to other commissioners: 'An Act of Parliament to keep the peace between the Army's Leader and his chief helpers! I feel humiliated beyond words!'[7] The 'opposition' pamphlet continued with some prescient paragraphs:

Why should the Parliament of today shackle the hands of reformers of tomorrow? What is more difficult than to repeal an Act of Parliament? At the recent Conference of Commissioners there were 19 votes cast for further modification of the General's powers, against 23 on the other side. The significance of this vote cannot be over-estimated, since it reflects a very decided progressive opinion amongst the leading officers of the Army.

Why, then, should the way be thus blocked for other and perhaps more useful reforms than those now proposed? If, for example, the next Commissioners' Conference should desire to set up a body of Managing Trustees instead of a company of Custodian Trustees, why should the Army be put to the trouble and expense of having to promote a Bill in Parliament necessitating the repeal of a previous Act?

Again, if the High Council desired to vary the retiring age of the next General from 70 to 65 or 75 years of age, why fetter the Council with the necessity of having to promote a Bill in Parliament to do so? Don't!

Parliament was required to refer all parliamentary Bills dealing with charities to the Attorney General, and Sir William Jowitt once again found himself occupying centre stage. Sir William noted that 'there were two changes in the provisions of the Army's trust deeds which are not only desirable but imperative if the work of the charity is to continue peacefully and efficiently in the future. They are an alteration in the present procedure for the appointment of the General and the vesting of the property in a trustee company.' He added: 'I am satisfied that these changes cannot be made in such a way as to be legally binding upon the General, officers, and members of The Salvation Army without the authority of Parliament.'[8]

The Attorney General, however, suggested that the clauses dealing with the age of retirement and the Board of Arbitration should be deleted from the Bill as these matters could be handled internally by the Army.

This advice was accepted and the two clauses were dropped. The two reforms that remained in the Bill were the formation of a trustee company and the election of future Generals.

The amended Bill was then debated in the House of Commons and was approved by 221 votes to 31. The measure had yet to go to the House of Lords, where it was considered by the Select Committee on Private Bills during five sittings in the period 29 June to 3 July 1931.

Written submissions against the Bill were made to the Select Committee in the House of Lords by Mrs Booth, Commissioner Catherine Bramwell-Booth, Commissioner David Lamb and, in a joint presentation, 105 officers and soldiers. Among those giving testimony in person were Commissioner Allister Smith, Major Carvosso Gauntlett (later lieut-commissioner), Major Wilfred Kitching (later General) and the indefatigable Mr Maurice Whitlow.

General Higgins testified on behalf of the Bill in the Select Committees of both the House of Commons and the House of Lords. On 3 July 1931 the Bill was endorsed by the Select Committee, its chairman, Viscount Chelmsford, noting that 'in their opinion the Promoters had no other choice than to proceed by Bill'. On 31 July 1931 the Act of Parliament received the Royal Assent and became law.

In a letter to leaders General Higgins commended to them the changes effected by 'the Salvation Army Act 1931', adding: 'It has been a matter of the deepest regret to me that unanimity of views as to the wisdom of the step taken was not possible of securement, and that a minority amongst us felt it necessary to endeavour to defeat the objects we were seeking by opposing the passage of the measure at its every stage.' He continued:

> I have all along refused to believe that the opponents were actuated by other than the purest of motives, and therefore felt it wise that liberty should be given to any officers to express his or her views, even to the extent of personally appearing before the committees of both Houses of Parliament to oppose the Bill ...
>
> I think, however, that the time has now arrived in which I must most clearly and definitely announce that the matter must be treated by us all as a settled and closed affair ... Our ranks must be closed and all must unite in seeking the great purposes of the Army's existence – purposes which are the very same today as they were 50 or five years ago.[9]

Reform through additions to orders and regulations

The question of a fixed retirement age for the General and the establishment of a Board of Arbitration had yet to be settled. As Parliament had declined to make these a matter of law, they had to be governed by the Army's internal orders and regulations. The problem was that it was the General who issued all orders and regulations, and it had always been understood that he himself stood above them and was not subject to them. How could his compliance to one of his own orders and regulations be guaranteed without legal backing?

On 1 February 1932 General Higgins met this challenge by issuing two 'special' orders and regulations.

The first was a *Special Order and Regulation Governing the Age of Retirement of the General,* in which the retirement age for Generals was set at 73 – the age he had originally preferred. Its draconian wording reflected the very real fear at the time that some future General would simply refuse to retire at the stipulated time. The *Special Order and Regulation* brought for the first time the Army's second authority – the commissioners – into the matter of changing orders and regulations. Signed by General Edward Higgins, it read:

> Until the present order and regulation shall be rescinded or varied by a further order and regulation made by the General with the previous consent in writing of not less than two in three of the commissioners, the General shall vacate the office of General on attaining the age of 73 years.
>
> I and every succeeding General shall by the very fact of acceptance of office be deemed to have pledged my and his (or her) faith and honour and loyalty to every other member of The Salvation Army to accept and abide by and give effect to such order and regulation, and to admit and acknowledge that if I or he (or she) should for any reason whatsoever fail or neglect so to do I or he (or she) would be unfit for office and ought to be removed therefrom.

The second document was a *Special Order and Regulation as to the Establishment and Maintenance of a Panel for the Settlement of Differences.* Through this order, any 'difference, misunderstanding or grievance' between the General and a commissioner, territorial commander, chief secretary or head of department at International Headquarters directly responsible to the General, could be referred for arbitration to a group of five officers. The General committed himself to keep permanently in being a panel of 20 officers of the rank of lieut-colonel upwards. From this panel, should a 'difference' arise, the General would select two officers, the other party would select two further officers, and this group of four would choose the fifth member. The determination of the group would be binding on both parties.

As with the special order governing the age of retirement of the General, this special order for the 'settlement of difference' could only be revoked or varied with the consent of two thirds of the commissioners. The historical record does not tell us whether anyone ever availed themselves of this somewhat extreme provision, which so clearly reflected a particular historical situation, or at what point the special regulation was revoked.

The constitution of The Salvation Army was now contained in three documents: the original Deed of Constitution of 1878 (with half of its six clauses – clauses 4, 5 and 6 – revoked by Parliament); the Supplementary Deed of 1904 (as amended by the Deed of Variation 1930), and the Salvation Army Act 1931.[10]

Thus ended the constitutional crisis of 1929, a crisis which had begun already in November 1928 with the calling of the High Council and which had not fully ended until February 1932 when General Higgins issued his two 'special' orders and regulations.

Yet it was not the end of reform.

Chapter Twenty

Ongoing Reform

THE constitutional crisis had been about reform, but reform did not stop in 1932. As the Army continued to evolve so did the process of reform – often in small incremental steps but each adding something significant. The story told in this book would not be complete without those steps being briefly charted. This also gives opportunity to trace the personal histories of some of the chief actors in the human drama we have surveyed.

General Edward Higgins had established the retirement age for Generals at 73, but after completing five years in office decided that he himself would retire at the age of 70. These two facts taken together enabled Commander-in-Chief Evangeline Booth, who had been asked by General Higgins to continue in active service after reaching her 65th birthday in 1930, to accept nomination at the 1934 High Council even though she would shortly reach 69 years of age.

The 1934 High Council with its revised membership had only 47 members. There were five candidates: Commissioner Catherine Bramwell-Booth, Commander Evangeline Booth, Commissioner Samuel Hurren, Commissioner David Lamb and Commissioner Henry Mapp. The Commander was in the lead from the first ballot, with Commissioner Henry Mapp in second place, and achieved the necessary two-thirds majority in the fifth ballot. Commissioner Catherine Bramwell-Booth had the support of four members of the Council throughout the balloting.

General Evangeline Booth did not introduce further reforms during her term of office. The Army was still settling down from the upheaval of the 1929 crisis.

However, a process was about to begin whereby the powers of the General were gradually to be further 'modified' – that is to say 'restricted' – in some way or other. These limitations of powers were sometimes imposed but were mostly voluntarily proposed by successive Generals themselves.

The 1939 High Council brought about an imposed restriction by deciding that questions could be addressed to the candidates before election. Mr William Frost had been consulted and had advised that questions about a candidate's views and intentions could be asked. The answers would not bind the candidate legally if elected General. Often it is only *after* entering office that a General becomes aware of all the facts and all the ramifications of given issues. 'Nothing can legally deprive the General of his right and duty', advised Mr Frost, 'to exercise his own final judgment and discretion from moment to moment in his administration of his trust.'

Mr Frost nevertheless counselled that candidates might be asked to give specific promises and pledges. These again would only have 'an honourable and moral value'. However, 'if a General, after appointment, were to dishonour his pledges, a High Council could be summoned to depose him'.[1]

At all High Councils from that time onwards questions have been addressed to candidates. The answers given impose a certain restriction, even if only of 'honourable and moral value', upon a General's freedom of action.

At the 1939 High Council Commissioner David Lamb also returned to his favoured concept of a 'General in Council', proposing that this council should consist of five to seven senior commissioners who would have no other appointments. The council would be in continual session as a 'think tank' and would be in attendance as a 'cabinet' whenever the General conducted business. The council would not be able to overrule the General. The General would always have the last word,[2] but in 1939 the time for a 'council' of any kind had not yet arrived, and the idea was not pursued.

The 1939 High Council elected Commissioner George Carpenter as General with 35 votes out of 51. In the final ballot Commissioner

Catherine Bramwell-Booth was in second place with eight votes. Her highest vote in a previous ballot had been nine.

The Advisory Council to the General

With the onset of the Second World War any further thinking about reform was of necessity placed on the back burner. However, in preparation for the 1946 High Council, Commissioner Albert Orsborn, the British Commissioner, circulated a lengthy paper on possible further reforms.

His main proposal was that an Advisory Council to the General should be established. This was a development of Commissioner Lamb's proposal, though unlike the 'General in Council' concept the members of the Advisory Council would not function as a 'cabinet' with the General in the chair. The General would in fact not be present at the deliberations of the council in order not to sway the discussion in any direction. He would submit issues in writing for the consideration of the council and would then receive written responses. Members of the Advisory Council to the General would hold other mainstream appointments, membership of the council being *additional* to these. As the name of the council clearly announced to the world, it would be advisory only.

The 1946 High Council elected Commissioner Albert Orsborn to be General with 36 out of 48 votes. Commissioner Catherine Bramwell-Booth had the support of four members.

The first meeting of the Advisory Council to the General was held on 17 March 1947. In constituting such a council, General Albert Orsborn voluntarily accepted for himself and his successors a restriction on his freedom of action. By official minute he undertook to consult the council on a range of substantial issues including proposed senior appointments and promotions and any major changes to orders and regulations before he took decisions on these matters.

The working of the Advisory Council evolved with time. At first it consisted of seven London-based commissioners who met weekly, but with the new possibilities opened by air travel the council eventually became a council of 10 members, five of whom were based in London and five of whom came from overseas. They met only three times a year but for several days each time.

With the council being advisory only, the General was constitutionally free not to accept the advice received. The degree to which Generals overrode the advice of the Advisory Council was to vary with the personalities of successive Generals and the particular issues under consideration. General Frederick Coutts reckoned in 1976 that 'all but a dozen of the more than 800 recommendations placed before the General in the last quarter of a century have been accepted by him'.[3] The fact that all Generals agreed to give an explanation to the council when they did not accept its advice was in itself a further voluntary restraint on their freedom of action.

Generals did not receive advice only from the Advisory Council to the General. The Commissioners' Conference of 1930 has been followed by many more, and there is now an established pattern whereby Generals meet frequently with senior colleagues in international conferences of leaders as well as in zonal conferences. Air travel has revolutionised the way that Generals interact with their senior leaders.

All such conferences are advisory, but it is not unusual for the General to ask for a show of hands to test opinion on some matter being discussed. A conference, however, is not a decision-making body and cannot overrule or outvote the General. The Commissioner's Conference of 1930 remains unique in that respect. Yet the 'honourable and moral' pressure exerted by such gatherings rightly and strongly affects the decision-making process.

The Booth family

The 1946 High Council was the last which Commissioner Catherine Bramwell-Booth attended. She had remained Leader of the Women's Social Work for 14 years, with a break of one year starting March 1930 to write the biography of her father. In 1940 she was appointed Principal of the International Training College but was prevented by circumstances from fulfilling that appointment. In 1942 she took up literary work at International Headquarters before being appointed International Secretary for Europe in 1946. She retired from active service in 1948.

Following the Second World War Mrs General Bramwell Booth settled in 'North Court', a large Victorian house in Finchampstead, Berkshire, together with her daughters Catherine and Mary. Colonel Mary Booth had served successively as territorial commander for Germany, Denmark and Belgium. During the war she spent two and a half years in Nazi prisons and internment camps, but was able to return to England and enter into retirement in 1943. Lieut-Colonel Olive Booth and Senior-Major Dora Booth joined the family in 'North Court' as they in turn entered into retirement.

Colonel Bernard Booth held various London appointments and retired as the staff secretary of The Salvation Army Assurance Society in 1954. He and his wife took up residence in the lodge attached to 'North Court'.

Wycliffe, the youngest son of Bramwell and Florence Booth, rose to become the territorial commander for France and then, with the rank of commissioner, for Norway followed by Canada, where he was the leader for nine and a half years. He was a candidate for the Generalship at the High Council in 1954 when General Wilfred Kitching was elected, and again in 1963 when General Frederick Coutts became General. In retirement he and his wife also settled in Finchampstead.

Mrs General Bramwell Booth was promoted to Glory on 10 June 1957 at the age of 96. She had survived her husband by 28 years.

Set term of office

In 1975 General Clarence Wiseman, following a conference of commissioners and territorial commanders, instituted another reform which indirectly limited the power of future Generals. He established that future Generals would serve for a set term of five years, retiring before completing the term if and when they reached the decreed retirement age. The retirement age for Generals, governed by the special order and regulation, had twice been revised with the consent of two-thirds of the commissioners, and had come down from 73 to 70 and then to 68 – where it stands today. There was widespread relief that such adjustments could be made without having to return to Parliament.

Having a set term of office for Generals had been the subject of fierce debate during the 1929 crisis, with the then Commander Evangeline Booth openly advocating it. Yet its adoption in 1975 caused no outcry. The principal motivation at that time was not so much to limit the authority of the General as to encourage High Councils to elect younger Generals. It was felt that High Councils were deterred from electing younger Generals because they would remain in office for too long. A set term of office was seen as a way of resolving that dilemma.

In establishing set terms, General Wiseman and the commissioners reactivated a provision of the revoked 1875 constitution in which William Booth had decreed that future General Superintendents would 'be appointed for a term of five years'.

Extension of term

In 1986 General Jarl Wahlström revived a further feature of the revoked 1875 constitution by making provision for Generals to be re-elected. The 1875 constitution permitted General Superintendents to be re-elected for another term of five years. Since 1986 there has been provision for a General's term to be extended – for one, two, or three years – by means of a postal ballot of the currently eligible members of the High Council. A proposal for extension can be initiated by the Chief of the Staff with seven other commissioners not married to each other, or by 10 commissioners without the Chief of the Staff.

Agreeing to such a postal ballot has an element of risk for Generals in office. They must achieve an immediate two-thirds majority, failing which they must retire when their term expires – possibly nursing a feeling of rejection. General Eva Burrows is the only General thus far to have experienced a postal ballot of the High Council, and in the secret vote the proposal that her term be extended for two years was overwhelmingly approved.

The system the Army has arrived at marries well the need for freedom and flexibility on the one hand with the need for accountability and control on the other. Should another William or Catherine Booth arise in our midst, he or she could be elected General at an early age, could serve for a term of five years, and could then have his/her term extended by postal ballot of the High Council for up to three years. After this maximum interval of eight years the High Council would have to physically meet. It would, however, be constitutionally possible for the outgoing General to be nominated and elected again at that High Council, and five years later to have his/her term extended for up to three years by a postal ballot of the High Council. There would be no constitutional bar to this cycle of election and extension being repeated until the General concerned reached the mandatory retirement age.[4]

Salvation Army Act 1980

'I think there will be no more constitutional changes of a drastic nature in our beloved Army,' wrote General Albert Osborn in 1958. 'It is certain there cannot be any without another Act of Parliament, and that is not a possibility within the lifetime of anyone now living.'[5]

The remembered pain of getting the 1931 Act through Parliament was such that another Act 'within the lifetime of anyone now living' was unthinkable. Yet within 22 years of the General penning those words that is exactly what happened. The Army was back in Parliament and the Salvation Army Act 1980, a far bigger legislative measure than the 1931 Act, was the result.

By 1980 the atmosphere had changed to an almost incredible degree. Though some leaders at first wondered whether another Act was really necessary, there was no rush to man the barricades. Few took sides on the issues and no one actually opposed the Act in Parliament. In the end it was generally accepted that another Act of Parliament was a most commendable idea.

The change in atmosphere was partly because the Salvation Army Act 1980 was more about constitutional tidying-up than constitutional reform, and partly because the link with Parliament had become an acceptable fact of life for Salvationists. The 1931 Act had even been amended on technical points in 1963 and 1968 without anyone demurring. Considering the trauma that had attended the passage of the 1931 Act, the difference in attitude in 1980 was nothing short of astounding.

The problem with the Army's constitution was that it had become immensely complex and by 1980 was contained in six separate documents: the Deed of Constitution of 1878 (as amended by the 1931 Act), the Supplementary Deed of 1904 (as varied by the 1930 Deed of Variation and a further Deed of Variation in 1965), the Salvation Army Act 1931, and the amending Act of 1968. One almost needed a special briefcase to carry the constitution around and the brain of a constitutional lawyer to understand it!

In the early 1970s, at the suggestion of the Charity Commissioners – the regulating authority for charities in Britain – the then Chief of the Staff, Commissioner Arnold Brown, undertook to examine the possibility of preparing a new and simplified constitutional document. When he later returned to International Headquarters as General he was able to bring this project to fruition. The draft text was considered paragraph by paragraph by the commissioners during an international conference of leaders held in 1979 in Toronto, Canada.

The Salvation Army Act 1980 started virtually from scratch. By it all previous constitutional deeds were revoked. Consigned to the historical museum were the Foundation Deed of 1878 and the Supplementary Deed of 1904 together with the variation deeds. Also repealed or amended were certain provisions of the Salvation Army Acts 1931 to 1968. Such was the change in attitude towards constitutional reform that, what would have been considered either as impossible or as rank heresy in 1929 raised hardly an eyebrow in 1980.

The 1980 Act is firmly based on what the Army has developed into since its inception in 1878 and what the General's role since then has become. Central to the constitution remains the provision that 'the Army shall be under the oversight, direction and control of the

General'. However, the General is granted wide powers 'to delegate such powers, duties and discretion as he thinks best' to the Chief of the Staff and 'other officers'.

Significantly, by the provisions of the 1980 Act the *Custodian* Trustee Company of the 1931 Act became a *Managing* Trustee Company. The General was relieved of his responsibility for the day-to-day management of British funds and property, and the responsibility for managing the assets was entrusted to the directors of The Salvation Army Trustee Company.

An important feature of the Salvation Army Act 1980 is that the provisions in its main schedules (appendices) can be varied by the General 'with the written approval of more than two-thirds of the commissioners' without the Army having to return to Parliament. Details relative to the vacation of office by a General and the High Council are governed by such schedules – and are therefore open to variation without recourse to Parliament.

The Salvation Army Act 1980 revoked the provisions in the Supplementary Deed 1904 whereby a General could be removed from office by a 'write-in' of the commissioners without them meeting – by four in five for mental or physical incapacity, and by nine in 10 for misconduct. Under the 1980 Act only the High Council can remove a General from office.

An adjudicatory High Council can be requisitioned by the Chief of the Staff with seven commissioners, or by 10 commissioners without the Chief of the Staff. The number of requisitioners needed to trigger a High Council was raised to these figures in 1995 when the membership of the High Council was increased as a result of the ruling by General Paul A. Rader that all married women officers – including the spouses of commissioners – would hold rank in their own right. Because of this ruling, the schedule now also includes a proviso that 'no two requisitioners shall be married to each other'.

Further reform factors
In 1990 General Eva Burrows used the powers of delegation granted her in the Salvation Army Act 1980 to separate the international and

British administrations and appoint a territorial commander responsible for all aspects of the Army's work in the United Kingdom. This was a further voluntary restriction of authority in that aspects of the Army's work that had previously come directly under the General were now delegated to a territorial commander.

The creation of two separate Salvation Army trustee companies in Britain also changed the dynamics. The General has a constitutional relationship with both the United Kingdom Trustee Company and the International Trustee Company. However, the bulk of British property holdings and all of British funds are controlled by the UK Trustee Company, of which the chairman is the UK territorial commander. At the time of the separation of administrations, nearly 80 per cent of the total assets became the responsibility of the United Kingdom Trustee Company.

The same administrative reforms in 1990 resulted in the creation of the International Management Council at International Headquarters – another voluntary restriction of the General's authority. Commissioner David Lamb would have been delighted, for the International Management Council – comprised of all commissioners serving on International Headquarters – is very close to his 'General in Council' concept.

The International Management Council is the General's 'cabinet'. The International Management Council cannot outvote or over-rule the General, for that would be inconsistent with the constitutional requirement that the Army shall be under the oversight, direction and control of the General. Nevertheless, it would be a rare event for a General to decide on a policy or embark on a venture that did not have the support of the International Management Council.

In 2001 General John Gowans brought about a major change to the working of the Advisory Council to the General, which is also part of this story of ongoing reform. If the advent of air travel had made international representation on the council possible, the advent of electronic communication opened the way to extending the circle of advisers. In a bold move – illustrative of the powers that a General still retains – General Gowans changed the Advisory

Council to the General with its small membership into the General's Consultative Council, of which all leaders eligible for the High Council are members. The number of advisers rose at a stroke from 10 to nearer 100.

The meetings of the General's Consultative Council have evolved into thrice-yearly residential meetings lasting several days, which are attended by around 30 members – those coming from outside International Headquarters on a rotating basis. The agenda is sent to *all* the members electronically, and all can contribute to the discussion by that means, and all receive the minutes of meetings. The members also have access to the electronic database of the General's Consultative Council which enables newly appointed members to read all material going back to the inception of the new-style council in 2001.

General Shaw Clifton has instituted two further changes to the working of the General's Consultative Council. First, he has extended the circle of advisers even further by making the spouses of territorial commanders with the rank of colonel, and officers commanding and their spouses – who are not members of the High Council – 'correspondents' of the General's Consultative Council. As such they receive copies of agenda items, discussion papers and minutes, and are invited to contribute to the discussion electronically.

Second, General Clifton has turned the previous sub-committee of the General's Consultative Council that used to consider proposed senior appointments and promotions into a fully-fledged International Appointments Board, thus, among other things, resolving the problem of revolving and therefore uncertain membership.

A key difference between the General's Consultative Council and the former Advisory Council to the General is that at the General's Consultative Council the General is present and chairs its proceedings. The advantage of that arrangement is that the General can hear and take part in the discussion on the various issues. It is often in the cut and thrust of debate that the way ahead becomes clear. The potential disadvantage is that opinions might be expressed less freely, but should he wish, the General may withdraw from the discussion at any point.

The means whereby the General of The Salvation Army receives advice and shares in consultation continue to develop and expand. Had the reformers of 1929 been able to see into the future, they would have been delighted.

Reflections

As one reflects on the story told in this book the mind is drawn to certain surprising aspects relative to William Booth, Bramwell Booth and the reformers.

With regard to William Booth, the greatest surprise is that he deliberately chose to set his 1878 constitution in stone. As we have seen, his 1875 constitution could be varied or even revoked with the concurrence of two thirds of the evangelists, and *had* to be reviewed for relevance after five years and then at 10-yearly intervals. Three years later he made use of those provisions to annul it totally.

At that same point, 1878, William Booth made his next constitution unchangeable. He no doubt had very good reasons for doing so, and we have looked at some of these. However, the fact that he deliberately chose not to include a clause permitting him to vary or annul the constitution still remains a surprise – and perhaps a warning to all founders of religious movements. Had the constitution included such a clause it would never have acquired the almost sacred status it later attained – and the course of Salvation Army history would have been different.

As far as Bramwell Booth is concerned, the greatest surprise is that he was not willing to institute the reforms that he could have brought about without changing the constitution of 1878.

Given the conservative streak in his character, to which even his father had drawn his attention, it is not surprising that he looked on the 1878 constitution as a sacred and unchangeable trust. Yet, as we have seen, all the reforms that were eventually instituted by recourse to Parliament in 1931 could have been achieved *within the terms of the 1878 constitution* if Bramwell Booth had been prepared to accept certain limitations. The fact that he did not do what the 1878 constitution fully permitted him to do therefore made him vulnerable to the charge of dynastic intent.

With regard to the reformers, the great surprise – as much for them as for later observers – is the unforeseen manner in which the locked door to reform was eventually opened.

As will be recalled, the reformers were 'helpless' when it came to initiating reform. Only the General could take the initiative. All the reformers could do was to step up the pressure on the General for him to take action.

Had General Bramwell Booth's health not broken in 1928, or had he returned to office after a few months of rest, it is likely that the reformers would have tried to increase the pressure on the General to call a commissioners' conference or to set up a special council to discuss reform. Had he still refused, it is possible that seven intrepid commissioners might have been found to trigger a High Council on the ground that his continued opposition to constitutional reform was sufficiently unreasonable as to constitute an 'other circumstance' that made him 'unfit for office'. In such a scenario, though, securing a three-in-four majority for his deposition at the High Council would have been much more difficult.

As events actually unfolded, it was the General's health breakdown and continued absence from office that became the key that unlocked the door to reform. In the end it was *on the ground of health* that General Bramwell Booth was removed from office by the High Council, and it was as a side-effect to this action that the door to reform was opened. This turn of events was as surprising to the reformers as it remains to later students of the crisis.

Standing well back and surveying the scene from afar, perhaps the 1929 crisis was a necessary rite of passage for the still fledgling Salvation Army. As Commissioner Gunpei Yamamuro in retrospect put it: 'Just as thoughtful parents can make the mistake of underestimating a child's growth, with their overprotection being unwelcome to the grown-up child, so the protection by General Bramwell Booth and his family of "their baby" – The Salvation Army – was no longer appropriate or welcomed by a weaned and grown Army.'[6] In 1929 The Salvation Army came of age.

One cannot help but feel great human sympathy for Bramwell Booth who at a time of declining health and diminishing natural powers found himself at the very vortex of these events. However, Bramwell Booth's place in history is secure. He was not only the Army's second General, but next to William Booth the greatest General the Army has yet seen or is ever likely to see again.

The Army came through its rite of passage strengthened and reanimated. Edward Higgins was exactly the 'storm pilot' the Army needed to guide it through the troubled waters. The officers and soldiers of the day rose to the occasion by refusing to be distracted from the task to which they had been called, and concerns about the effects of the reforms soon dissipated. As General Frederick Coutts in his own masterful way sums it up in the official history of The Salvation Army:

> There were those who genuinely feared that 'the introduction of the principle of election as a permanent means of appointing future Generals must bring a decay of a General's independence of action, unhealthy rivalry and intrigue, and the eventual disruption of the Army as an international body'. But time has proved these fears unfounded. The international unity and solidarity of the Army is now as strong, if not stronger, than ever. Wisdom was justified of her children.[7]

With the constitutional reforms resulting from the 1929 crisis and the ongoing reforms since then, the scene today has been transformed out of all recognition from that which obtained pre-1929. The foundation principle that the Army shall always be under the 'oversight, direction and control of some one person' has been retained. This enables swift and decisive action to be taken when needed. The Army is not led by a committee but by a General. Yet the foundation principle has been supplemented by wise safeguards against the frailties of human nature and by the establishment of formal channels for input from a much wider circle to inform the decision-making process.

Retention of the foundation principle at the highest level has enabled it also to be kept at the three other command levels within the Army. Neither territories, divisions nor corps or social centres are run by committees. Each has a 'commander', and each unit retains the capacity for speedy action for which the Army is rightly renowned.

The 'commander', though, does not rule alone or arbitrarily. The development of territorial and divisional boards and councils parallels that which has taken place at the highest level, as do corps councils and meetings of local officers in corps. Leadership at all levels has become consultative. The contours have softened. It is not coincidental that the initials 'CO' which used to stand for 'Commanding Officer' now also stand for 'Corps Officer'.

William Booth would approve.

Epilogue
A Life Concluded

'AS it has pleased God to promote our comrade Commissioner Catherine Bramwell-Booth to the home prepared for her in Heaven ...'

The voice of Commissioner Francy Cachelin rang out clearly in the crisp autumn air as the small family group stood around the flag-draped coffin adorned by a large bonnet in the Finchampstead cemetery on Friday 9 October 1987.

The funeral and meeting of thanksgiving for the life of Commissioner Catherine Bramwell-Booth had been held the previous evening in the Regent Hall in Oxford Street, London. A capacity congregation of Salvationists had praised God for her life in 'good old Army' style in which laughter was as natural as tears. A message from the Queen was read. At the request of the family, the burial was to be a private service. Commissioner Francy Cachelin, until recently the British Commissioner but now an International Evangelist and the General's Representative, was a member of the family through his marriage to Geneviève Booth, daughter of Commissioner and Mrs Wycliffe Booth.

Commissioner Catherine Bramwell-Booth had lived a long and full life. After she retired in 1948 she had disappeared from public view, living in virtual seclusion with her mother and sisters at 'North Court' in Finchampstead, Berkshire. There she devoted herself to writing a major biography of her grandmother Catherine Booth, the Army Mother.

When in 1957 Commissioner Catherine Bramwell-Booth conducted the funeral of her mother, Mrs General Bramwell Booth, a new generation of Salvationists watched with fascination as the Booth family emerged into view again. After that one-day event, the family retired to 'North Court' once more – with Commissioner Catherine Bramwell-Booth as its new head – and yet again, apart from attending Wokingham Corps on Sundays, seemed to vanish from sight.

Then, 20 years later, when in her mid-90s, Commissioner Catherine Bramwell-Booth made a remarkable comeback and became the best-known Salvationist in Britain.[1] It began with the making of a Salvation Army film entitled *Catherine Bramwell-Booth* in which she was interviewed by Ronald Allison. Wherever Salvationist audiences saw the film they greeted it with a standing ovation. When the film was offered to television, the television companies were so intrigued by Catherine Bramwell-Booth that they arranged for her to appear on their own interview programmes. With her pungent style that had audiences roaring with laughter she became an instant hit – a TV celebrity.

She was interviewed on television by Malcolm Muggeridge, Peter France, Russell Harty, Michael Parkinson and other well-known British TV personalities. Her exchange with Michael Parkinson was typical. After some introductory comments he said: 'I read this week that you have said that you would like to live to be older than Moses.'

'I said no such thing – no such thing,' she shot back.

'Well,' stuttered Michael looking at his notes, 'I just read something here ...'

'No, no, no,' interrupted the old warrior, 'I said that I would like to come to the end of my days *like* Moses – but I can't. Scripture says that his sight was unabated. I have cataracts!'

'Oh, Commissioner,' interjected Michael Parkinson lightly to the delight of the audience, 'if it was between you and Moses I'd put my money on you any day.'

'What do you mean?' asked Catherine Bramwell-Booth sternly, to the great amusement of the crowd.

'Well, if there was a book running ...'

'A book? A book?' interrupted Catherine. 'I hope you're not a betting man, Mr Parkinson!'

As the audience shrieked with laughter Michael Parkinson's blush showed up even on black-and-white television. Yet he rated Catherine Bramwell-Booth as one of the greatest personalities he had ever interviewed; in fact, as he said, 'one of the most extraordinary human beings I have ever encountered.' At the end of the 13 weeks' TV series he paid her the compliment of showing again the whole of his interview with her.

One thing led to another. The Toastmasters' Guild presented her with the Best Speaker of the Year award in 1977. In what was supposed to be a five-minute response she instead had the audience laughing uncontrollably for five minutes before embarking on a full-length warning about the danger of alcohol – all of which was televised. Shortly afterwards, Variety Clubs International presented her with the Humanitarian Award. Wherever she went television crews and radio reporters from home and abroad awaited her arrival, and she was in constant demand for international press and radio interviews.

After she had appeared on television, Salvationists would be stopped in the street the next day to be told by passers-by that they had seen 'your lady' on TV. One said: 'I saw your General on TV last night!' She was awarded a CBE in recognition of her Army service, spoke at the International Congress in London in 1978, and on her 100th birthday was admitted to the Order of the Founder – the Army's highest award – for 'her permanent contribution to the Army's history and advance'.

On her centenary birthday she said: 'It's a very strange experience, living so near to death as I do now. I know it must be just next door, tomorrow perhaps, today perhaps. But still I am in love with life and I'm in love with the world.'

Death had now come. As the small group of family members stood by the graveside no television cameras rolled. This was a personal farewell to a loved one who had become a matriarchal figure to everyone in that group.

'We now commit her body to the grave,' intoned Commissioner Cachelin. 'Earth to earth, ashes to ashes, dust to dust; in the certainty of the resurrection to eternal life through our Lord Jesus Christ.'

As the coffin was slowly lowered into the open grave, did some member of the family wonder what might have been?

Catherine Bramwell-Booth died at the age of 104. Had she succeeded her father in 1929, and had the constitution remained unchanged, she would have been the General of The Salvation Army for 58 years.

Sources and Acknowledgments

IN writing this book I have been able to draw on a wide range of historical material, constitutional documents and correspondence – some of which has previously been published (though not always in a form readily accessible to the general reader) and some of which sees the light of day for the first time.

Published sources
The primary published sources regarding the 1929 High Council are the three books that appeared already that year. These have been mentioned in the text as they each in their own way affected the course of events. The three publications were: *The Clash of the Cymbals* by F. A. Mackenzie (Brentano's Ltd), *The Betrayal of Bramwell Booth* by Frank Smith (Jarrolds Publishers) and *A Statement by Mrs Booth* (a privately published booklet).

In the autumn of 1929 General Edward Higgins completed the manuscript of a work entitled *The History of the High Council.* Sadly for the historian, the General in the end decided not to go ahead with its publication, and the manuscript is no longer extant. General Higgins was among those who burnt all their papers relating to the 1929 High Council and the manuscript was probably destroyed at that time.

In May 1933 appeared Catherine Bramwell-Booth's life of her father *Bramwell Booth* (Rich and Cowan), in which the final chapter is devoted to the 1929 crisis and the death of her father.

In 1934 St John Ervine, a distinguished author and playwright, published his monumental two-volume biography of William Booth under the title *God's Soldier* (William Heinemann Ltd). He concluded the book with an epilogue entitled 'Bramwell Booth becomes General and is deposed'. The epilogue, which includes 17 appendices of historical documents, is itself of book-length and until now has been the most comprehensive account of the crisis. As well as having access to key documents and correspondence, St John Ervine was able to interview or correspond with many of the participants.

Subsequent writers on the constitutional crisis have in the main based their accounts on material drawn from the five books mentioned above. Among books that include brief surveys of the crisis are:

Portrait of a Prophet – Samuel Logan Brengle by Clarence W. Hall, 1933 edition (National Headquarters, USA);

Salvation Dynasty by Brian Lunn (William Hodge, 1936);

General Evangeline Booth by P. W. Wilson (Charles Scribner's Sons, 1948);

The House of My Pilgrimage by Albert Orsborn (SP&S Ltd, 1958);

The History of The Salvation Army, Volume 6, by Frederick Coutts (Hodder and Stoughton, 1973);

No Discharge in This War – A One Volume History of The Salvation Army, by Frederick Coutts (Hodder and Stoughton, 1974);

Marching to Glory – The History of The Salvation Army in the United States by Edward H. McKinley (Harper and Row, 1980);

Storm Pilot – The Life of General Edward Higgins by William G. Harris (SP&S Ltd, 1981);

Catherine Bramwell-Booth by Mary Batchelor (Lion Publishing plc, 1986);

A Man of Peace in a World at War – The Story of General George L. Carpenter by Stella Carpenter (published privately in Australia, 1993);

Turning Points by Allen Satterlee (Crest Books, 2004);

Soldiers of the Cross – David Lamb: Pioneer of Social Change by Norman Murdoch (Crest Books, 2006).

In 1961 *Four Bonnets to Golgotha* by Garry Allighan – a former officer who for a time was a Member of Parliament – was published by MacDonald's & Co Ltd but was almost immediately withdrawn on a legal issue. This study of Bramwell Booth's relationship with his mother, wife, sister Evangeline and daughter Catherine touches on the constitutional crisis, but belongs to the genre of faction – part fact, part fiction.

In 1999 Lieut-Colonel John Kirkham, a keen Australian student of the constitutional crisis, published privately a short work entitled *Deposed but not Despised*. With its many appendices it is a fine introduction to the subject.

Much of what was said at the High Council is available in published sources. For example, in her *Statement by Mrs Booth*, Mrs Booth quotes freely from what she herself said at the Council and reproduces in full the text of Commissioner Catherine Bramwell-Booth's main speech. Commissioner David Lamb had his key speech printed in the form of a commemorative booklet following the High Council. Other extracts from speeches subsequently appeared in print, either quoted by the speakers themselves or by their hearers.

A number of the territorial commanders present at the High Council – including Commissioner James Hay, the President of the High Council – recorded their personal impressions of the event in *The War Cry* of their respective territories, and these accounts have provided helpful insights and useful quotes. Commissioner William McIntyre was especially prolific, writing a five-part series for the *The War Cry* of the USA Southern Territory. I am grateful to all territorial commanders and territorial archivists who have provided copies of such material, especially where translation into English has been involved.

Commissioner Gunpei Yamamuro not only wrote for the Japanese *War Cry*, but such was the public interest in that country that he also published a booklet entitled *The New Epoch for The Salvation Army – The True Story of the High Council*. Commissioner Yamamuro based much of his writing on the personal diary he kept in which he recorded his personal day-to-day impressions of the High Council. I am indebted to Commissioner Makoto Yoshida, the territorial commander for Japan, for making extracts from these sources available to me in English.

Through endnotes in the text I have drawn attention to historical documents that have been made accessible to students by their inclusion as appendices in published works.

Other sources

The archives in the International Heritage Centre have been the main source for unpublished material, and I am grateful to all members of the team, especially Major Stephen Grinsted, Mr Gordon Taylor, Commissioner Karen Thompson, Captain Heather Coles and Mr Alex von der Becke, for their unfailing graciousness and skill in unearthing relevant material and tracing needed facts.

The centre has well-stocked boxes of documents, letters and press cuttings relating to the 1929 crisis and these records have been central to my research. Much material has also been drawn from the papers of individual participants held in the archives.

Included in the material kept at the International Heritage Centre is the result of General Albert Osborn's request to surviving members of the 1929 High Council to record their recollections of the event and what led up to it. Though the yield from that exercise was small, one very valuable result was a 20-page document from Commissioner James Hay in which he reflected on the event in which he himself played such a prominent part.

Also held at the Centre is a series of unpublished articles written for the April 1929 edition of *The Staff Review*. The editor asked six members of the High Council to record their personal impressions of the High Council. The contributors were Commissioners James Hay, Charles Jeffries, Samuel Brengle, Johanna van de Werken, Lieut-Commissioner Gunpei Yamamuro and Colonel Charles Baugh. The articles were typeset but were never published.

With so much of the resource material coming from the International Heritage Centre, the *absence* of an endnote reference in the text indicates that the source is the International Heritage Centre. This has significantly reduced the number and length of endnote references.

In the archives of International Headquarters are the official minutes of the High Council, handwritten by Commissioner John Carleton. The minutes, though, simply record the events of each session, the wording of resolutions and texts of letters sent and received by the Council, and the names of those who spoke – but not what they said. Some speakers read from prepared scripts, some spoke from notes, and others addressed the Council extemporaneously – but no verbatim record of what was spoken was kept.

However, a second document in the archives containing what might be described as 'minute jottings' provides pointers to what the speakers said. These jottings were probably made by Colonel Gerald Freeman, the assistant recorder. Most of these notes consist of fragmentary phrases, with what must sometimes have been quite lengthy interventions reduced to a phrase or two. Some key speeches, however, are recorded more fully and include quotable material.

The impression that speakers made on the Council and some of the actual words they spoke are also to be found in unpublished letters written by those present.

Another key source for unpublished material has been the National Archives of The Salvation Army at National Headquarters in Alexandria, Virginia, near Washington DC, USA. The reform movement created a steady flow of correspondence across the Atlantic in both directions, and much of what was lost on the European side of the ocean when International Headquarters was destroyed by fire has been preserved on the American side. I am greatly indebted to Susan Mitchem, the National Archivist, who has spent many hours tracing relevant material as well as engaging in her own research, especially to establish the identity of William L. Atwood and to track down legal correspondence related to the 1929 High Council.

Unexpected discoveries are the joy of any researcher. I mention but two. I can still recall my delight at discovering the photograph of the 1929 High Council crowded together in the council chamber at Sunbury Court. I found a framed copy of this treasure hanging on the wall of the Army's museum in Seoul, Korea, moments after I had declared the centre open when visiting the territory as General.

Imagine my elation when I discovered that Captain Stewart Grinsted – a great-grandson of Commissioner Theodore Kitching – had inherited from General Wilfred Kitching, his great-uncle, the handwritten document dated 29 September 1879 by which William Booth appointed Bramwell Booth – still only 23 years old – to be his eventual successor. To unexpectedly come across the document that had been in the first 'sealed envelope', an envelope whose very existence had hitherto only been a matter of conjecture for historians, was joy indeed.

Finally

My very special thanks to Freda, my wife, encourager-in-chief and main proofreader, and to my sister, Lieut-Colonel Miriam Frederiksen, for applying her editorial expertise to the manuscript. I am also grateful to Colonel Laurence Hay for his in-depth checking of the text, and to General John Gowans (Retired) and Commissioner Gisèle Gowans, and Commissioner Keith Banks who read the book in draft form and whose comments I have greatly valued. I record also my appreciation for the valuable 'younger generation' perspective offered by our sons Karl and Kevin following their reading of the draft manuscript. I furthermore express my warm thanks to Lieut-Colonel Charles King, Literary Secretary at International Headquarters, for his much-valued support for this project at every stage.

Appendix I

The Deed of Constitution 1978

TO ALL TO WHOM THESE PRESENTS SHALL COME

I WILLIAM BOOTH of 3 Gore Road Victoria Park Road Hackney in the County of Middlesex Minister of the Gospel the Founder and General Superintendent for the time being of the Christian Mission send greeting.

WHEREAS in the year 1865 the said William Booth commenced preaching the Gospel in a Tent erected in the Friends Burial Ground Thomas Street in the Parish of Whitechapel in the County of Middlesex and in other places in the same neighbourhood

AND WHEREAS a number of people were formed into a community or Society by the said William Booth for the purpose of enjoying Religious fellowship and in order to continue and multiply such efforts as had been made in the Tent, to bring under the Gospel those who were not in the habit of attending any place of worship by preaching in the open air, in Tents, Theatres, Music Halls, and other places and by holding other religious services or meetings

AND WHEREAS at the first the said Society was known by the name of the East London Revival Society and afterwards as the East London Christian Mission

AND WHEREAS other Societies were afterwards added in different parts of London and a Society was also formed at Croydon

AND WHEREAS the names of these united Societies was then altered to that of 'The Christian Mission'

AND WHEREAS divers Halls or Meeting houses School-rooms Vestries lands buildings and appurtenances situate lying and being in various parts of Her Majesty's dominions and elsewhere have been or are intended to be and hereafter may be given and conveyed to certain persons in such gifts and conveyances named and to be named upon trusts for the purposes therein and herein mentioned or any of them and generally for promoting the objects of the said Christian Mission under the direction of the General Superintendent

AND WHEREAS in order to render valid and effectual such trusts, to remove doubts and prevent litigation in the interpretation thereof or as to the terms used therein, to ascertain what is the name or title and what are and shall be for ever the doctrines of the said Christian Mission, and also in order to preserve the system of the said Christian Mission generally by means of a General Superintendent it has been deemed expedient to make and execute these presents

NOW THESE PRESENTS WITNESS that for the purposes aforesaid I the said William Booth DO HEREBY DECLARE:

FIRSTLY, that the name style and title by which the said religious community or mission hereinbefore described hath during the last nine years been called known and recognised is 'The Christian Mission'.

SECONDLY, that the religious doctrines professed believed and taught by the Members of the said Christian Mission are and shall for ever be as follows:-

1. We believe that the Scriptures of the Old and New Testaments were given by inspiration of God, and that

348

they only constitute the Divine rule of Christian faith and practice.

2. We believe there is only one God, who is infinitely perfect, the Creator, Preserver, and Governor of all things, and who is the only proper object of religious worship.

3. We believe that there are three persons in the Godhead – the Father, the Son and the Holy Ghost, undivided in essence and co-equal in power and glory.

4. We believe that in the person of Jesus Christ the Divine and human natures are united, so that He is truly and properly God and truly and properly man.

5. We believe that our first parents were created in a state of innocency, but by their disobedience they lost their purity and happiness, and that in consequence of their fall all men have become sinners, totally depraved, and as such are justly exposed to the wrath of God.

6. We believe that the Lord Jesus Christ has by His suffering and death made an atonement for the whole world so that whosoever will may be saved.

7. We believe that repentance towards God, faith in our Lord Jesus Christ, and regeneration by the Holy Spirit, are necessary to salvation.

8. We believe that we are justified by grace through faith in our Lord Jesus Christ and that he that believeth hath the witness in himself.

9. We believe that continuance in a state of salvation depends upon continued obedient faith in Christ.

10. We believe that it is the privilege of all believers to be 'wholly sanctified', and that 'their whole spirit and soul

and body' may 'be preserved blameless unto the coming of our Lord Jesus Christ' (1 Thess. v. 23).

11.   We believe in the immortality of the soul; in the resurrection of the body; in the general judgment at the end of the world; in the eternal happiness of the righteous; and in the endless punishment of the wicked.

THIRDLY, that the said Christian Mission is and shall be always hereafter under the oversight direction and control of some one person who shall be the General Superintendent thereof whose duty it shall be to determine and enforce the discipline and laws and superintend the operations of the said Christian Mission and to conserve the same to and for the objects and purposes for which it was first originated.

The General Superintendent shall have power to expend on behalf of The Christian Mission all moneys contributed for the general purposes of the said Christian Mission or for any of the special objects or operations thereof but he shall annually publish a Balance Sheet (duly audited) of all such receipts and expenditure.

The General Superintendent shall have power to acquire by gift purchase or otherwise any Hall or Meeting-house School-room Vestry land building and appurtenances and any seats fittings furniture or other property whatsoever which may in his judgment be required for the purposes of the said Christian Mission and to build upon such land or alter or pull down any such buildings, and to hire on lease or otherwise any land or buildings and to lend give away let sell or otherwise dispose of any such property land or buildings as he may deem necessary in the interests of the said Christian Mission wherein all Trustees shall render him every assistance, and he may in all such cases as he shall deem it expedient so to do nominate and appoint Trustees or a Trustee of any part or parts respectively of such property and direct the conveyance or transfer thereof to such

Trustees or Trustee with power for the General Superintendent to declare the Trusts thereof and from time to time if it shall seem expedient to him so to do to revoke any such Trusts or the appointment of such Trustees or Trustee and upon such revocation the same property shall be conveyed or transferred to such persons or person and upon such trusts as he may direct but only for the benefit of the said Christian Mission.

FOURTHLY, that the said William Booth shall continue to be for the term of his natural life the General Superintendent of the Christian Mission unless he shall resign such Office.

FIFTHLY, that the said William Booth and every General Superintendent who shall succeed him shall have power to appoint his Successor to the Office of General Superintendent and all the rights powers and authorities of the Office shall rest in the person so appointed upon the decease of the said William Booth or other General Superintendent appointing him or at such other period as may be named in the document appointing him.

SIXTHLY, that it shall be the duty of every General Superintendent to make in writing as soon as conveniently may be after his appointment a statement as to his Successor or as to the means which are to be taken for the appointment of a Successor at the decease of the General Superintendent or upon his ceasing to perform the duties of the Office such statement to be signed by the General Superintendent and delivered in a sealed envelope to the Solicitor for the time being of The Christian Mission but such statement may be altered at will by the General Superintendent at any time during his continuance in office upon a new statement being signed by him and delivered as before mentioned to such Solicitor as aforesaid.

IN WITNESS whereof I the said William Booth have hereunto subscribed my name and affixed my Seal this seventh day of August in the year of Redemption One thousand eight hundred and seventy-eight.

WILLIAM BOOTH

Signed Sealed and Delivered by the said William Booth in the presence of

THOS. WHTTINGTON
3 Bishopsgate Street.
Without, Solr.
J. E. BILLUPS

THIS DEED was duly presented to and approved by the persons assembled at a General Meeting of the Christian Mission held at No. 272 Whitechapel Road in the County of Middlesex And we the undersigned William Booth and George Scott Railton do hereby in the name of the Christian Mission set our hands hereto in ratification of and for perpetuating testimony of this Deed.

Dated this same seventh day of August 1878.

WILLLAM BOOTH
General Superintendent
G. S. RAILTON
Secretary of the Christian Mission

Witnesses to both signatures
THOS. WHITTINGTON
J. E. BILLUPS

Enrolled in the High Court of Justice (Chancery Division) the thirteenth day of August in the year of our Lord 1878 (being first duly stamped) according to the tenor of the Statutes made for that purpose.

ENDORSEMENT

BE IT REMEMBERED and entered as of RECORD that WHEREAS the Society called and known previously to the end of the year One thousand eight hundred and seventy-eight as 'The Christian Mission' was on or about the first day of January One thousand eight hundred and seventy-nine with a view to the more beneficially extending of its operations renamed and has been since that time and is now usually known as 'The Salvation Army'

NOW I WILLIAM BOOTH the General of The Salvation Army (and also the General Superintendent of The Christian Mission) do hereby by virtue of all and every powers and authority in me vested declare that the said Society formerly known and in the within written Deed described as The Christian Mission is now and is intended to be hereafter called and known or described for all public purposes of its operations as 'The Salvation Army' and that the expression 'The Christian Mission' in the within Deed contained shall be taken to mean 'The Salvation Army' and that everything in the within Deed contained relating or referring to The Christian Mission shall be taken as relating or referring to 'The Salvation Army'.

IN WITNESS whereof I have hereto set my hand this twenty-fourth day of June One thousand eight hundred and eighty.

WILLIAM BOOTH

Witness
THOS. WHITTINGTON

Enrolled in the Central Office of the Supreme Court of Judicature the twentieth day of April in the year of our Lord 1906.

Appendix II

Members of the 1929 High Council

(in alphabetical order)

Colonel Joseph BARR	Territorial Commander, Korea
Colonel Charles BAUGH	Territorial Commander, Northern India
Commissioner Arthur BLOWERS	International Secretary for India, Ceylon and the Eastern Missionary Section
Mrs General Bramwell BOOTH	International Headquarters
Commander Evangeline BOOTH	National Commander, USA
Commissioner Catherine BOOTH	Leader, Women's Social Work, UK
Colonel Mary BOOTH	Territorial Commander, Germany
Commissioner Mrs BOOTH-HELLBERG	International Travelling Commissioner
Commissioner Samuel BRENGLE	Spiritual Campaigner, USA
Colonel Thomas CLOUD	Territorial Commander, West Indies (West)
Colonel Edward COLES	Territorial Commander, Ceylon
Commissioner John CUNNINGHAM	International Secretary for Europe
Brigadier William EBBS	Officer Commanding, Italy

Lieut-Commissioner Stanley EWENS	Territorial Commander, Western India
Lieut-Commissioner Bruno FRIEDRICH	Territorial Commander, Czechoslovakia
Commissioner Adam GIFFORD	Territorial Commander, USA (Western)
Commissioner Johannes de GROOT	Territorial Commander, South Africa
Lieut-Commissioner Reinert GUNDERSEN	Territorial Commander, Finland
Lieut-Commissioner William HAINES	Managing Director, The Salvation Army Assurance Society
Lieut-Colonel William HANCOCK	Officer Commanding, Burma
Commissioner James HAY	Territorial Commander, New Zealand
Commissioner Edward HIGGINS	The Chief of the Staff
Commissioner Robert HOGGARD	International Travelling Commissioner
Lieut-Commissioner Richard HOLZ	Territorial Commander, USA (Eastern)
Lieut-Commissioner Julius HORSKINS	On furlough
Commissioner William HOWARD	Territorial Commander, Switzerland
Commissioner Samuel HURREN	The British Commissioner
Commissioner Charles JEFFRIES	International Training Garrison
Brigadier Karl JOHANSON	Officer Commanding, Latvia and Estonia
Lieut-Commissioner George JOLLIFFE	Governor, Men's Social Work, UK

356

Commissioner Theodore KITCHING	Editor-in-Chief
Commissioner David LAMB	International Social Secretary
Commissioner Karl LARSSON	Territorial Commander, Norway
Commissioner John LAURIE	Chancellor of the Exchequer
Brigadier Alfred E. LINDVALL	Officer Commanding, South America (West)
Lieut-Colonel Charles MACKENZIE	Officer Commanding, Eastern India
Lieut-Commissioner William McINTYRE	Territorial Commander, USA (Southern)
Lieut-Commissioner William McKENZIE	Territorial Commander, China
Lieut-Commissioner John McMILLAN	Territorial Commander, USA (Central)
Commissioner Henry MAPP	International Secretary for USA and British Dominions
Lieut-Colonel Albert MARPURG	Chief Secretary 'in charge', Denmark
Lieut-Commissioner William MAXWELL	Territorial Commander, Canada (East)
Commissioner George MITCHELL	Territorial Commander, Sweden
Colonel Narayana MUTHIAH	Territorial Commander, Madras and Telegu, India
Lieut-Commissioner William PALMER	International Travelling Commissioner
Lieut-Commissioner Wiebe PALSTRA	Territorial Commander, Dutch East Indies
Commissioner Albin PEYRON	Territorial Commander, France

357

Lieut-Commissioner Charles RICH	Territorial Commander, Canada (West)
Commissioner Wilfred SIMPSON	International Travelling Commissioner
Commissioner Allister SMITH	International Travelling Commissioner
Colonel George SOUTER	Territorial Commander, West Africa
Commissioner George SOWTON	Territorial Commander, Australia (East)
Lieut-Colonel Robert STEVEN	Territorial Commander, Brazil
Colonel Mrs Annie TROUNCE	Territorial Commander, Southern India
Lieut-Commissioner Barnard TURNER	Territorial Commander, South America (East)
Lieut-Colonel Wilfred TWILLEY	Territorial Commander, West Indies (Eastern)
Lieut-Commissioner Isaac UNSWORTH	International Travelling Commissioner
Lieut-Commissioner Bouwe VLAS	Territorial Commander, Holland
Commissioner Johanna van de WERKEN	On furlough
Commissioner Hugh WHATMORE	Territorial Commander, Australia (South)
Commissioner Richard WILSON	Salvationist Publishing & Supplies Ltd
Lieut-Colonel Thomas WILSON	Territorial Commander, East Africa
Lieut-Commissioner Gunpei YAMAMURO	Territorial Commander, Japan

Notes

The source of any documents not referenced in these endnotes is the International Heritage Centre of The Salvation Army in London.
Publishers of books are listed in the endnotes only at the first appearance of each book.

Prologue

1 *The News Chronicle*, 12 August 1912.
2 The plans included two quadrangles of houses on either side of the tower and assembly hall, with capacity for 350 cadets each. The quadrangle on the Denmark Hill side was never completed.
3 Catherine Bramwell-Booth, *Bramwell Booth* (Rich and Cowan, 1933), page 520. The events and dialogue of that day are based on her account.
4 William Booth, *A Talk with Mr Gladstone at his own Fireside* (International Headquarters, 1897), page 33.

Chapter 1 – Laying the Foundation

1 Bramwell Booth, *Echoes and Memories* (Salvationist Publishing and Supplies Ltd, 1925), page 174.
2 Robert Sandall, *The History of The Salvation Army*, Volume 1 (Thomas Nelson and Sons Ltd, 1947), page 178.
3 Recorded by Robert Sandall in *The History of The Salvation Army*, Volume I, page 198.
4 Ibid, page 198.
5 *The Christian Mission Magazine*, July 1877.
6 The 1875 constitution is reproduced in full in St John Ervine's *God's Soldier* (William Heineman Ltd, 1934), Appendix I.
7 Robert Sandall, *The History of The Salvation Army*, Volume 1, page 235.
8 *The Christian Mission Magazine*, September 1878.
9 Quoted by Robert Sandall in *The History of The Salvation Army*, Volume 1, page 187.
10 Ibid, page 237.

[11] If this was the first 'sealed envelope' it means that for 13 months the Army would have been in a vulnerable position with regard to the succession had William Booth died during that time. The historical record does not tell us whether there was an earlier, holding 'sealed envelope'. If so, the only possible interim name would have been that of Catherine Booth, the Army Mother, who, if she had become the General Superintendent, would have nominated Bramwell for the leadership when she deemed that he was ready.

Chapter 2 – Second Thoughts

[1] International Headquarters, 1897.

[2] Recounted by Brindley Boon in an article entitled 'It Started with a Bomb' in *Salvationist*, 16 July 1994.

[3] Quoted in a letter from Messrs Waterhouse & Co, legal advisers to Bramwell Booth's executors, to Mr William Frost, 29 June 1929.

[4] Ibid.

[5] The Supplementary Deed 1904 is reproduced in full in St John Ervine's *God's Soldier*, Appendix 6.

[6] Letter from Lieut-Colonel Theodore Kitching to Dr Washington Ranger, 16 May 1904.

[7] Recorded by Commissioner Karl Larsson, who was present on the occasion, in his autobiography *Under Order (Under Orders)*, Volume III (Territorial Headquarters, Sweden), page 26.

Chapter 3 – A Smooth Transition

[1] *The War Cry*, 13 July 1929.

[2] The letters are reproduced in full in St John Ervine's *God's Soldier*, Appendix 7.

[3] *The War Cry*, 19 October 1882.

[4] *Orders and Regulations for Officers*, 1925.

[5] Albert Orsborn, *The House of my Pilgrimage* (Salvationist Publishing and Supplies Ltd, 1958), page 102.

[6] St John Ervine, *God's Soldier*, page 921. Letter dated 29 December 1918.

Chapter 4 – Warning Rumbles

[1] 'The First Blast of a Trumpet' is reproduced in full in St John Ervine's *God's Soldier*, Appendix 8, and in John Kirkham's *Deposed but not Despised*, Appendix A.

[2] William G. Harris, *Storm Pilot* (Salvationist Publishing and Supplies Ltd, 1981), page 61.

[3] *The War Cry*, Atlanta, USA, 13 April 1929.

[4] William G. Harris, *Storm Pilot*, page 60.

[5] St John Ervine, *God's Soldier*, page 902.

[6] F. A. Mackenzie, *Booth Tucker, Sadhu and Saint* (Hodder and Stoughton, 1930), page 235.

[7] In Appendices IX – XI of *God's Soldier*, St John Ervine reproduces not only Bulletin No 1 but also Bulletin No 2 and the first edition of *The International Salvationist.*

[8] Clarence Hall, *Samuel Brengle – Portrait of a Prophet,* 1933 edition (National Headquarters, USA), page 356.

[9] Ibid, page 359.

[10] Letter dated 3 September 1927, quoted by St John Ervine in *God's Soldier.*

[11] Diaries of Commissioner Alexander Damon, 27 March 1927 and Major John Milsaps, 4 January 1928. USA National Archives.

[12] Letter dated 21 March 1927 to Colonel Robert Sandall, Editor-in-Chief, USA Southern Territory.

[13] Edward H. McKinley, *Marching to Glory, The History of The Salvation Army in the United States* (Harper and Row, *1980),* page 265, endnote 7.

[14] 5 February 1929.

[15] George Carpenter's personal papers, quoted by Stella Carpenter in *A Man of Peace in a World at War* (private publication, 1993), page 147.

[16] Ibid, page 153.

[17] Ibid, page 160.

[18] St John Ervine, *God's Soldier,* page 882.

Chapter 5 – Confrontation

[1] St John Ervine, *God's Soldier,* page 907.

[2] William G. Harris, *Storm Pilot,* page 62.

[3] St John Ervine, *God's Soldier,* page 922. Letter dated 26 November 1927.

[4] William G. Harris, *Storm Pilot,* page 2.

[5] Albert Orsborn, *The House of my Pilgrimage,* page 101.

[6] Letter to Commissioner John McMillan, Territorial Commander, USA Central Territory, dated 28 December 1927. USA National Archives.

[7] Letter 25 March 1928.

[8] Letter from Commissioner John Carleton to Commander Evangeline Booth, December 1927, USA National Archives.

[9] Undated excerpt from letter by Commissioner John Carleton to Commander Evangeline Booth. USA National Archives.

Chapter 6 – Pressure

[1] Catherine Bramwell-Booth, *Bramwell Booth,* page 503.

[2] Mrs Bramwell Booth, Booklet: *A Statement by Mrs Booth* (private publication, 1929), page 15.

[3] Catherine Bramwell-Booth, *Bramwell Booth*, page 500.
[4] St John Ervine, *God's Soldier*, page 930.
[5] Ibid, page 930.
[6] William Frost in a letter to *The Times*, 24 January 1930.

Chapter 7 – Breakdown
[1] Mrs Bramwell Booth, Booklet: *A Statement by Mrs Booth*, page 16.
[2] Ibid, page 17.
[3] Ibid, page 18.
[4] Clarence Hall, *Portrait of a Prophet*, 1933 edition, page 360. Letter dated 19 March 1928.
[5] Mrs Bramwell Booth, Booklet: *A Statement by Mrs Booth*, page 16.
[6] Ibid, page 20.
[7] Letter to Commissioner John McMillan, Territorial Commander, USA Central Territory, 14 April 1928.
[8] Letter to Commissioner John J. Allan, Chief of the Staff, 25 November 1947.
[9] USA National Archives.
[10] Letter to Colonel William S. Barker, Chief Secretary, USA Western Territory, 17 April 1928.
[11] St John Ervine, *God's Soldier*, page 938.
[12] Letter dated 14 May 1928.
[13] Mrs Bramwell Booth, Booklet: *A Statement by Mrs Booth*, page 21.
[14] Ibid, page 22.
[15] Ibid, page 18.
[16] Ibid, page 18. Letter dated 29 April 1928.

Chapter 8 – The Gathering Storm
[1] Catherine Bramwell-Booth, *Bramwell Booth*, page 107.
[2] Jenty Fairbank, *For Such a Time, The Story of Young Florence Booth*, page 145 (Salvation Books, IHQ, 2007).
[3] Notes of High Council speech.
[4] Mrs Bramwell Booth, Booklet: *A Statement by Mrs Booth*, page 21.
[5] Catherine Bramwell-Booth, *Bramwell Booth*, page 515.
[6] Mrs Bramwell Booth, Booklet: *A Statement by Mrs Booth*, page 24.
[7] Catherine Bramwell-Booth, *Bramwell Booth*, page 515.
[8] Mrs Bramwell Booth, Booklet: *A Statement by Mrs Booth*, page 25.
[9] Ibid, page 24.
[10] Ibid, page 25.
[11] Based on correspondence in the USA National Archives.

[12] Letter to Mr George W. Wickersham dated 11 September 1928. USA National Archives.

[13] Commissioner Charles Jeffries to Commander Evangeline Booth, 30 October 1928 – referring to the meeting with the Chief of the Staff that took place in September. USA National Archives.

[14] Letter dated 27 September 1928. USA National Archives.

[15] Letter dated 21 September to Commissioner Henry Mapp. USA National Archives.

[16] Letter dated 27 September 1928. USA National Archives.

[17] USA National Archives.

[18] Letter dated 4 January 1929.

[19] USA National Archives.

[20] USA National Archives.

[21] St John Ervine, *God's Soldier*, page 942 ff.

[22] Account dated 13 November 1932, quoted by St John Ervine, *God's Soldier*, page 945.

[23] Ibid, page 945.

[24] USA National Archives.

Chapter 9 – Battle for Hearts and Minds

[1] Letter dated 16 November 1929. USA National Archives.

[2] Cable dated 16 November 1929. USA National Archives.

[3] Albert Orsborn, *The House of My Pilgrimage*, page 138.

[4] Unpublished article written for *The Staff Review*.

[5] Letter dated 18 November 1928.

[6] Letter dated 27 December 1928.

[7] Two of the communications are dated 26 November 1928 and the third 10 December 1928. The pamphlet is dated 8 December 1928. These documents are reproduced in full in *Deposed but not Despised* by John Kirkham, the pamphlet in the text of the book and the other communications in Appendices F, G and H.

[8] Letter dated 3 December 1928. USA National Archives.

[9] *The Times,* 24 December 1928.

Chapter 10 – Countdown

[1] *Daily News,* 29 December 1928.

[2] USA National Archives, 28 December 1928.

[3] USA National Archives. The letter is dated 3 December 1928 but this is clearly an error as the events the Commander describes took place after her arrival in London on 28 December 1928.

[4] Letter to Colonel W. F. Jenkins, 14 January 1929. USA National Archives.
[5] Japanese *War Cry*, 13 April 1929.
[6] Unpublished article written for *The Staff Review*.
[7] *Bramwell Booth*, by Catherine Bramwell-Booth, page 514.
[8] Letter dated 14 January 1929.
[9] *Bramwell Booth*, by Catherine Bramwell-Booth, page 521.
[10] *The Times*, 4 January 1929.
[11] *The War Cry*, 12 January 1929.

Chapter 11 – The Council Meets

[1] Letter dated 1 January 1929.
[2] This and other references are taken from the 'Statement about the 1929 High Council' that Commissioner James Hay prepared in 1948 in response to a request from General Albert Orsborn.
[3] James Hay, *Aggressive Salvationism* (published privately by Gordon Hay, 1951), page 76.
[4] These and numerous other references that follow are drawn from the official minutes of the High Council together with some 'minute jottings' – see notes on Sources and Acknowledgments.
[5] Letter to Colonel W. F. Jenkins, 14 January 1929. USA National Archives.
[6] Letter dated 17 January 1929.
[7] Unpublished article written for *The Staff Review*.
[8] Notes of speech.
[9] Unpublished article written for *The Staff Review*.
[10] *Daily Mail*, 10 January 1929.
[11] *Daily Mail*, 11 January 1929.
[12] *Daily Chronicle*, 11 January 1929.

Chapter 12 – A Deputation of Seven

[1] F. A. Mackenzie, *The Clash of the Cymbals* (Brentano Ltd, 1929), page 125.
[2] Unpublished article written for *The Staff Review*, April 1929.
[3] Letter to Commissioner John J. Allan, Chief of the Staff, 6 February 1948.
[4] 'Statement about the 1929 High Council' by Commissioner James Hay.
[5] 19 January 1929.
[6] 'Statement about the 1929 High Council' by Commissioner James Hay.
[7] Letter to British staff officers dated 17 January 1929.
[8] Letter to Colonel W. F. Jenkins, 14 January 1929. USA National Archives.

Chapter 13 – The Council Acts

1 14 January 1929.
2 12 January 1929.
3 Both dated 14 January 1929.
4 14 January 1929.
5 14 January 1929.
6 *The Times*, 16 January 1929.
7 16 January 1929.
8 *Daily News*, 18 January 1929.
9 Notes of speech.
10 F. A. Mackenzie, *The Clash of the Cymbals*, page 137.
11 The full text of Commissioner Catherine Booth's speech was subsequently published by her mother in the booklet *A Statement by Mrs Booth*. The text of the speech is also to be found in Appendix I of *Deposed but not Despised* by John Kirkham.
12 In 1929 the platform was at the end of the room nearer to the River Thames. At that time the door by the platform led to a small adjoining room.
13 Letter to Colonel W. F. Jenkins, 21 January 1929. USA National Archives.
14 *Daily Chronicle*, 17 January 1929.

Chapter 14 – Black Friday

1 *Evening News*, 18 January 1929.
2 Letter to Colonel W. F. Jenkins, 22 January 1929. USA National Archives.
3 Letter to Colonel W. F. Jenkins, 23 January 1929. USA National Archives.
4 Ibid.
5 *Daily Express*, 19 January 1929.
6 Submission to Mr Justice Eve.
7 *Orders and Regulations for Soldiers of The Salvation Army*, 1927 edition.
8 Letter to Colonel W. F. Jenkins, 23 January 1929.
9 *The New Age*, 24 January 1929.
10 Letter dated 18 January 1929.
11 Letter dated 19 January 1929.
12 Letter dated 19 January 1929.
13 Letter to Colonel W. F. Jenkins, 23 January 1929.

Chapter 15 – Booth versus Hurren and Others

1 30 January 1929.
2 *Daily Herald*, 26 January 1929.

[3] *The Times,* 30 and 31 January 1929. The account of the court hearing draws on these reports, which are reproduced in full in *The History of The Salvation Army,* Volume 6, by Frederick Coutts (Hodder and Stoughton, 1973), Appendices B and C.

[4] The *Daily Express,* 30 January 1929, printed the text virtually in full.

Chapter 16 – The Council Waits

[1] Letter to Colonel W. F. Jenkins, 3 February 1929. USA National Archives.

[2] *Daily Telegraph* and *Daily Chronicle,* 1 February 1929.

[3] John C. Waite, *Dear Mr Booth* (Territorial Headquarters, New Zealand, c.1964), page 23.

[4] Cyril R. Bradwell, *Fight the Good Fight* (A. W. & A. H. Reed Ltd, 1982), page 5.

[5] The Supplement itself is dated Wednesday 6 February 1929.

[6] Letter dated 6 February 1929.

[7] Position paper prepared for the High Council.

[8] Letter dated 3 February 1929. USA National Archives.

[9] *Daily Herald,* 4 February 1929. *Daily Chronicle,* 5 February 1929.

[10] *Daily Express,* 13 February 1929.

Chapter 17 – Day of Decision

[1] The full texts of the speeches by Commissioners Lamb and Wilson were subsequently included in a booklet for private circulation commemorating the events of the day.

[2] Estimates of the length of his address vary greatly. The press and later *The War Cry* said that he spoke for 'over two hours', a piece of information that has been repeated in most subsequent accounts of the High Council. However, Commissioner James Hay recalls in his 'Statement about the 1929 High Council' that 'it was not a long address – I should say from recollection and my notes, not beyond 15 minutes'. It is difficult to reconcile these two extremes. The mention of 'over two hours' may have referred to the *total* time that Mr Jowitt addressed the Council during the day, as it is hard to see how a two-hour address could have been slotted into the timetable of the morning session. One also wonders whether an address of that length would not have been counterproductive to his case.

[3] In his diary, Commissioner Gunpei Yamamuro reports Mr Jowitt as saying that though it was true that the 1904 Supplementary Deed was executed in order to make it possible to remove a General on the grounds of mental or physical unfitness, lack of capacity or misconduct, the words 'or other circumstances' were not in the original draft of the deed. These words, he said, were probably

added by the legal team in their final shaping up of the document, and it would be unfair to apply them to the present case.

4 'Statement about the 1929 High Council' by Commissioner James Hay.

5 *Daily Express,* 14 February 1929.

6 'Statement about the 1929 High Council' by Commissioner James Hay.

7 Ibid.

8 Unsigned copy of report by one of the USA territorial commanders present.

9 'Statement about the 1929 High Council' by Commissioner James Hay.

10 *The War Cry,* USA Southern Territory, 11 May 1929.

11 *Daily Chronicle,* 14 February 1929.

12 'Statement about the 1929 High Council' by Commissioner James Hay.

13 Ibid.

14 St John Ervine, *God's Soldier,* page 998, and letter by Commissioner Samuel Hurren to British staff officers, 14 February 1929.

15 P. W. Wilson, *General Evangeline Booth* (Charles and Scribner's Sons, 1948), page 219.

16 William G. Harris, *Storm Pilot,* page 2.

17 Letter dated 15 February 1929. USA National Archives.

18 Letter to Colonel W. F. Jenkins, 15 January 1929. USA National Archives.

19 *Daily Telegraph,* 14 February 1929.

20 Ibid.

21 Ibid.

Chapter 18 – An Unexpected Sequel

1 Hebrews 10:23 and 24, *Authorised Version.*

2 *Daily Telegraph,* 14 February 1929.

3 *The Times,* 15 February 1929.

4 *The War Cry,* 23 February 1929.

5 *The War Cry,* 23 February 1929.

6 Albert Orsborn, *The House of my Pilgrimage,* page 139.

7 *Daily Telegraph,* 26 February 1929.

8 *The War Cry,* USA Eastern Territory, 23 March 1929. USA National Archives.

9 P. W. Wilson, *General Evangeline Booth,* page 219.

10 Letter dated 15 March 1929. USA National Archives.

11 Catherine Bramwell-Booth, *Bramwell Booth,* page 529.

12 *The War Cry,* 13 July 1929.

13 Letter dated 18 March 1929. USA National Archives.

14 Letter dated 20 April 1929 from Commissioner Henry Mapp, Chief of the Staff, to leaders.

15 Catherine Bramwell-Booth, *Bramwell Booth,* page 529.

[16] *Daily News,* 30 October 1929. Interview with General Higgins.

[17] Frederick Coutts, *The History of The Salvation Army,* Volume 6, page 94.

[18] *The War Cry,* 13 July 1929.

[19] USA National Archives.

[20] Letter dated 15 August 1929 from Messrs Waterhouse & Co, legal advisers to the three trustees, to Mr William Frost.

[21] Update on the legal position sent by the Chief of the Staff to leaders on 30 October 1929.

[22] Strictly speaking the booklet has no title. The cover simply says 'Strictly Private and Confidential – Not for Publication'. The title used in this book to identify the booklet is the title of its second and longest section, *A Statement by Mrs Booth.*

[23] Internal International Headquarters memorandum.

[24] Letter dated 17 January 1930. USA National Archives.

[25] The account of the court hearing draws on the report in *The Times,* 22 January 1930, which is reproduced in full in *The History of The Salvation Army,* Volume 6, Appendix E.

[26] *Daily News,* 25 January 1930.

Chapter 19 – Towards Reform

[1] Minute by the General, 20 February 1930.

[2] *The Times,* 4 November 1930.

[3] 'Memorandum on the Government of The Salvation Army' presented to the 1939 High Council.

[4] Letter to General Edward Higgins dated 12 June 1929.

[5] Preliminary Report of the Advisory Commission on Reform, 29 October 1930.

[6] The father of Mrs Commissioner Pauline Hunter.

[7] Letter dated 29 November 1930. USA National Archives.

[8] *The Times,* 13 March 1931.

[9] Letter dated 11 August 1931.

[10] For completeness, the Salvation Army Act 1931 includes as schedules the Deed of Constitution of 1878, the Supplementary Deed of 1904, the Deed of Variation of 1930, and a draft of the proposed Memorandum and Articles of Association of The Salvation Army Trustee Company.

Chapter 20 – Ongoing Reform

[1] 'Constitutional Notes' prepared by Mr William Frost for the 1939 High Council.

[2] 'Memorandum on the Government of The Salvation Army' by Commissioner David Lamb.

[3] Frederick Coutts, *No Continuing City* (Hodder and Stoughton, 1976), page 103.

[4] In such a hypothetical and unprecedented scenario it is likely that *Orders and Regulations Governing The Age of Retirement of The General and An Extension of the General's Term in Office* would need to be amended in order to take the new situation into account.

[5] Albert Orsborn, *The House of my Pilgrimage*, page 141.

[6] Gunpei Yamamuro, Booklet: *The New Epoch of The Salvation Army – The True Story of the High Council* (Japan Territory, 1929).

[7] Frederick Coutts, *The History of The Salvation Army*, Volume 6, page 101.

Epilogue

[1] I am indebted to Colonel John Bate, the then Director of Salvation Army Information Services at International Headquarters, for many of the details in what follows, as contained in his unpublished memoirs.

Index

374

Y